W9-CDD-493

Magnolia Table

— VOLUME 3 —

JOANNA GAINES

PHOTOGRAPHY BY AMY NEUNSINGER

MAGNOLIA
PUBLICATIONS

wm
WILLIAM MORROW
An Imprint of HarperCollins*Publishers*

also by Joanna Gaines

THE MAGNOLIA STORY

MAGNOLIA TABLE, VOLUME 1

HOMEBODY

WE ARE THE GARDENERS

MAGNOLIA TABLE, VOLUME 2

THE WORLD NEEDS WHO YOU WERE MADE TO BE

THE STORIES WE TELL

MAGNOLIA TABLE, VOLUME 3. Copyright © 2023 by Joanna Gaines. All rights reserved. Printed in the United States of America. No part of this book may be used or reproduced in any manner whatsoever without written permission except in the case of brief quotations embodied in critical articles and reviews. For information, address HarperCollins Publishers, 195 Broadway, New York, NY 10007.

HarperCollins books may be purchased for educational, business, or sales promotional use. For information, please email the Special Markets Department at SPsales@harpercollins.com.

FIRST EDITION

Designed by Kelsie Monsen
Photography by Amy Neunsinger

Library of Congress Cataloging-in-Publication Data has been applied for.

ISBN 978-0-06-282017-4

23 24 25 26 27   WOR   10 9 8 7 6 5 4 3 2 1

For my dad,

You have always been one of my favorite people to cook for. Growing up, I loved making your lunches for work every day. You always brought home an empty lunch pail and praise for every last bite. Nowadays, it's a warm dinner or pan of fresh cinnamon rolls that I enjoy surprising you with, and then that picture you send when you've cleared the plate. My love for cooking has always been about the moments that unfold after the meal is made—the connection, the gift it is to nourish the people I care for—and that love took root with you.

It will always be a great joy of mine to cook for you, Dad.

Contents

Introduction

My parents were married on the front steps of a San Francisco courthouse. It was 1972, a Saturday afternoon, and only a few hours earlier my mom had landed in America for the very first time. She wore jean shorts and sandals. My dad donned a white tank top and denim bell-bottoms.

They met during my dad's service in South Korea and fell in love long-distance, through a year of letters that were read to them by a translator. Twelve years after their wedding day, they wanted to renew their vows with a more formal ceremony—one with friends and food and a traditional wedding cake—so invitations were mailed out and my two sisters and I were the flower girls.

My mom had ordered this elegant white cake for the reception. The cake felt like it was half my six-year-old size, five tiers tall with smooth icing on top.

My Korean mother made a point to embrace a few American wedding traditions, which included preserving the top tier of the reception cake for the first anniversary. So when the party was over, my mom covered the cake in plastic wrap and slid it onto the bottom shelf of our kitchen freezer.

Just low enough for me to reach.

I can't explain what came over me, but that first night, once everyone was asleep, I tiptoed down the hallway and into the kitchen. In one hand I held a fork, and with the other I carefully opened the freezer. You can put together the rest.

I can still place myself there now, standing barefoot on our carpeted kitchen floor. Nothing but the refrigerator light casting a glow in the dark. And that *taste*: White vanilla cake, thick buttercream icing. Perfectly chilled. After a few bites, I washed the fork, placed it back in the drawer, and rewrapped the cake. Until a couple nights later, and a few more after that.

The day of their anniversary came the following year, and when my mom went to grab the cake, what was left was basically the plastic she'd wrapped it in, which I'd stuffed behind bags of frozen peas. My poor mom—she immediately burst into tears. I can't remember another time she was more mad than at that moment when I confessed it was me who had eaten her wedding cake. I regretted it instantly, of course. It was out of character for me to be sneaky like that. But that small act of rebellion sparked within me a love of taste. It's the earliest memory I have of truly savoring something delicious. I don't remember the price I paid, but I never forgot the taste of that single tier of white wedding cake.

I can count a few other memories like this one, moments I can still feel, that are *part of me* because I remember intimately the way they tasted. The chocolate chip cookies I'd bake with my dad on Saturday afternoons. Sundays at my grandparents' house, sharing plates of rolled grape leaves. Watching my mom cook alongside my grandmother—the scent of Korean food filling our kitchen. Every time my grandfather on my dad's side let me roll out the dough for his famous Syrian donut recipe, and the way my hands would carry the scent of cinnamon and sugar for days after. The hospital chicken cordon bleu Chip and I shared after our first son was born.

More than any of the other senses, it seems that taste is what sticks with me. It's what I remember minutes, months, years later. It's what I carry forward. Flavor is how I mark the changing of seasons. Give me spring veggies, crisp and bright. Summer berries, juicy and dripping. Give me autumn's harvest to pickle and preserve and make those flavors last. Give me a winter filled with tradition: casseroles and Christmas candy. Give me a taste of something meaningful, and I know to savor it.

I've chased that word a thousand times over: *savor*. The definition is "to enjoy completely." Imagine that. Imagine unfettered delight. Imagine breathing, deeply, until it sinks in fully. Imagine a wholehearted moment. Taste that truly satisfies. Imagine saving the best of something—a moment, a sound, a feeling, and carrying it forward.

Savor has only ever come naturally to me when I'm cooking. I've chalked this up to food being a love language of mine. I've been chopping and whisking for decades. I've said it a million times before—my kitchen is my favorite place to be. It hasn't always been this way, but it gets truer with time. It's become second nature to relish flavors and think curiously about ingredients. Over the years, my kitchen itself has become a place I crave. And my island, an anchor.

It's this space that keeps my feet firmly planted despite a world turning. Despite the instinct to give myself in pieces in every direction. I've looked to the kitchen and the food I make here to ground me, upholding the promise of pulling all my senses into harmony.

Here, I am only the moment in front of me. I can slow down long enough to enjoy completely what's unfolding: the pulling out of a well-loved recipe, a favorite among the bellies I feed daily. Anticipation for the meal to come, and the voices it inevitably draws to the table, one and then another, always with stories to tell about their day. The familiar smells rising from the stove as I catch the timer tick to its finish.

And I can feel it: the weight of an ordinary moment becoming something more.

I can feel its charge brimming at the edge. *Savor this*. It's equal parts tangible and intangible, sometimes dissipating as fast as it forms. But I've learned not to brush it off. Not to move on to whatever is next. Not yet. Because moments like this are often only noticed in pause. Where we can glean the gold worth carrying forward: connection, communion, *delight*.

It's a fragile thing, in a world filled with interruptions. A world filled with expectations. Where what's ahead is promised to be better than what's present. A world where one look toward a distraction can abandon even our best-laid plans. I have half a lifetime's experience of letting worthy moments slip through my fingers.

I love to create, always have. Watching something go from nothing to something, and being part of it, really fuels me. In the garden, in the kitchen. In my work, especially. And in some ways, I feel like I was made for this side of life. To work with my hands. To build and help things prosper. But beyond the kitchen, I haven't always been so great at the harvesting part, in savoring what I've sown. Relishing the process, or even celebrating the finish. Instead, I've been quick to move on to whatever is next, ready to set my mind to something new.

And it's tempting, isn't it? To think there's always something better waiting around the corner. And maybe there is, but our hands were made to hold only one moment at a time. So I'm learning to hold on tight while it's mine. In a gentle whisper I remind myself as often as I think to: *enjoy this completely*.

I'm still a work in progress, but the practice is what I'm after. When it feels like too much is slipping through my fingers, I know I can always return to my island. Where instinct tells me to slow down. With hands mixing and pots of water bubbling, the life that resounds on this three-by-eight-foot table draws me in. And I feel it once again, that inner rebellion, this time to risk the interruptions and the distractions for the *right now*, the *right here*. To quiet everything around me so I can enjoy this completely.

I hope you sense that intention throughout the book. That what you find in the recipes and stories will feel like an invitation to pause. That they might pave the way for more connection and delight. Whether it's in the making, the gathering, or where it all began for me, the taste of something truly delicious, this is a collection I hope you'll savor.

The recipes, yes. But also the moments they shape.

Enjoy!

Joanna

CHAPTER ONE

Breads

LET IT REST, WATCH

IT RISE, SAVORING GROWTH

THAT'S EARNED GRADUALLY

Popovers

PREP: *10 minutes*   COOK: *30 minutes*   COOL: *5 minutes*

I doubt I'm the only one who gets excited when the bread basket arrives at the table of a good restaurant. Typically, I'll reach for any kind of bread that's in front of me, but traditional popovers have never been my favorite. I always found that the tried-and-true recipe tasted more like crust and the insides seemed just too hollow. So I thought we'd create a recipe that brings together the best of what bread has to offer: a crispy, flaky exterior and delicious, bready insides.

1 tablespoon coarse salt

2 teaspoons fresh rosemary, left whole or roughly chopped

1½ cups whole milk, at room temperature

1⅓ cups all-purpose flour

4 large eggs, at room temperature

1 teaspoon kosher salt

½ cup grated Parmesan cheese (about 2 ounces)

3 tablespoons unsalted butter, melted

Nonstick baking spray

Softened butter and/or jam, for serving (optional)

1. Position a rack in the middle of the oven and preheat the oven to 425°F. Place a popover pan or muffin tin in the oven while it is preheating. Once the oven reaches about 350°F, start mixing the popover batter.

2. In a small bowl, stir together the coarse salt and rosemary and set aside.

3. In a blender, combine the milk, flour, eggs, and kosher salt and blend for 30 to 45 seconds. (The more air is incorporated into the batter, the better the rise.) Add the Parmesan and melted butter, and blend for about 10 more seconds.

4. Carefully remove the hot pan from the oven and spray with nonstick baking spray. Pour the batter into the wells until they are about two-thirds full. Sprinkle with the rosemary salt and carefully return the pan to the oven.

5. Bake for 20 minutes, then lower the oven temperature to 350°F and bake until deeply golden brown, another 10 minutes. Do not open the oven during baking, as this could deflate the popovers. Allow the popovers to cool for 3 to 5 minutes before serving. Repeat as needed with the remaining batter.

6. Serve with butter or jam, if you like.

7. Store in a sealed bag at room temperature for up to 2 days.

Makes 10 to 12 popovers

Garlic-Cilantro Naan

PREP: *2 hours*   **COOK:** *20 minutes*   **COOL:** *none*

I love the discovery that comes with cooking. Over the years, I've come to love naan, a traditional Indian bread, more and more. I've started to pair it with any dish that has a rich sauce base, or I'll use it to make a wrap with meat and veggies. I've learned that baking it in the oven tends to give it a hard and crispy texture while cooking it on the stove at a high temperature for less time allows the bread to stay soft.

2 tablespoons warm water (about 110°F)

1 tablespoon active dry yeast

1 teaspoon sugar

3 cups all-purpose flour, plus more for dusting

⅓ cup full-fat plain Greek yogurt

¼ cup plus 1 teaspoon olive oil

3 teaspoons kosher salt

Cooking spray

4 tablespoons (½ stick) unsalted butter, melted

2 teaspoons chopped fresh cilantro

2 garlic cloves, minced

1. In a small bowl, stir together the warm water, yeast, and sugar. Let stand until foamy, about 5 minutes. (If the yeast mixture does not foam, your water was too hot or too cold, or your yeast was expired.)

2. In a stand mixer fitted with the dough hook, combine the flour, ⅔ cup of water, the yogurt, ¼ cup of the olive oil, and 2 teaspoons of the salt on low speed. With the mixer still on low speed, slowly add the yeast mixture, then increase the speed to medium. Continue to mix until the dough is smooth, about 5 minutes. Remove the dough from the bowl and shape into a ball. Lightly grease a large bowl with the remaining teaspoon olive oil, add the dough, and cover with plastic wrap. Allow the dough to proof for 2 hours, preferably in a warm area of the kitchen.

3. Heat a 10-inch skillet over medium heat and spray lightly with cooking spray. On a lightly floured surface, portion the dough into 8 pieces. Using a rolling pin, roll each piece into an oval shape about ¼ inch thick. Place a single rolled-out piece into the pan and cook until both sides are deep golden brown, about 1 minute per side, adjusting the temperature as needed. Transfer the cooked naan to a wire rack. Repeat, spraying again lightly before adding more dough, until all are cooked.

4. In a small bowl, stir together the butter, cilantro, garlic, and the remaining 1 teaspoon salt. Brush the tops of each naan with the garlic butter and serve immediately.

5. Store in an airtight container at room temperature for up to 2 days. Reheat in a nonstick skillet over medium-high heat for about 10 to 25 seconds per side.

Makes 8 naan

French Bread

PREP: *55 minutes*   **COOK:** *30 minutes*   **COOL:** *15 minutes*

There are no limits to the ways you can eat a fresh loaf of French bread. Whether paired with an assortment of appetizers, used as a vessel for my favorite—butter—or simply eaten warm and straight from the oven, it's a comforting staple. This recipe is my go-to. I never tire of its crunchy exterior that gives way to a soft, bready inside.

2 cups warm water
(about 110°F)

1 tablespoon plus 1 teaspoon
active dry yeast

1 tablespoon sugar

5 cups all-purpose flour,
plus additional for dusting

2 teaspoons kosher salt

Cooking spray

Tomato Butter or Burrata,
(page 14), for serving
(optional)

1. In a small bowl, stir together the warm water, yeast, and sugar. Let stand until foamy, about 5 minutes. (If the yeast mixture does not foam, your water was too hot or cold, or the yeast was expired.)

2. In a stand mixer fitted with the dough hook, stir together 3 cups of the flour and the salt. Add the yeast mixture and mix on medium speed. With the mixer still running, slowly add the remaining 2 cups flour. Once a dough starts to form, continue mixing until it is slightly tacky but pulls away from the sides of the bowl, about 5 minutes.

3. On a lightly floured surface, gently knead the dough into a ball. Spray a large bowl with cooking spray and place the dough in it. Cover the bowl with a towel and set in a warm spot for 30 minutes.

4. Preheat the oven to 375°F. Place a small, rimmed pan on the bottom rack of the oven. Line a large, rimmed baking sheet with parchment paper.

5. Lightly punch down the dough to release the air. On a lightly floured surface, split the dough into two equal balls and press each ball into a rectangle about 1 inch thick. Starting with the long end, roll each rectangle into a 12-inch-long log, making sure to press out the air bubbles as you roll. Pinch the seams together to seal and place the loaves seam side down about 4 inches apart on the lined baking sheet.

6. Using a sharp razor blade, score the top of the loaves with shallow angled lines about 2 inches apart. Cover the dough with a towel and let it rest at room temperature for 25 minutes.

7. Place the loaves in the oven on a rack above the empty pan. Place three ice cubes in the empty pan and shut the oven door. (This creates steam, which will help harden the crust.)

8. Bake until golden brown, 25 to 30 minutes. Let cool for at least 15 minutes before slicing. Serve with tomato butter or burrata (if using).

9. Store in a sealed bag at room temperature for up to 3 days.

Makes 2 loaves

Tomato Butter

PREP: *10 minutes*   COOK: *20 minutes*   COOL: *60 minutes*

8 ounces cherry
   or grape tomatoes

1 cup (2 sticks) unsalted butter,
   at room temperature

1 garlic clove, minced

¼ teaspoon kosher salt

¼ teaspoon dried basil leaves

1 loaf French Bread
   (page 13)

1. Preheat the oven to 425°F.

2. Place the tomatoes on a small baking sheet and roast until they release their juices, 20 minutes. Let cool for at least 30 minutes.

3. Puree the cooled tomatoes in a food processor or blender until smooth, about 30 seconds.

4. In a stand mixer fitted with the whisk attachment, whip the butter on medium-high speed until pale and fluffy, about 3 minutes.

5. Reduce the speed to medium-low and slowly add in the tomato puree, garlic, salt, and basil. Mix on medium-low until incorporated, about 2 minutes. Let stand at room temperature 30 minutes before serving with the French bread.

6. Store in an airtight container in the refrigerator for up to 1 week.

Makes 6 to 8 servings

Simple Burrata

PREP: *5 minutes*   COOK: *none*   COOL: *none*

2 balls burrata

1 tablespoon olive oil

Kosher salt and freshly
   cracked black pepper

1 loaf French Bread
   (page 13)

Place the burrata in a serving dish and gently slice the top open. Drizzle with the olive oil and sprinkle with a pinch of salt and pepper. Serve with the French bread.

TIP: Top with thyme, rosemary, or your favorite fresh herb. Or try Jo's favorite burrata variation (page 115).

Makes 6 to 8 servings

Roasted Garlic Parmesan Toast

PREP: *10 minutes*   **COOK:** *1 hour 5 minutes*   **COOL:** *20 minutes*

1 garlic head

½ teaspoon olive oil

1 cup (2 sticks) unsalted butter,
   at room temperature

1 tablespoon dried parsley
   leaves

½ teaspoon kosher salt

½ cup finely shredded
   Parmesan cheese
   (about 2 ounces)

1 loaf French Bread
   (page 13)

1. Preheat the oven to 400°F. Line a baking sheet with foil.

2. Peel the excess papery skin off the head of garlic and trim the top, exposing the garlic cloves. Drizzle with the olive oil. Wrap the garlic in foil, keeping the top exposed.

3. Roast directly on the oven rack for 45 minutes, then carefully remove the garlic from the foil and let cool for about 15 minutes. Squeeze the cloves into a small bowl, discarding the skin.

4. Using a stand mixer fitted with the paddle attachment, whip the butter on medium-high speed until pale and fluffy, about 2 minutes. Add the roasted garlic cloves, parsley, and salt, and continue mixing on high for about 1 minute to fully incorporate the flavors. Slowly add the Parmesan and mix on medium-low speed until incorporated.

5. Slice the bread in half lengthwise and place it cut side up on the lined baking sheet. Divide the butter mixture between the halves and spread evenly.

6. Bake for 15 minutes, then broil on high for about 1 minute to make the edges crispy. Allow the toast to cool for about 5 minutes. Cut into slices and serve.

7. Store in an airtight container at room temperature for up to 3 days.

Makes 6 to 8 servings

Truffle Butter Rolls

PREP: *1 hour 30 minutes*   **COOK:** *20 minutes*   **COOL:** *5 minutes*

I love everyday dinner rolls, but when I want to bring something a little more special to the table, I will serve these. The truffle butter is so distinct and delicious, it often becomes the star of the meal. You might guess the recipe would be difficult to put together, but an especially endearing part of this recipe is its ease. Even if I decide late in the day to whip up these rolls, I can have them ready to serve by dinnertime.

DOUGH

1 cup warm whole milk
(about 110°F)

One ¼-ounce packet active
dry yeast

1 teaspoon sugar

3¼ cups all-purpose flour,
plus more for rolling

4 tablespoons (½ stick)
unsalted butter,
at room temperature

2 tablespoons honey

1 tablespoon white truffle oil

½ teaspoon kosher salt

1 large egg

Cooking spray

FILLING

2 tablespoons unsalted butter,
melted

2 teaspoons truffle oil

½ cup grated Parmesan
cheese (about 2 ounces)

TOPPING

2 tablespoons unsalted butter,
melted

Coarse sea salt, for garnish

Truffle zest, for garnish

Chopped fresh parsley,
for garnish

1. To make the dough: In a small bowl, stir together the milk, yeast, and sugar. Let stand until foamy, about 5 minutes. (If the yeast mixture does not foam, your water was too hot or too cold, or your yeast was expired.)

2. In a stand mixer fitted with the dough hook, combine the flour, butter, honey, truffle oil, salt, and egg on low speed. Pour in the yeast mixture, increase the speed to medium, and mix the dough for about 3 minutes. The dough should be tacky and slightly sticky to the touch. Spray a medium bowl with cooking spray and place the dough in the bowl. Cover with plastic wrap and set in a warm spot for 1 hour.

3. Remove the plastic wrap and lightly punch down the dough to release the air.

4. Turn the dough onto a heavily floured surface. Split the dough into two equal halves. Using a rolling pin, roll each half into a 9 × 5-inch rectangle, about ⅓ inch thick.

5. Preheat the oven to 350°F. Line a baking sheet with parchment paper.

6. To make the filling: In a small bowl, stir together the melted butter and truffle oil. Brush the butter mixture onto the top of each rectangle and cut each into six 1½ × 5-inch strips. Sprinkle about 2 teaspoons of Parmesan in a line down the center of each strip. Starting with the short end, gently roll each strip of dough into a tight coil. Place the rolls, seam side down, about 2 inches apart on the lined baking sheet. Let the rolls rest, uncovered, for 30 minutes.

7. Transfer the rolls to the oven and bake until golden brown, 16 to 20 minutes.

8. When the rolls come out of the oven, immediately brush them with the melted butter and sprinkle with the salt, truffle zest, and parsley. Allow the rolls to cool on the baking sheet for 5 minutes before serving.

9. Store in a sealed bag at room temperature for up to 2 days.

Makes 12 rolls

Hush Puppies

WITH HOMEMADE TARTAR SAUCE

PREP: *25 minutes*   **COOK:** *15 minutes*   **COOL:** *1 hour*

When hush puppies are cut too large, they tend to end up with what my kids call "mushy middles." I prefer to cut them on the smaller side, so they'll keep a firm consistency all the way through. Hush puppies are delicious on their own, but I can't imagine serving fried fish without them. On those occasions, I'll have a plate prepped and ready to fry right before dinnertime so I can serve them my favorite way—piping hot.

TARTAR SAUCE

¾ cup mayonnaise

5 tablespoons dill pickle relish

1 tablespoon chopped fresh dill

1 tablespoon dried onion flakes

2 teaspoons fresh lemon juice

1½ teaspoons freshly cracked black pepper

1 teaspoon garlic powder

Kosher salt

HUSH PUPPIES

Vegetable oil, for deep-frying

1½ cups cornmeal

1 cup frozen whole kernel corn

½ cup all-purpose flour

¼ cup finely diced onion

2 teaspoons baking powder

1 teaspoon kosher salt

1 teaspoon garlic powder

½ teaspoon baking soda

½ teaspoon onion powder

½ teaspoon sugar

1 cup whole-milk buttermilk

1 large egg

2 teaspoons chopped fresh parsley

Lemon wedges, for serving

1. To make the tartar sauce: In a medium bowl, stir together the mayonnaise, relish, dill, onion flakes, lemon juice, pepper, garlic powder, and salt. Cover and refrigerate for at least 1 hour.

2. To make the hush puppies: Pour about 2 inches of oil into a Dutch oven. Have ready a baking sheet lined with paper towels to use for draining. Heat the oil over medium-high heat until it reaches 350°F on a deep-fry thermometer.

3. Meanwhile, in a large bowl, whisk together the cornmeal, corn, flour, onion, baking powder, salt, garlic powder, baking soda, onion powder, and sugar. Add the buttermilk and egg and mix together until just fully combined.

4. Using a small (2-tablespoon) scoop, scoop 6 balls of the batter into the hot oil and fry for 1½ minutes. Flip and cook until dark golden brown, crispy, and cooked throughout, about 1½ more minutes. Place the cooked hush puppies on the prepared baking sheet. Repeat with the remaining batter. Garnish with parsley and serve with lemon wedges and chilled tartar sauce.

5. Store hush puppies in an airtight container at room temperature for up to 2 days. Store tartar sauce in an airtight container in the refrigerator for up to 5 days.

Makes 4 servings

Honey Oat Bread

PREP: *2 hours 30 minutes*   **COOK:** *45 minutes*   **COOL:** *45 minutes*

Fresh bread doesn't last very long in our house. While it takes about four hours to make this honey oat bread from start to finish, it seems to take just minutes for my kids to slice it up, only pausing to quickly top it with a light layer of butter and preserves or honey—which makes this sweet bread even sweeter.

¼ cup warm water
   (about 110°F)

One ¼-ounce packet
   active dry yeast

1 teaspoon sugar

2 cups all-purpose flour,
   plus more for dusting

1½ cups whole wheat flour

½ cup plus 2 tablespoons
   rolled oats

1 teaspoon kosher salt

1 cup whole milk

1 large egg, lightly beaten

¼ cup plus 1 tablespoon
   honey

Cooking spray

1 tablespoon unsalted
   butter, melted

1. In a small bowl, stir together the warm water, yeast, and sugar. Let stand until foamy, about 5 minutes. (If the yeast mixture does not foam, your water was too hot or too cold, or your yeast was expired.)

2. In a stand mixer fitted with the dough hook, combine the all-purpose flour, whole wheat flour, ½ cup of the oats, and the salt on low speed. Slowly pour in the milk, beaten egg, ¼ cup of the honey, and the yeast mixture. Raise the speed to medium and mix until a dough forms, then continue mixing for an additional 4 to 5 minutes. (This will allow the gluten to form and create a stable dough.) The dough should be tacky to the touch but pull away from the sides of the bowl.

3. Remove the dough from the bowl and shape it into a ball. Spray the bowl with cooking spray, set the dough back in the bowl, and cover with plastic wrap or a towel. Allow the dough to rest in a warm spot for about 30 minutes.

4. Turn the rested dough onto a lightly floured surface and press into a 9 × 9-inch square. Evenly roll the dough into a log, fold under each side, and press the seams together. Spray a 9 × 5-inch loaf pan with cooking spray and place the dough seam side down into the pan. Cover with a towel or plastic wrap and allow the dough to proof in a warm spot for 2 hours.

5. Preheat the oven to 350°F.

6. For the topping, stir together the remaining tablespoon of honey and the melted butter. Gently brush the top of the loaf with the mixture and sprinkle with the remaining 2 tablespoons oats.

7. Bake until the internal temperature reaches 190°F, about 45 minutes.

8. Let cool in the pan for 20 minutes, then carefully remove the loaf from the pan and place on a wire rack. Continue cooling for another 25 minutes before slicing.

9. Store in a sealed bag at room temperature for up to 5 days.

Makes 1 loaf

Beer Bread

PREP: *10 minutes*   **COOK:** *45 minutes*   **COOL:** *55 minutes*

When the weather outside is cool and dinner has been simmering on the stove for the better part of the day, it's unlikely that I won't also start pulling out ingredients for this bread. The beer acts as a yeast, making this similar to a quick bread, and the honey balances the beer with a subtle sweetness. If you're craving comfort and warmth, this bread offers plenty of both.

Nonstick baking spray

12 ounces dark beer

8 tablespoons (1 stick) unsalted butter, melted, plus additional softened butter for serving

¼ cup honey

3 cups all-purpose flour

1 tablespoon baking powder

1½ teaspoons kosher salt

1. Preheat the oven to 375°F. Generously spray a 9 × 5-inch loaf pan with nonstick baking spray.

2. In a large mixing bowl, whisk together the beer, 5 tablespoons of the melted butter, and the honey until well combined. Add the flour, baking powder, and salt and whisk until well combined. (The mixture will be very sticky.)

3. Evenly spread the dough in the prepared loaf pan.

4. In the loaf pan pour the remaining 3 tablespoons melted butter over the top of the dough. Bake until a toothpick inserted in the center comes out clean, 40 to 45 minutes.

5. Let cool for 10 minutes in the pan, then carefully remove the loaf from the pan and place on a wire rack. Continue cooling for 45 more minutes. Slice and serve with softened butter.

6. Store in an airtight container at room temperature for up to 5 days.

Makes 1 loaf

Lemon Blueberry Bread

PREP: *30 minutes*   **COOK:** *60 minutes*   **COOL:** *55 minutes*

This bread is simple and subtly sweet, and often the perfect thing to drop off on a friend's porch—sometimes for no reason other than to say "I'm thinking about you."

CRUMB

½ cup all-purpose flour

3 tablespoons sugar

2 tablespoons unsalted butter, melted

1 tablespoon freshly grated lemon zest

LEMON BLUEBERRY BREAD

1½ cups plus 1 tablespoon all-purpose flour

2 teaspoons baking powder

½ teaspoon kosher salt

1 cup sugar

8 tablespoons (1 stick) unsalted butter, melted and slightly cooled

3 large eggs, at room temperature

1 teaspoon pure vanilla extract

1 cup sour cream

⅓ cup fresh lemon juice

2 tablespoons freshly grated lemon zest

1 cup fresh or frozen blueberries

Nonstick baking spray

1. To make the crumb: In a small bowl, stir together the flour, sugar, melted butter, and zest until pebbly. Refrigerate until ready to use.

2. To make the bread: Preheat the oven to 375°F. Spray a light-colored 9 × 5-inch loaf pan with cooking spray.

3. In a medium bowl, stir together 1½ cups of the flour, the baking powder, and salt. In a large bowl, whisk together the sugar, melted butter, eggs, and vanilla.

4. Add the flour mixture to the sugar mixture in two additions, alternating with the sour cream, stirring until combined. Gently stir in the lemon juice and lemon zest.

5. Toss the blueberries in the remaining tablespoon of flour and fold into the batter using a spatula.

6. Pour the batter into the prepared loaf pan. Evenly sprinkle the crumb topping over the top of the batter.

7. Bake until a toothpick inserted in the center comes out clean, 50 to 60 minutes, tenting with foil to prevent excess browning after 40 minutes if needed. Let cool in the pan for 10 minutes, then transfer to a wire rack to cool for another 45 minutes before slicing.

8. Store in an airtight container or sealed bag at room temperature for up to 3 days, or place in the freezer for up to 1 month.

Makes 1 loaf

Jo's Pear Bread

SERVED AT
MAGNOLIA TABLE
WACO . TX

PREP: *25 minutes*   **COOK:** *45 minutes*   **COOL:** *20 minutes*

After we planted our pear trees at the farm, it felt as though I was waiting forever for them to bear fruit. Now, years later, we find ourselves completely overwhelmed with pears most autumns, and I try to add this crisp fruit anywhere I can—salads, preserves, desserts. One of my favorite discoveries is a twist on my classic banana bread. I swap pears for bananas and walnuts for pecans, and add a pinch of cinnamon. The walnuts tone down the sweetness of the pears, and bring a crunch that I find myself craving every fall. This recipe always reminds me of the value of trusting my gut and having fun in the kitchen—sometimes an experiment will become a family staple.

Nonstick baking spray (optional)

1½ pounds ripe Bosc pears (about 4)

1 cup packed light brown sugar

12 tablespoons (1½ sticks) unsalted butter, melted and cooled, plus softened butter for serving

2 large eggs, beaten

1½ teaspoons pure vanilla extract

1¾ cups all-purpose flour

1 teaspoon ground cinnamon

1 teaspoon baking soda

1 teaspoon kosher salt

½ cup walnuts, chopped

1 to 2 tablespoons turbinado sugar, as needed

1. Preheat the oven to 350°F. Spray an 8 × 8-inch pan with nonstick baking spray or line it with parchment paper.

2. Peel, core, and roughly chop the pears, then place them in a food processor or blender and puree until smooth, making approximately 2 cups of puree.

3. In a stand mixer fitted with the paddle attachment (or in a large bowl with an electric mixer), beat the brown sugar, melted butter, eggs, and vanilla on medium speed until well blended, about 30 seconds. Add the pear puree and mix until combined, another 30 seconds.

4. In a medium bowl, whisk together the flour, cinnamon, baking soda, and salt. Add the dry ingredients to the wet ingredients and beat until just combined, 1 minute. Add the walnuts and mix until combined, 15 seconds.

5. Pour the batter into the prepared pan and spread out evenly with a spatula. Evenly sprinkle the top of the batter with the turbinado sugar. Bake until a toothpick inserted in the center comes out clean, 40 to 45 minutes.

6. Let cool for 20 minutes. Serve warm or at room temperature topped with softened butter.

7. Store in an airtight container at room temperature for up to 2 days.

Makes 12 servings

Earl Grey Tea Cake

PREP: *20 minutes*   **COOK:** *60 minutes*   **COOL:** *30 minutes*

TEA CAKE

Nonstick baking spray

1 cup plus 2 tablespoons
  superfine sugar

2 large eggs

¾ cup plain whole-milk
  Greek yogurt

1½ tablespoons Earl Grey
  tea leaves

2½ teaspoons grated fresh
  tangerine zest

2½ teaspoons fresh tangerine
  juice

1 teaspoon orange extract

1 teaspoon pure vanilla extract

¾ cup vegetable oil

1½ cups all-purpose flour

1 teaspoon kosher salt

½ teaspoon baking soda

½ teaspoon baking powder

3 thin slices tangerine

COCONUT
WHIPPED CREAM

2 cups nondairy coconut
  whipping cream, chilled

½ cup powdered sugar

1 teaspoon orange extract

1 teaspoon pure vanilla extract

1. To make the tea cake: Position a rack in the middle of the oven and preheat the oven to 350°F. Spray a 9 × 5-inch loaf pan heavily with nonstick baking spray. Line the pan with parchment paper, allowing the paper to hang over the sides to use as handles later. Spray the bottom and sides of the exposed parchment paper.

2. In a stand mixer fitted with the whisk attachment, whisk the sugar and eggs until the mixture is thick, pale yellow, and falls in thick ribbons when the whisk is lifted, 2½ to 3½ minutes. Add the yogurt, tea leaves, tangerine zest and juice, orange extract, and vanilla and whisk on low for 30 seconds. With the mixer still on low speed, slowly stream in the oil.

3. In a medium bowl, combine the flour, salt, baking soda, and baking powder.

4. Add the dry ingredients to the egg mixture one-third at a time, mixing on medium speed until just combined, being careful not to overmix.

5. Pour the batter into the prepared pan and top with the tangerine slices.

6. Bake until a toothpick inserted in the center has crumbs clinging to it, 50 to 60 minutes. Cover with foil the last 10 or 15 minutes to prevent overbrowning. Let cool in the pan for 30 minutes.

7. To make the coconut whipped cream: While the cake cools, in a stand mixer fitted with the whisk attachment, whip the cream until it becomes slightly thick, 3 to 4 minutes. Add the sugar, orange extract, and vanilla and whip until well combined, 30 seconds. If necessary, refrigerate until ready to use.

8. Carefully remove the loaf from the pan by using the parchment handles. Cut the loaf into 8 slices and top with coconut whipped cream as desired.

9. Store the tea cake in an airtight container at room temperature for 3 to 5 days. Store the whipped cream in an airtight container in the refrigerator for up to 2 days.

TIP: This cake is also excellent when served slightly warmed and buttered, with hot tea or coffee.

Makes 8 servings

Apple Cinnamon Walnut Bread

PREP: *20 minutes*   **COOK:** *38 minutes*   **COOL:** *15 minutes*

There are certain flavors that can instantly transport me to a specific time and place. Apples and cinnamon top that list, and when the scent of this bread baking fills the kitchen, it can feel like a brisk October day—even if we're nowhere near autumn. If you prefer muffins more than bread, this recipe serves well both ways.

BREAD

Nonstick baking spray

1 cup packed light brown sugar

8 tablespoons (1 stick) unsalted butter, melted, plus softened butter for serving

2 large eggs

2 teaspoons pure vanilla extract

1¼ cups unsweetened applesauce

1¾ cups all-purpose flour

2 teaspoons ground cinnamon

1 teaspoon baking soda

1 teaspoon baking powder

½ teaspoon kosher salt

1 large Granny Smith apple, cored and diced

1 cup chopped walnuts (optional)

TOPPING

⅓ cup packed light brown sugar

¼ cup all-purpose flour

2 tablespoons unsalted butter, at room temperature

1 teaspoon ground cinnamon

1. To make the bread: Preheat the oven to 350°F. Spray an 8 × 8-inch baking pan with nonstick baking spray.

2. In a stand mixer fitted with the paddle attachment, combine the brown sugar, melted butter, eggs, and vanilla on medium speed until well blended, about 1 minute. Add the applesauce and mix until just combined.

3. In a medium bowl, whisk together the flour, cinnamon, baking soda, baking powder, and salt. Add the dry ingredients to the wet ingredients and beat on low speed until just combined. Using a spatula, fold in the diced apple and chopped walnuts (if using) and mix until combined.

4. To make the topping: In a small bowl, press together the brown sugar, flour, butter, and cinnamon with a fork until crumbly.

5. Pour the batter into the prepared pan and spread evenly. Evenly sprinkle the streusel topping over the top of the batter.

6. Bake until a toothpick inserted in the center comes out clean, 35 to 38 minutes. Let cool for about 15 minutes before serving. Slice and serve warm with softened butter.

7. Store in an airtight container at room temperature for up to 3 days.

Makes 12 servings

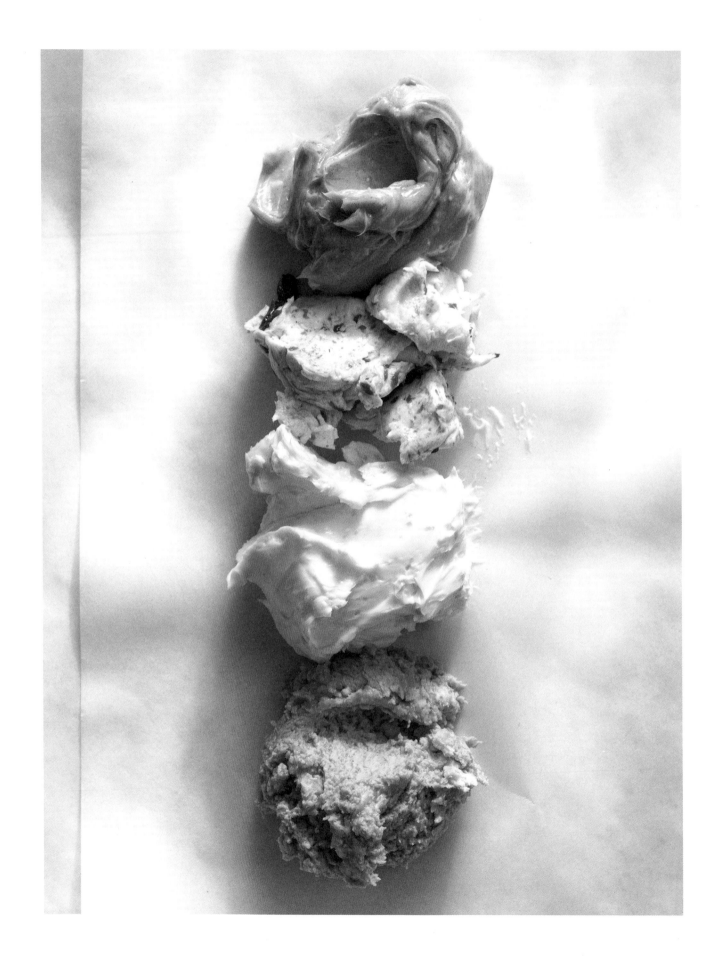

Flavored Butter Flight

SERVED AT MAGNOLIA TABLE WACO · TX

PREP: *20 minutes*   **COOK:** *none*   **COOL:** *none*

I will happily take butter in any form. But ever since our restaurant, Magnolia Table, started serving these butter flights, I've come to see how much curiosity and conversation it generates around the table. That's really what I love about cooking—with a little creativity you can make something as simple as butter feel special. As written, this recipe will make enough for a party, so when you decide how many people you'll be serving, you can scale the amounts accordingly. Or, like me, make a full batch and keep it in the fridge to enjoy all week long!

2 pounds (8 sticks)
   unsalted butter,
   at room temperature

CINNAMON BUTTER

¼ cup powdered sugar

¼ cup honey

2 tablespoons ground
   cinnamon

BERRY CITRUS BUTTER

3 tablespoons four-berry
   preserves (or Strawberry
   Raspberry Preserves,
   page 59)

1 tablespoon fresh orange juice

LEMON BUTTER

Grated zest of 1 large lemon

PUMPKIN BUTTER

½ cup pumpkin puree

⅓ cup powdered sugar

1 tablespoon honey

¾ teaspoon pumpkin pie spice

¾ teaspoon ground cinnamon

¾ teaspoon kosher salt

1. In a stand mixer fitted with the whisk attachment, beat the butter on high until light and fluffy, 7 to 10 minutes.

2. Meanwhile, mix together the ingredients for each flavor of butter in four separate medium bowls.

3. Divide the whipped butter equally among the four bowls. Individually whisk together each flavored butter until well combined.

4. Serve with your favorite rolls or biscuits.

5. Store in an airtight container in the refrigerator for up to 7 days or the freezer for up to 4 months.

Makes approximately 1½ cups of butter per flavor

CHAPTER TWO

Breakfast

FIRST LIGHT, THE START

OF DAY, THIS IS WHERE WE BREAK

OUR FAST, WHERE WE FILL UP

AGAIN, NOURISHMENT FOR BODY

AND SOUL

Bananas Foster Pancakes

PREP: *35 minutes*   **COOK:** *35 minutes*   **COOL:** *none*

BANANA PANCAKES

2 cups all-purpose flour

3 tablespoons granulated sugar

1 tablespoon baking powder

2 teaspoons ground cinnamon

1 teaspoon baking soda

½ teaspoon kosher salt

1½ cups whole milk

2 large eggs, lightly beaten

3 tablespoons unsalted butter, melted, plus 4 teaspoons unsalted butter

1 teaspoon banana extract

1½ bananas, mashed

Flavored whipped cream (page 270), for serving (optional)

BANANAS FOSTER SAUCE

4 tablespoons (½ stick) unsalted butter

½ cup packed light brown sugar

2 teaspoons rum extract or rum

1½ bananas, sliced ¼ inch thick

½ cup chopped toasted pecans

1. To make the banana pancakes: In a medium bowl, whisk together the flour, sugar, baking powder, cinnamon, baking soda, and salt. Add the milk, eggs, 3 tablespoons melted butter, and banana extract, and whisk until the ingredients are thoroughly combined. Fold in the mashed bananas.

2. In a 12-inch nonstick skillet, melt 1 teaspoon of the butter over medium-high heat. Using a ½-cup measure for each pancake, add batter to the pan to make three pancakes at a time, avoiding overcrowding. Cook until the pancakes begin to bubble on top, 1½ to 2 minutes. Flip and cook until the other side is slightly browned, 1 minute. Place the cooked pancakes on a wire rack. Repeat, adding 1 teaspoon of butter to the pan between batches.

3. To make the bananas foster sauce: Wipe out the skillet used for the pancakes, then melt the butter over medium-high heat. Add the brown sugar and stir until the sugar has dissolved and the sauce thickens, about 1½ minutes. Add the rum extract, let simmer for about 30 seconds, then add 1 tablespoon of water. Carefully add the sliced bananas and pecans to the pan. Stir until the bananas and pecans are well coated and warmed through, about 30 seconds.

4. Distribute the pancakes among 4 plates and top with a dollop of whipped cream (if using). Pour the sauce over the pancakes and serve immediately.

5. Store pancakes (without whipped cream and sauce) in a sealed bag in the refrigerator for up to 3 days. Store leftover sauce in an airtight container in the refrigerator for up to 3 days.

TIP: To make Bananas Foster as a dessert: In a 10-inch skillet, melt 4 tablespoons unsalted butter over medium-high heat. Stir in ½ cup packed light brown sugar, 1 teaspoon vanilla, and ½ teaspoon cinnamon. Continue stirring until the sugar has dissolved, about 1½ minutes. Add 2 sliced bananas and ¼ cup chopped toasted pecans to the pan and stir into the sauce until they are fully coated, 15 seconds. Remove from the heat. Pour ¼ cup rum into the pan. Carefully use a lighter to light the rum on fire and gently jiggle the pan while the fire burns out naturally, about 15 seconds. Portion 2 pints of ice cream into 4 bowls and top with the banana mixture. Serve immediately.

Makes 4 servings

Black-and-White Bagels

PREP: *1 hour 35 minutes*   **COOK:** *45 minutes*   **COOL:** *3 to 24 hours*

For each of our kids' tenth birthdays, they get to choose a trip somewhere, just the two of us—the boys with Chip and the girls with me. When Emmie turned ten, she chose New York, simply because she wanted a good bagel. Emmie's go-to is an everything bagel with cream cheese and a fried egg between, and she's managed to get the whole family hooked.

BAGEL DOUGH

1¾ cups warm water (110°F)

One ¼-ounce packet active
    dry yeast

2 tablespoons unsulfured
    molasses

5 cups all-purpose flour

5 teaspoons sugar

2 teaspoons kosher salt

Cooking spray

1 large egg

2 teaspoons baking soda

BLACK-AND-WHITE TOPPING

1 cup white sesame seeds

1 cup black sesame seeds

EVERYTHING TOPPING

¼ cup poppy seeds

2 tablespoons dried
    minced onion

2 tablespoons dried
    minced garlic

2 tablespoons black
    sesame seeds

2 tablespoons white
    sesame seeds

2 tablespoons kosher or sea salt

1. To make the bagel dough: In a medium bowl, stir together the warm water, yeast, and 1 tablespoon of the molasses. Let stand until foamy, about 5 minutes. (If the yeast mixture does not foam, your water was too hot or too cold, or your yeast was expired.)

2. In a stand mixer fitted with the paddle attachment, add 2 cups of the flour and the yeast mixture. Mix on medium-low speed for 2 minutes to combine. Cover the bowl with plastic wrap and let rest at room temperature until the mixture has doubled in volume, 30 minutes.

3. Attach the dough hook to the stand mixer. Add the remaining 3 cups flour, the sugar, and salt and mix on low speed until there is no more dry flour, about 2 minutes. Slowly increase the speed to medium and mix until the dough is firm and moist and the sides of the bowl are clean, 10 minutes.

4. Meanwhile, line two large baking sheets with parchment paper. Spray the paper generously with cooking spray, then loosely cover with plastic wrap.

5. Remove the dough from the bowl and place it onto an unfloured countertop. Immediately portion the dough into 12 equal parts. Roll each portion into a ball by placing it on the counter, doming your hand over the top, and moving in small quick circles until the dough forms a smooth, tight ball. As you finish each one, immediately place it on the prepared baking sheets, spacing the balls 2 inches apart, and cover with the plastic wrap to keep from drying out. Refrigerate the covered baking sheets for 20 minutes.

6. Working one at a time, shape the chilled dough by poking your forefinger and thumb through the center of a dough ball, making a hole. Using a forefinger on either side of the bagel hole, rotate and stretch the dough until the hole is 1½ inches in diameter. Quickly place the shaped dough back under the plastic. Repeat with the remaining dough balls. Let rest in a warm spot in the kitchen for about 20 minutes.

CONTINUED

CONTINUED FROM PAGE 41

7. Perform a "float test": Take one rested, shaped dough and place it in a bowl of cool water. If the dough sinks, place it back on the pan and allow it to rest for another 10 minutes before repeating the test. (There is no need to float-test them all.) If the dough floats, return it to the pan, cover it again, and refrigerate for 2 hours. Bake the bagels anytime within the following 24 hours.

8. Move the refrigerated, shaped dough to the countertop.

9. Position a rack in the middle of the oven and preheat the oven to 425°F. Place wire racks onto the two large baking sheets.

10. Make one of the toppings (unless you want plain bagels): In a small bowl, mix together either the black-and-white or everything topping. In another small bowl, whisk together the egg and 1 tablespoon of water to make an egg wash. Set aside.

11. In a large Dutch oven, bring 4 quarts of water to a boil over high heat. Stir in the remaining 1 tablespoon molasses and the baking soda and reduce the heat to medium-high.

12. If the holes in the dough have nearly closed, use the same two-finger shaping method to open them up again before boiling. Place three raw bagels into the boiling solution and cook, undisturbed, for 1 minute. Flip the bagels and cook for 1 more minute before transferring to one of the prepared baking sheets. Repeat with the next three bagels.

13. Using a pastry brush, lightly brush the tops of the first six bagels with egg wash while they are still hot. If you want plain bagels, continue to the next step. If you want black-and-white or everything bagels, dip the bagels into the desired topping, then return them to the wire rack, flavored side up. Allow the bagels to cool for 2 minutes.

14. Bake the bagels for 9 minutes. Rotate the pan 180 degrees and continue to bake until the bagels appear dark, another 9 minutes.

15. Meanwhile, boil the remaining bagels in sets of three and place on the second prepared rack. When you remove the first batch from the oven, bake the second batch.

16. Let cool completely on the wire racks before cutting into them, at least 30 minutes.

17. Store in an airtight container at room temperature for up to 3 days.

Makes 12 bagels

Daybreak Juice

PREP: *5 minutes*   **COOK:** *none*   **COOL:** *none*

While I'm not a fan of straight carrot juice, the simple combination of carrot and apple with the balancing brightness of lemon transforms it into a drink I crave at the start of the day. I reach for Granny Smith or Honeycrisp apples—varieties with a tart taste.

6 medium carrots, trimmed
  (not peeled)

2 Honeycrisp apples, cored
  and sliced (not peeled)

1 lemon, peeled

1. Place the carrots, apples, and lemon in a juicer and process according to the manufacturer's instructions. Stir until well combined. Serve promptly.

2. Store in a jar in the refrigerator for 1 day.

Makes 2 servings

Kick-Start Juice

PREP: *5 minutes*   **COOK:** *none*   **COOL:** *none*

With spinach as an anchor in this recipe, you just know you are getting the good stuff—iron, potassium, and vitamin A, to name a few. Whenever I eat breakfast at Magnolia Table, it's my favorite drink to order. True to its name, this juice is a great way to kick-start my day.

2 cups fresh spinach

1 cup pineapple chunks

5 celery stalks, including
  leaves

½ Honeycrisp apple, cored
  and sliced (not peeled)

1 lime, peeled

½ jalapeño, seeded (optional)

1. Place the spinach, pineapple, celery, apple, lime, and jalapeño (if using) in a juicer and process according to the manufacturer's instructions. Stir until well combined. Serve promptly.

2. Store in a jar in the refrigerator for 1 day.

Makes 2 servings

Sticky Bun Casserole

PREP: *30 minutes*   **COOK:** *40 minutes*   **COOL:** *30 minutes*

DOUGH

¼ cup warm water (110°F)

1 tablespoon active dry yeast

1 tablespoon granulated sugar

4 cups all-purpose flour,
plus more for dusting

1 cup warm whole milk (110°F)

½ cup canola oil

2 large eggs

1 teaspoon kosher salt

Cooking spray

TOPPING

¾ cup packed light brown sugar

4 tablespoons (½ stick)
unsalted butter

3 tablespoons honey

1 tablespoon light corn syrup

FILLING

½ cup granulated sugar

½ cup packed light brown sugar

2 teaspoons ground cinnamon

5 tablespoons unsalted butter,
melted

GLAZE

1 cup powdered sugar

6 tablespoons heavy cream

2 teaspoons pure vanilla
extract

½ cup chopped pecans
(optional)

1. To make the dough: In a small bowl, stir together the warm water, yeast, and sugar. Let stand until foamy, about 5 minutes.

2. In a stand mixer fitted with the dough hook attachment, combine the flour, warm milk, oil, eggs, and salt. With the mixer on low speed, add the yeast mixture. As the dough comes together, slowly increase the speed to medium-high and let mix for 5 minutes. (The dough will be sticky.)

3. Spray a large bowl with cooking spray. Shape the dough into a ball and place it in the bowl. Cover with a towel and let rise in a warm spot until doubled in size, about 90 minutes.

4. To make the topping: In a medium saucepan, combine the brown sugar, butter, honey, and corn syrup over medium-low heat. Cook, stirring occasionally, until the butter has melted and the sugar has dissolved, about 5 minutes. Generously spray a 9 × 13-inch baking pan with cooking spray. Pour the topping into the bottom of the prepared pan.

5. To make the filling: In a small bowl, stir together both sugars and the cinnamon.

6. Punch down the dough to release the air. On a lightly floured surface, using a rolling pin, roll out the dough into a 12 × 18-inch rectangle. Using a pastry brush, brush the dough with the melted butter and sprinkle with the cinnamon-sugar mixture, leaving a ½-inch border.

7. Beginning on the long end, roll the dough into a log and pinch the seam together to seal. Position the log seam side down. Cut the log into 2-inch rolls, then turn each roll face up and cut into quarters. Evenly place the quartered pieces in the bottom of the pan, filling in any empty spots. Cover the pan loosely with a towel and let rest at room temperature for 25 minutes.

8. Preheat the oven to 350°F.

9. Bake until the surface is deeply golden brown, 35 to 40 minutes. Let cool slightly, about 7 minutes, then flip the casserole out onto a large baking sheet or serving platter. Let cool for another 20 minutes.

10. To make the glaze: In a medium bowl, whisk together the powdered sugar, heavy cream, and vanilla until smooth. Evenly pour over the top of the casserole and sprinkle with pecans (if using).

11. Store in an airtight container at room temperature for up to 2 days.

Makes 12 servings

Old-Fashioned Glazed Cake Donuts

PREP: *20 minutes*   **COOK:** *20 minutes*   **COOL:** *1 hour 10 minutes*

When we first opened Magnolia, Chip and I would drive to trade days in Canton, Texas, looking for unique pieces to sell at the shop. One of the food trucks there sold the most delicious cake donuts that just melted in your mouth. This recipe is a nod to those early days when Magnolia was just beginning.

DONUTS

2½ cups cake flour, plus more for dusting

2 teaspoons baking powder

1 teaspoon ground nutmeg

1 teaspoon kosher salt

3 tablespoons unsalted butter, at room temperature

¼ cup granulated sugar

¼ cup packed light brown sugar

½ cup sour cream

2 large egg yolks

1 teaspoon pure vanilla extract

¼ cup whole-milk buttermilk

Vegetable oil, for deep-frying

GLAZE

2 cups powdered sugar

½ cup plus 2 tablespoons half-and-half

1 tablespoon light corn syrup

½ teaspoon pure vanilla extract

¼ teaspoon kosher salt

1. To make the donuts: In a medium bowl, sift together the cake flour, baking powder, nutmeg, and salt.

2. In a stand mixer fitted with the paddle attachment, combine the butter, sugar, and brown sugar on medium speed until smooth, about 3 minutes. Reduce the speed to low and slowly add the sour cream, egg yolks, and vanilla. With the mixer still on low, slowly add the flour mixture until just combined. Scrape down the sides and bottom of the bowl with a spatula. Add the buttermilk and mix on low until incorporated. Remove the paddle, cover the bowl with plastic wrap, and refrigerate for 1 hour. The dough should be slightly tacky to the touch.

3. Pour 1½ to 2 inches of oil in a large high-sided cast-iron pan or Dutch oven. Have ready a wire rack to use for draining. Heat the oil over medium heat until it reaches 350°F on a deep-fry thermometer. Line a baking sheet with parchment paper.

4. On a lightly floured surface, using a rolling pin, roll the dough ¼ inch thick. Using a donut cutter (or a 3-inch round cutter and 1-inch round cutter for the holes), cut out donuts and holes and place on the prepared baking sheet. Reroll scraps to cut out additional donuts. Refrigerate the cut donuts and holes until the oil is hot.

5. Carefully place a few donuts at a time in the oil and fry, flipping once, until deep golden brown all over, about 1 minute on each side for the donuts and 30 seconds for the donut holes. Transfer to the rack while frying the remaining donuts. Let cool for 5 minutes before glazing.

6. To make the glaze: In a medium bowl, whisk together the powdered sugar, half-and-half, corn syrup, vanilla, and salt. (For a thinner glaze, dilute with water until you reach the desired consistency.)

7. Dip the tops of each donut into the glaze. Place the donuts glaze side up on the wire rack to set, about 5 minutes.

8. Store leftovers in an airtight container at room temperature for up to 2 days.

Makes 24 donuts

Apple Fritters

PREP: *25 minutes*   **COOK:** *20 minutes*   **COOL:** *20 minutes*

My dad and I are alike in many ways, one being that we both have a sweet tooth. When I was younger, I loved whipping up my take on his favorite desserts. To this day, I get so much joy from being able to crack the code on a cookie he loves, or in this case, an apple fritter just like the one he orders at his favorite donut shop.

FRITTERS

2 cups all-purpose flour

⅓ cup granulated sugar

1 tablespoon baking powder

1 teaspoon ground cinnamon

½ teaspoon ground nutmeg

¼ teaspoon kosher salt

¾ cup whole-milk buttermilk, at room temperature

2 large eggs, at room temperature

3 tablespoons unsalted butter, melted

2 teaspoons pure vanilla extract

1 pound Granny Smith apples, cored, peeled, and cut into ¼-inch dice (about 2½ cups)

Vegetable oil, for deep-frying

GLAZE

1½ cups powdered sugar

½ cup heavy cream, plus more as needed

1 teaspoon pure vanilla extract

1. To make the fritters: In a medium bowl, whisk together the flour, granulated sugar, baking powder, cinnamon, nutmeg, and salt. In a large bowl, whisk together the buttermilk, eggs, melted butter, and vanilla. Slowly stir the flour mixture, ½ cup at a time, into the buttermilk mixture until all ingredients are well mixed. Using a spatula, fold in the apples. Let the batter sit at room temperature, uncovered, while the oil heats up.

2. Pour 1½ to 2 inches of oil into a large high-sided cast-iron skillet or Dutch oven. Have ready a baking sheet lined with paper towels to use for draining. Heat the oil over medium until it reaches 335°F to 350°F on a deep-fry thermometer.

3. Scoop ¼ cup of the batter and carefully place in the hot oil. Repeat to cook three fritters at a time. Fry, flipping as needed, until golden brown and crispy all over and a knife inserted into the center of the fritter comes out clean, 3 to 4 minutes. Remove the fritters using tongs or a slotted spoon, and place on the prepared baking sheet. Repeat with the remaining batter. Let cool for about 10 minutes before glazing.

4. To make the glaze: In a medium bowl, whisk together the powdered sugar, cream, and vanilla. (If the glaze is too thick, add more cream, a teaspoon at a time, until you reach the desired consistency.)

5. Dip the tops of each fritter into the glaze. Place the fritters glaze side up on a wire rack to set, about 10 minutes.

6. Store in an airtight container at room temperature for up to 2 days.

NOTE: Apple fritters are also delicious dusted with cinnamon sugar instead of this glaze. In a large bowl, stir together 1½ cups sugar and 4 teaspoons cinnamon, then toss in the warm fritters to coat all sides.

Makes 16 fritters

Dutch Baby

PREP: *20 minutes*   **COOK:** *25 minutes*   **COOL:** *none*

I like to describe a Dutch baby as an elevated pancake—same basic ingredients, just made with a little more intention. I prefer to keep the toppings simple—a light dust of powdered sugar or a squeeze of lemon usually does the trick.

½ cup all-purpose flour

½ cup whole milk

3 large eggs

1 tablespoon granulated sugar

2 teaspoons pure vanilla extract

½ teaspoon kosher salt

¼ teaspoon ground nutmeg

3 tablespoons unsalted butter

⅓ cup powdered sugar

1 small lemon, thinly sliced

¾ cup pure maple syrup, for serving

1. Preheat the oven to 425°F. Place a 10-inch oven-safe skillet into the oven to preheat as well.

2. In a medium bowl, whisk together the flour, milk, eggs, granulated sugar, vanilla, salt, and nutmeg until the batter is well combined and smooth. Let the batter rest for 5 minutes to allow the flour to absorb the liquid.

3. Carefully remove the preheated skillet from the oven and add the butter, moving it around to coat the pan while it melts. Once the butter has fully melted, pour the batter in the pan, and immediately place the pan in the oven.

4. Bake until the sides are dark golden brown and the center is fully cooked, 22 minutes. (Residual melted butter on top is okay.) If the edges are getting too dark before the center is cooked, gently cover the Dutch baby with foil and continue baking.

5. Serve immediately. Sift the powdered sugar over the Dutch baby. Place the lemon slices on top, cut into slices, and serve immediately with maple syrup.

TIP: Lemon can be substituted with any seasonal fruit or your pancake topping of choice.

Makes 6 to 8 servings

Lemon and Raspberry Muffins

PREP: *20 minutes*   **COOK:** *25 minutes*   **COOL:** *15 minutes*

Muffins might be so dependable—and accessible—that they can get overlooked for being basic or even boring. But these raspberry and buttermilk muffins are anything but ordinary. The combination of flavors is reminiscent of cheesecake, with just enough lemon to keep it bright and light—perfect for breakfast or an afternoon snack.

2½ cups all-purpose flour

1 tablespoon baking powder

½ teaspoon kosher salt

1 cup granulated sugar

8 tablespoons (1 stick)
   unsalted butter, melted

2 large eggs

1 teaspoon pure vanilla extract

1 cup whole-milk buttermilk

¼ cup fresh lemon juice

1 tablespoon freshly grated
   lemon zest

1½ cups fresh raspberries

½ cup sugar crystals
   or turbinado sugar

1. Preheat the oven to 375°F. Line muffin tins with cupcake liners.

2. In a medium bowl, stir together the flour, baking powder, and salt. In a large bowl, whisk together the granulated sugar, melted butter, eggs, and vanilla. In a small bowl, stir together the buttermilk, lemon juice, and lemon zest.

3. Add half the flour mixture to the sugar mixture, then add the buttermilk mixture, then add the remaining flour mixture, stirring after each addition until combined.

4. Using a fork, gently smash the raspberries on a cutting board, leaving some larger pieces. Using a spatula, fold the raspberries into the batter.

5. Scoop ¼ cup of batter into each cup of the prepared muffin tins. Sprinkle each muffin with about 1 teaspoon of the sugar crystals.

6. Bake until the muffins are lightly golden brown and a toothpick inserted into the center comes out clean, 21 to 23 minutes. Carefully remove from the muffin tin, let cool on a wire rack for about 15 minutes before serving. Repeat as needed with the rest of the batter and sugar crystals.

7. Store in an airtight container at room temperature for up to 4 days.

Makes 20 muffins

Chocolate Chocolate Chip Muffins

PREP: *25 minutes*   **COOK:** *20 minutes*   **COOL:** *15 minutes*

Some mornings call for fresh fruit or a bowl of oatmeal, but other mornings, I'll be honest, all I want is chocolate cake. I'm making this a muffin recipe, mostly because that makes me feel better about eating cake for breakfast, though these muffins are good any time of day. Usually after the first bite I don't care what we're calling it, it's just delicious. During the holidays, try topping them with Peppermint Whipped Cream (page 270).

1¾ cups all-purpose flour

⅔ cup unsweetened cocoa powder

2 teaspoons baking powder

1 teaspoon baking soda

1 teaspoon kosher salt

1¼ cups buttermilk

1 teaspoon instant coffee crystals

8 tablespoons (1 stick) unsalted butter, melted

1 cup granulated sugar

3 large eggs

2 teaspoons pure vanilla extract

1 cup semisweet chocolate chips

1 tablespoon white sanding sugar, sugar crystals, or turbinado sugar

1. Preheat the oven to 375°F. Line muffin tins with cupcake liners.

2. In a medium bowl, whisk together the flour, cocoa, baking powder, baking soda, and salt. In a small bowl, stir together the buttermilk and instant coffee crystals until the crystals dissolve.

3. In a stand mixer fitted with the paddle attachment, combine the melted butter and sugar on medium-high speed until well incorporated, about 1 minute. Reduce the speed to medium-low and add the eggs, one at a time, beating well after each addition.

4. Using a spatula, scrape down the sides and bottom of the bowl. Add the vanilla and the buttermilk mixture and mix on medium-low speed until combined. Reduce the speed to low and slowly add the flour mixture, mixing until well incorporated, then mix in the chocolate chips.

5. Scoop approximately ⅓ cup of batter into each cup of the prepared muffin tins and sprinkle with the sanding sugar.

6. Bake until a toothpick inserted into the center of a muffin comes out clean, 14 to 16 minutes. Let cool in the pans for 5 minutes, then turn out to cool on a wire rack for an additional 10 minutes. Repeat as needed with the rest of the batter and sanding sugar.

Makes 22 muffins

Honey Butter Layered Biscuit Bites

PREP: *30 minutes*   **COOK:** *15 minutes*   **COOL:** *50 minutes*

I've always believed butter is a magic ingredient, so it feels fitting that the secret to really good, light, and layered biscuits happens to be butter. Before I make this recipe, I cut cold butter into small pieces, about the size of a pea. This ensures that when the biscuits are baking, the butter melts and releases steam, which creates small pockets of air. Those pockets of air are what make the biscuits airy and flaky. It's impossible to eat only one.

BISCUITS

2½ cups all-purpose flour, plus more for rolling

1 tablespoon baking powder

1 teaspoon kosher salt

½ teaspoon baking soda

8 tablespoons (1 stick) unsalted butter, very cold, cubed

¾ cup cold buttermilk

¼ cup honey

1 large egg yolk

HONEY BUTTER

1 cup (2 sticks) unsalted butter, at room temperature

2 tablespoons honey

¼ teaspoon kosher salt

Small-Batch Preserves (page 59), for serving

1. To make the biscuits: Preheat the oven to 425°F. Line a baking sheet with parchment paper.

2. In a large bowl, combine the flour, baking powder, salt, and baking soda. Add the cold butter cubes and toss to coat. Using a pastry blender or your fingers, cut in the butter until it resembles coarse crumbs.

3. With a wooden spoon, slowly work in the buttermilk, honey, and egg yolk until a slightly sticky dough is formed. Turn the dough onto a lightly floured work surface and sprinkle with a little more flour.

4. Using a floured rolling pin, roll the dough into a ½-inch-thick rectangle. Starting from one short end, fold one-third of the dough upon itself, then repeat on the other end, like folding a letter. Repeat, rolling and folding the dough two more times. Wrap the dough in plastic wrap and refrigerate for about 15 minutes.

5. Roll the chilled dough about ¾ inch thick. Use a 2-inch round cookie cutter to cut out biscuits. Arrange them 1 inch apart on the prepared baking sheet. Gather and reroll the scraps once to cut out additional biscuits. (Leftover scraps can be baked as is or discarded.) Refrigerate the tray of biscuits for at least 30 minutes.

6. Bake until the tops are golden brown, 10 to 12 minutes. Allow the biscuits to cool for 5 minutes.

7. To make the honey butter: In a stand mixer fitted with the whisk attachment, whip the butter on medium-high speed until it is light and fluffy, about 2 minutes. Slowly drizzle in the honey and salt. Continue whisking until the ingredients are well combined, about 1 minute.

8. Serve the warm biscuits with honey butter or preserves on the side.

9. Store the biscuits in a sealed bag at room temperature for up to 2 days. Store the butter in an airtight container in the refrigerator.

Makes 14 to 16 biscuits

Small-Batch Preserves

PREP: *5 minutes*　　**COOK:** *20 minutes*　　**COOL:** *2 hours 15 minutes*

Whenever I spend an afternoon making preserves, my mind goes to a friend whose grandmother had a huge garden and made jars and jars of preserves for her grandchildren every season. The year her grandmother passed away, as my friend ate the preserves her grandmother had gifted her, she both mourned and savored memories of the woman who'd meant so much. And when she got to the last jar of her grandmother's preserves, she couldn't bring herself to open it. To this day, that jar sits in her pantry. I think this story moves me so much because it's the essence of how meaningful cooking can be. In what she made for others, my friend's grandmother defined a legacy, and every jar was a gift much greater than she probably knew. I don't assume that every jar of my preserves will mean quite that much to anyone, but I do love the idea that down the line, next week or perhaps next month, someone will open it and find joy in all the ingredients—fruit, love, and intention—I put in it today.

STRAWBERRY RASPBERRY

2 cups diced fresh strawberries

1 cup fresh raspberries

½ cup sugar

1 teaspoon fresh lemon juice

LEMON BLUEBERRY

3 cups fresh blueberries

½ cup sugar

1 teaspoon fresh lemon juice

1 teaspoon freshly grated lemon zest

1. To make either flavor: In a small saucepan, combine the fruit and sugar over medium heat. Cook, stirring occasionally, until the fruit begins to break down and release its juice, 6 to 7 minutes. Bring to a boil over medium-high heat. Cook, stirring occasionally, until the mixture thickens, 10 minutes.

2. Pour in the lemon juice. Reduce the heat to low and, using the back of a wooden spoon, crush the fruit until it reaches the desired consistency, 1 to 2 minutes. Remove from the heat and let the preserves rest in the pan for 15 minutes. For blueberry preserves, stir in the lemon zest.

3. Pour the preserves into a 2-cup jar with a lid and let cool on the counter for 1 hour. Refrigerate for 1 hour to set.

4. Serve with warm biscuits or muffins.

5. Store in a jar in the refrigerator for up to 3 months.

TIP: This also makes a delicious chicken marinade.

Makes about 1½ cups per flavor

Hash Brown Casserole

PREP: *20 minutes*   **COOK:** *1 hour 10 minutes*   **COOL:** *5 minutes*

I love the versatility of this recipe. It works well if I'm serving a big breakfast for a crowd, because it's so easy to throw together. I've also found it can be a great dish to serve for dinner alongside a steak. Another plus is that you can make this casserole ahead of time and freeze it, which I find especially nice around the holidays. When life gets busy, I like knowing I have a satisfying dish I can pull out of the freezer and serve alongside steak or eggs.

6 tablespoons unsalted butter

40 ounces frozen shredded hash browns, thawed

2 cups freshly shredded white sharp Cheddar cheese (about 8 ounces)

1 cup freshly shredded yellow sharp Cheddar cheese (about 4 ounces)

⅓ cup all-purpose flour

2 cups whole milk

1 teaspoon kosher salt

1½ teaspoons freshly cracked black pepper

1 teaspoon onion powder

2 cups sour cream

2 tablespoons sliced green onions (green part only)

1. Preheat the oven to 350°F. Melt 2 tablespoons of the butter. Grease a 9 × 13-inch baking dish with the melted butter.

2. Place the thawed hash browns on a clean kitchen towel and squeeze out as much liquid as possible.

3. In a large bowl, mix together the hash browns, 1 cup of the white Cheddar, and the yellow Cheddar until well combined.

4. In a medium saucepan, melt the remaining 4 tablespoons butter over medium heat. Add the flour and cook, stirring constantly, for 1 minute. Add the milk, salt, pepper, and onion powder and whisk constantly to dissolve any lumps, until thickened, 2 to 3 minutes. Add the sour cream and cook, stirring, for another 3 minutes.

5. Pour the sour cream mixture into the potato mixture and stir until well combined.

6. Add the potato mixture to the prepared baking dish and spread evenly. Cover with foil, leaving one corner loose to vent.

7. Bake for 45 minutes. Carefully remove the foil, sprinkle the remaining cup of white Cheddar over the top, and bake for an additional 15 minutes, allowing the top to bubble and brown. Broil for 1 to 3 minutes if you prefer a slightly browner top.

8. Top with the green onions. Let cool for 5 minutes before serving.

9. Store in an airtight container in the refrigerator for up to 5 days.

Makes 8 to 10 servings

Breakfast Puff Pastry Squares

PREP: *20 minutes*   **COOK:** *30 minutes*   **COOL:** *5 minutes*

¾ pound ground breakfast sausage

3 large eggs

One 17.3-ounce box puff pastry (2 sheets)

½ cup heavy cream

1½ teaspoons Dijon mustard

1 teaspoon garlic powder

½ teaspoon kosher salt

½ teaspoon freshly cracked black pepper

1 cup shredded Gruyère cheese (about 4 ounces)

Chopped fresh parsley or sliced green onions, for garnish (optional)

1. Preheat the oven to 400°F.

2. In a medium skillet, cook the sausage over medium-high heat, stirring often to break into small crumbles, until cooked through and browned, about 8 minutes. Drain the grease from the meat and set the cooked sausage aside to cool.

3. Make the egg wash by mixing 1 egg and 1 tablespoon water in a small bowl. Place one sheet of puff pastry on a clean, flat surface. Using a pastry brush, lightly brush the entire top with egg wash.

4. Place the second sheet of puff pastry next to the first sheet. Using a 1½- or 2-inch round cookie cutter, cut out 9 evenly spaced circles, in three rows of three. Place the sheet with the cutouts on top of the first sheet and press gently to seal. Using a knife, cut the pastry into 9 even squares, each with a single round cutout centered on its top layer. Transfer the squares and the circles to a nonstick baking sheet.

5. Brush the entire top of the squares with the egg wash. Bake until the pastry is puffed and lightly golden, 12 to 14 minutes.

6. Meanwhile, in a medium bowl, whisk together the remaining 2 eggs, cream, mustard, garlic powder, salt, and pepper. Stir in the sausage and ½ cup of the Gruyère and mix well to combine.

7. Carefully remove the pastries from the oven and reduce the oven temperature to 350°F. Using the back of a measuring cup, gently press down the bottom layer of pastry that has risen into the cut-out holes, to create space for the filling.

8. Distribute the sausage mixture equally among the holes, being careful not to overfill, and place the baking sheet back into the oven.

9. Bake until the mixture in the cups is set, about 15 minutes. The circles may cook faster than the squares, as they aren't filled.

10. Carefully top the pastries with the remaining ½ cup Gruyère cheese. Let cool for 5 minutes. Garnish with fresh parsley or sliced green onions, if you like, and serve warm.

11. Store in an airtight container in the refrigerator for up to 2 days. Reheat in a toaster oven (not the microwave) at 350°F until warm and toasty, about 4 minutes.

TIP: The plain circular cutouts are delicious with jam.

Makes 9 servings

Garden Vegetable Quiche

PREP: *25 minutes*   **COOK:** *50 minutes*   **COOL:** *1 hour 20 minutes*

I love the idea of letting a quiche cool after baking, but my secret is that I can never wait. I can't tell you how many times my kids have wandered into the kitchen because they can smell something delicious, only to find me eating a piping-hot slice of quiche over the stove. Next to that straight-from-the-oven slice, my second favorite way to eat a quiche is the day after it's baked, when all the ingredients have set. A quiche will rarely make it that long in our house, but when it does, it makes for a delicious lunch.

1 recipe pie crust (page 67, made through step 2) or 1 store-bought raw pie crust

2 tablespoons olive oil

1 cup frozen shredded hash browns

1 cup sliced mushrooms

½ cup diced red bell pepper

½ cup roughly chopped asparagus

¼ cup diced white onion

2 garlic cloves, minced

1 teaspoon freshly cracked black pepper

½ teaspoon kosher salt

5 large eggs

1 cup heavy cream

3 ounces Gruyère cheese, shredded (about ¾ cup)

3 ounces Asiago cheese, shredded (about ¾ cup)

1. Lightly dust the counter with flour. Using a rolling pin, roll the dough out to an 11½-inch round. Transfer the dough to a 9-inch pie plate and carefully ease it into the edges. Trim the dough to an even ½-inch overhang all around and fold it under itself on top of the rim. Using your fingers, carefully crimp the edges of the pie dough. Refrigerate for 1 hour.

2. Preheat the oven to 350°F.

3. In a large skillet, heat the olive oil over medium-high heat. Spread the hash browns evenly in the pan, stirring them every few minutes, until golden and crispy, about 10 minutes. Add the mushrooms, bell pepper, asparagus, onion, and garlic and cook, stirring occasionally, until the vegetables have slightly softened, about 4 minutes. Season the vegetables with pepper and salt and let cool for 10 minutes.

4. In a large bowl, whisk together the eggs and cream. Add the cheeses and cooled vegetables, stir to combine, then pour into the chilled pie shell. Place the pie on a baking sheet.

5. Bake until a toothpick inserted in the center comes out clean, 35 to 40 minutes. Let cool for 10 minutes before serving.

6. Store in an airtight container in the refrigerator for up to 3 days.

Makes 6 servings

Broccoli Cheddar Quiche

PREP: *30 minutes*   **COOK:** *45 minutes*   **COOL:** *2 hours 10 minutes*

I find quiches to be a great way to experiment with different herbs, meats, and vegetables, and this recipe is one of my favorite ways to get broccoli on the table. There's nothing complicated about the ingredients, and the combination of the crumbly crust, crisp vegetables, and creamy cheese make it well-loved in our family. Even though quiches are quick to put together, I make sure to take my time thoroughly whisking the eggs and cream so that they are more airy when they bake.

PIE CRUST

1¼ cups all-purpose flour, plus more for rolling

1 teaspoon kosher salt

8 tablespoons (1 stick) unsalted butter, chilled, cut into ½-inch cubes

¼ cup ice-cold water

BROCCOLI CHEDDAR FILLING

4 large eggs

1 cup heavy cream

One 5.2-ounce package Boursin Cheese Garlic & Fine Herbs, crumbled

1 teaspoon kosher salt

½ teaspoon ground white pepper

2 cups roughly chopped broccoli florets

1 cup shredded Cheddar cheese (about 4 ounces)

1. To make the pie crust: In a large bowl, whisk together the flour and salt. Scatter in the butter and use a pastry blender or your fingers to cut the butter into the flour until the biggest pieces are the size of small peas. Gradually drizzle the water on top, using a spatula or your hands to stir until the dough comes together. The dough should not be watery or wet.

2. Shape the dough into a flattened ball. Wrap it tightly in plastic wrap and refrigerate for at least 1 hour or up to overnight.

3. Lightly dust the counter with flour and roll the dough into an 11½-inch round. Transfer the dough to a 9-inch pie plate and carefully ease it into the edges. Trim the dough to an even ½-inch overhang all around and fold it under itself on top of the rim. Using your fingers, carefully crimp the edges of the pie dough. Refrigerate for 1 hour.

4. To make the filling: Preheat the oven to 375°F.

5. In a large bowl, whisk together the eggs, cream, Boursin, salt, and pepper until well combined and smooth. Add the broccoli and Cheddar and stir until evenly incorporated. Pour the mixture into the chilled pie shell.

6. Bake until a toothpick inserted into the center of the quiche comes out clean, 45 minutes. Let cool for 10 minutes before serving.

7. Store in an airtight container in the refrigerator for up to 3 days.

Makes 6 servings

Berry Blast Smoothie

PREP: *5 minutes*   **COOK:** *none*   **COOL:** *none*

This is a great breakfast smoothie, but at our house we prefer it as an afternoon snack. Once you get the base right, you can set the kids free to add their favorite flavors to the mix. It's such a fun thing to see how everyone customizes their own.

1 cup frozen strawberries

1 cup frozen blueberries

1 cup whole milk or almond milk, plus an additional ½ cup if needed

⅔ cup vanilla whole-milk Greek yogurt

⅓ cup rolled oats

1 tablespoon honey

Add the strawberries, blueberries, milk, yogurt, oats, and honey to a blender and blend for 2 minutes. Add an additional ½ cup of milk if you prefer a thinner smoothie. Serve promptly.

Makes 4 servings

Mikey's PB Banana Smoothie

PREP: *5 minutes*   **COOK:** *none*   **COOL:** *none*

My younger sister, Mikey, and I are always sharing tips about eating healthier and treating our bodies better. This is her go-to smoothie and has become my favorite as well. It's loaded with fiber and protein, but the peanut butter makes it feel like a treat.

1 cup unsweetened almond milk

2 tablespoons natural peanut butter

1 tablespoon unsweetened cocoa powder

5 pitted dates

1 banana, cut into 2-inch pieces and frozen

Add the almond milk, peanut butter, cocoa powder, dates, frozen banana, and a handful of ice cubes to a blender and blend until well combined, 2 to 3 minutes. Serve promptly.

TIP: Mix in chia or hemp seeds for a nutritional punch.

Makes 2 servings

Cold Brew

WITH SWEET CREAM FOAM

PREP: *5 minutes* **COOK:** *none* **COOL:** *12 hours*

In the mornings I usually prefer a cup of hot coffee, but this cold brew offers a nice change in routine, especially during a warm Texas summer. The recipe itself yields a generous amount, but I wouldn't recommend halving it. Every time I make a smaller batch because I think I'm the only one who will be drinking it, people magically appear and want a cup or two.

COLD BREW

1½ cups whole coffee beans

SWEET CREAM FOAM (PER SERVING)

2 tablespoons heavy cream

2 tablespoons whole milk

2 teaspoons vanilla syrup

1. To make the cold brew: Coarsely grind the coffee beans and transfer to a 1.5-liter jar with a lid. Add 6 cups tap water and put the lid on. Gently shake the jar to make sure the grounds are thoroughly saturated. Allow the coffee to steep in the refrigerator for at least 12 hours.

2. Line a strainer with cheesecloth and place inside a large bowl. Pour the coffee through the cheesecloth and discard the coffee grounds. Rinse out the jar, then return the cold brew to the jar.

3. To make the sweet cream foam for a single serving: Add the cream, milk, and vanilla syrup to a small mug. Using a handheld frother, whip the milk mixture until frothy, 20 to 30 seconds. Pour immediately over a glass of cold brew.

4. Cold brew can be stored in the refrigerator for up to 1 week. Make the foam fresh for each serving.

Makes 6 servings of cold brew, 1 serving of foam

White Chocolate and Cranberry Biscotti

PREP: *30 minutes*   **COOK**: *40 minutes*   **COOL**: *1 hour*

1 cup sugar

7 tablespoons unsalted butter, at room temperature

1 teaspoon almond extract

3 large eggs

3 cups all-purpose flour

4 teaspoons baking powder

14 ounces white chocolate chips

¾ cup dried cranberries

1½ tablespoons coconut oil

1. Preheat the oven to 350°F. Line a baking sheet with parchment paper.

2. In a stand mixer fitted with the paddle attachment, beat the sugar and butter on medium-high speed, until light and fluffy, about 3 minutes.

3. With the speed on medium, add the almond extract. Reduce the speed to low and add the eggs, one at a time, and mix until well incorporated.

4. In a medium bowl, sift together the flour and baking powder. With the speed on low, add the flour mixture to the butter mixture and mix until well incorporated. Add in ½ cup (3 ounces) of the white chocolate chips and the dried cranberries and mix until incorporated.

5. Divide the dough in half and roll each portion into a log. Pat each log into a rectangle, about 9 × 3 inches and 1 inch thick. Place the rectangles on the prepared baking sheet, spacing them far apart.

6. Bake until light blond and slightly golden around the edges, about 25 minutes. Let cool on the pan for about 20 minutes.

7. Transfer the rectangles to a cutting board. Using a very sharp serrated knife, cut each rectangle diagonally into about eight 1-inch-thick slices. Place each slice back on the baking sheet cut side down. Bake until golden brown, 12 to 15 more minutes.

8. Carefully transfer the biscotti to a wire rack to cool for 25 minutes. Keep the pan lined with parchment paper.

9. To make the white chocolate dip: In a medium microwave-safe bowl, add the coconut oil and remaining 11 ounces white chocolate chips. (For a thicker dip, omit the coconut oil.) Microwave on high in 30-second intervals, stirring thoroughly between intervals, until the mixture is completely melted and smooth.

10. Dip one end of each biscotto in the white chocolate dip, gently shake off any excess, and place on the prepared baking sheet. Refrigerate the pan to set the chocolate, about 15 minutes.

11. Store in an airtight container in a cool place for up to 5 days.

Makes 16 biscotti

"Blueberry Muffin" Overnight Oats

SERVED AT
MAGNOLIA PRESS
WACO · TX

PREP: *10 minutes*   **COOK:** *5 minutes*   **COOL:** *6 hours*

When I first learned the trick to overnight oats, it felt like I'd uncovered a best-kept secret. Pulling together a few ingredients and letting the flavors come together while I sleep is the easiest way I know how to gift myself time in the mornings. I like to make the streusel ahead and keep it stored in the pantry. When the oats are ready, all we have to do is add the topping and go.

OVERNIGHT OATS

½ cup rolled oats

½ cup unsweetened vanilla almond milk

1 teaspoon honey

1 teaspoon chia seeds

¼ teaspoon pure vanilla extract

½ cup blueberries, fresh or frozen

2 tablespoons vanilla whole-milk Greek yogurt

STREUSEL TOPPING

2 tablespoons plus 1 teaspoon light brown sugar

1 tablespoon plus 1 teaspoon all-purpose flour

1 tablespoon cold unsalted butter, cubed

⅛ teaspoon ground cinnamon

Kosher salt

1. To make the overnight oats: In a ¼-liter WECK jar (or any other short 2-cup jar with a lid), stir together the oats, almond milk, honey, chia seeds, and vanilla. Slightly mash ¼ cup of the blueberries and add to the oat mixture along with the Greek yogurt. Stir well to combine.

2. Cover and refrigerate for at least 6 hours or overnight.

3. To make the streusel topping: Preheat the oven to 350°F. Line a small baking sheet with parchment paper.

4. In a small bowl, use your fingers to rub together the brown sugar, flour, butter, cinnamon, and a pinch of salt until the butter is coated and the mixture resembles coarse crumbs. Spread out the crumbs on the prepared baking sheet and bake for 5 minutes. Let cool.

5. When ready to eat, stir the oats, then top with the streusel and remaining ¼ cup blueberries.

6. Store oats in an airtight container in the refrigerator for up to 5 days. Streusel can be made ahead of time and stored in an airtight container at room temperature.

Makes 1 serving

Chunky Blackberry Applesauce

PREP: *15 minutes*   **COOK:** *25 minutes*   **COOL:** *1 hour*

We've jokingly referred to this recipe as applesauce for grown-ups, but that's exactly what it is! The blackberries offer a deeper flavor and texture, and part of the fun is telling a table full of adults that you're serving them chunky applesauce but pairing it in unexpected ways—for example, as a topping on ice cream, alongside fried chicken, or beside a plate of warm biscuits. Watch as they dive right in, perhaps remembering all the reasons they once loved this food, too.

1½ pounds Honeycrisp apples (about 3 large)

2 tablespoons fresh lemon juice

½ cup fresh blackberries

1 tablespoon honey

½ teaspoon ground cinnamon

Kosher salt

One 3-inch cinnamon stick

1. Peel and core the apples. Slice them ½ inch thick, then cut the slices into 1-inch pieces.

2. In a medium pot, add the apples, ¼ cup of water, and the lemon juice and bring to a boil over medium-high heat. Cook, stirring occasionally, until the apples release their juice, 5 minutes. Reduce the heat to medium-low, cover, and simmer until the apples are soft, 15 minutes.

3. Stir in ¼ cup of the blackberries, the honey, cinnamon, and a pinch of salt. Cover and continue to simmer until the blackberries begin to break down, 5 minutes. Stir in the cinnamon stick. Let cool for at least 1 hour.

4. Stir in the remaining ¼ cup blackberries.

5. Store in an airtight container in the refrigerator for up to 5 days.

Makes 4 servings

French Toast Crunch

SERVED AT MAGNOLIA TABLE WACO · TX

PREP: *35 minutes*   **COOK:** *50 minutes*   **COOL:** *80 minutes*

I've always preferred waffles or pancakes over French toast, mostly because I didn't like the texture of the bread with syrup. But then, on a trip to New York City, at one of our favorite breakfast spots, a friend ordered French toast with a caramel crunch topping. I took one bite and immediately realized the delicious texture had changed my mind about French toast. We came up with our own version to serve at Magnolia Table, and when I make it at home, I always whip up an extra batch of the topping— it's like a favorite cereal you want to snack on by the handful.

CARAMEL CRUNCH

8 cups cornflakes

1½ cups sugar

¼ teaspoon cream of tartar

6 tablespoons unsalted butter, cubed

½ cup heavy cream

¼ teaspoon kosher salt

1 tablespoon ground cinnamon

FRENCH TOAST

4 large eggs

1 cup heavy cream

1 teaspoon pure vanilla extract

12 slices thick-sliced sandwich bread

6 tablespoons unsalted butter

Pure maple syrup, for serving

Sliced strawberries, for serving (optional)

Flavored whipped cream (page 270), for serving (optional)

1. To make the caramel crunch: Preheat the oven to 375°F. Line a baking sheet with parchment paper.

2. Evenly spread the cornflakes on the baking sheet. Bake until the edges brown lightly, 6 to 8 minutes. Let cool.

3. In a medium heavy-bottomed saucepan, combine the sugar, ¼ cup of water, and the cream of tartar. Gently stir until the sugar is wet. Turn the heat to medium-high. Using a wooden spoon or heat-resistant spatula, slowly stir to dissolve the sugar, continuing until the mixture boils. Stop stirring and continue boiling until the mixture becomes an amber color, 8 to 10 minutes.

4. Immediately remove the mixture from the heat and carefully stir in the butter. Once the butter melts, slowly stir in the heavy cream and salt. Let cool for about 10 minutes.

5. Line two baking sheets with parchment paper.

6. In a large mixing bowl, using a spatula, gently fold together the cornflakes, caramel sauce, and cinnamon until the cornflakes are coated. Divide the caramel crunch between the two prepared pans and spread into a single layer. Let cool for about 1 hour. (Once completely cooled, the caramel crunch can be stored in an airtight container for about 12 hours.)

7. To make the French toast: Preheat the oven to 200°F. Set a wire rack inside a baking sheet.

8. In a medium shallow bowl, lightly crush approximately 6 cups of the caramel crunch, creating both large and small pieces.

9. In another medium shallow bowl, whisk together the eggs, heavy cream, and vanilla until smooth.

CONTINUED FROM PAGE 79

10. Working one piece at a time, dip both sides of a piece of the bread into the egg mixture, allowing the excess to drip off, then dip it into the caramel crunch, making sure to fully coat each side. Set on a clean baking sheet. Repeat with the remaining toast.

11. In a large nonstick skillet, melt 1 tablespoon of the butter over medium heat. Place two slices of coated bread in the skillet and cook until deeply golden brown, 2 to 3 minutes per side. Place the finished French toast on the prepared baking sheet and place in the oven to keep warm. Repeat the process with the remaining butter and bread.

12. To serve, cut each slice of French toast diagonally, place six wedges on a plate, and sprinkle with the reserved caramel crunch. Top with maple syrup and, if you like, strawberries and a dollop of whipped cream. Serve immediately.

Makes 4 servings

Blended Peach Sunrise

PREP: *5 minutes*   **COOK:** *none*   **COOL:** *none*

One 1-pound bag frozen
   peaches

2 cups peach nectar

3 cups fresh orange juice

1 tablespoon fresh lemon juice

1½ cups sparkling white
   grape juice

½ cup mixed berries,
   for garnish

1. Place the frozen peaches, peach nectar, 1 cup of the orange juice, and the lemon juice in a blender and process until smooth.

2. Add the peach mixture to a large pitcher and gently stir in the grape juice and remaining 2 cups orange juice.

3. Divide among 6 to 8 cups and garnish with the fresh berries. Serve promptly.

4. Store in an airtight container in the refrigerator for 2 to 3 days.

Makes 6 to 8 servings

Mini Chicken and Waffles

PREP: *40 minutes*   **COOK:** *1 hour 10 minutes*   **COOL:** *4 hours 15 minutes*

While the waffle side of this duo naturally puts this dish in the breakfast category, it really has a place at any mealtime. When making it for a crowd, I've found it can be easiest to make large waffles that are easily cut into four pieces. Even though I prefer it with the hot honey drizzle, I always offer the traditional option of warm maple syrup.

HOT HONEY

1 cup honey

1 tablespoon sriracha

1 teaspoon crushed
   red pepper flakes

CHICKEN NUGGETS

1 cup buttermilk

1 large egg

2½ pounds boneless, skinless
   chicken breasts (about 5)

Canola oil, for deep-frying

3 cups all-purpose flour

¼ cup cornstarch

2 tablespoons garlic powder

1 tablespoon onion powder

1 tablespoon paprika

1 tablespoon freshly
   cracked black pepper

1 tablespoon kosher salt

2 teaspoons dried parsley

2 teaspoons baking powder

1½ teaspoons garlic salt

1. To make the hot honey: In a small saucepan, stir together the honey, sriracha, and pepper flakes. Cook over medium heat, stirring continuously, until the honey is very thin and runny, about 2 minutes. Let cool for 10 minutes.

2. To make the chicken nuggets: In a medium bowl, whisk together the buttermilk and egg.

3. Pat the chicken dry with a paper towel. Using a meat tenderizer, pound the chicken to an even thickness, then cut into 1-inch pieces. Place the cubed chicken in the bowl with the buttermilk mixture and stir to coat. Cover and refrigerate for 4 hours.

4. To make the waffles: Preheat a Belgian-style waffle maker to medium. Preheat the oven to the lowest setting.

5. In a large bowl, whisk together the buttermilk, milk, oil, egg yolks, and vanilla. Sift in the flour, sugar, baking powder, and salt, and whisk just until fully incorporated.

6. In a large bowl, beat the egg whites with an electric mixer until they hold a stiff peak when you pull the beater out of the bowl, about 2 minutes. Using a spatula, gently fold the beaten egg whites into the batter until no streaks remain.

7. Spray the waffle iron with cooking spray. Spoon ½ cup batter onto the waffle iron and cook until the waffle is golden brown and releases easily, 4 to 6 minutes. Place the cooked waffle on a baking sheet, cover with foil, and transfer to the preheated oven until ready to eat. Repeat with the remaining batter.

8. To cook the chicken: Pour 3 inches of oil into a Dutch oven. Have ready a baking sheet with paper towels to use for draining. Heat the oil over medium-high heat until it reaches 350°F on a deep-fry thermometer.

CONTINUED

CONTINUED FROM PAGE 83

WAFFLES

1 cup whole-milk buttermilk

1 cup whole milk

½ cup vegetable oil

2 large eggs, separated

1 teaspoon pure vanilla extract

2 cups all-purpose flour

⅓ cup sugar

2 teaspoons baking powder

½ teaspoon kosher salt

Cooking spray

9. Meanwhile, in a large bowl, whisk together the flour, cornstarch, garlic powder, onion powder, paprika, pepper, salt, parsley, and baking powder until thoroughly combined.

10. Working one piece at a time, remove the chicken from the buttermilk mixture and allow any excess liquid to drip off, then dredge in the seasoned flour. Working in small batches, gently place the coated chicken in the oil and cook, flipping once, until the nuggets are golden and reach an internal temperature of 165°F, 4 to 5 minutes. Place the cooked chicken nuggets on the prepared baking sheet and sprinkle with the garlic salt. Repeat until all the chicken has been fried. Let cool for about 5 minutes before serving.

11. Cut each waffle into 4 equal pieces, place a chicken nugget on top of each waffle quarter, and secure it with a toothpick. Place the hot honey in a small bowl for dipping.

12. Store the hot honey in an airtight container at room temperature for up to 10 days. Store the waffles and chicken in an airtight container in the refrigerator for up to 3 days.

TIP: To make spicy nuggets: Add ½ cup hot sauce to the buttermilk brine before marinating the chicken, and add 2 tablespoons cayenne pepper and 2 teaspoons pepper flakes to the dredging mixture.

Makes 6 to 8 servings

CHAPTER THREE

Appetizers & Starters

SIMPLE STARTS, SMALL PLATES,

RETURNING US TO THE

RHYTHM OF BEING TOGETHER

Sausage-Stuffed Mushrooms

PREP: *20 minutes*   **COOK:** *30 minutes*   **COOL:** *15 minutes*

When you're having dinner guests, it seems as if no matter how much you prepped and stayed on track, you always need those few minutes when people start arriving to finish the final details of the meal. This is a great appetizer to keep guests occupied while you're still busy in the kitchen. The mushrooms are easy to pull together yet feel hearty and decadent. When I make them, I sometimes wonder if 35 are too many—but history has shown me that 35 mushrooms sometimes aren't enough.

Cooking spray

1 pound ground breakfast sausage

4 ounces cream cheese

½ cup grated Parmesan cheese (about 2 ounces)

3 garlic cloves, minced

1 teaspoon Italian seasoning

1 teaspoon kosher salt

½ cup panko bread crumbs

2 tablespoons unsalted butter, melted

2 pounds large white button mushrooms (about 35), wiped clean, stems removed

1. Preheat the oven to 375°F. Line a baking sheet with foil and spray with cooking spray.

2. In a large nonstick skillet, cook the sausage over medium heat, stirring often to break up into small pieces, until browned, 6 to 8 minutes. Stir in the cream cheese, ¼ cup of the Parmesan, 2 of the minced garlic cloves, the Italian seasoning, and salt. Mix until the cream cheese and Parmesan melt and completely coat the sausage, about 2 minutes. Remove from the heat and let cool for 10 minutes.

3. To make the topping: In a small bowl, stir together the panko, remaining ¼ cup Parmesan, the melted butter, and remaining minced garlic clove.

4. Place a heaping tablespoon of the sausage mixture into the cavity of each mushroom, completely filling it. Place the filled mushrooms on the prepared baking sheet, spacing them an inch apart. Sprinkle each mushroom with the panko topping.

5. Bake until a golden crust forms, 20 minutes. Let cool for 5 minutes before serving promptly.

6. Store in an airtight container in the refrigerator for up to 2 days.

Makes 5 to 7 servings

Balsamic-Glazed Prosciutto Flatbread

PREP: *15 minutes*   **COOK:** *15 minutes*   **COOL:** *10 minutes*

There are some meals you know are special because of the time they require or the long list of ingredients they call for. Other times, I find joy in recipes that can be as creative or straightforward as I want. The base of this recipe offers that flexibility. Flatbread is delicious with a simple, traditional hummus or dip, but I also love piling on veggies from the garden, or as this recipe calls for, a little bit of prosciutto and arugula.

2 cups all-purpose flour, plus more for rolling

½ cup whole milk

5 tablespoons unsalted butter, melted

1 garlic clove, minced

1 teaspoon kosher salt

½ teaspoon dried basil

1 tablespoon plus 1 teaspoon olive oil

8 ounces fresh mozzarella cheese, sliced

2 cups arugula

3 ounces prosciutto, very thinly sliced

¼ cup store-bought balsamic glaze

1. In a medium bowl, mix together the flour, milk, melted butter, garlic, salt, and basil until a dough forms. Using your hands, knead the dough on a lightly floured surface for about 2 minutes. Using a rolling pin, roll out the dough to about a ¼-inch thickness.

2. Preheat the oven to 400°F. Line a baking sheet with parchment paper.

3. Heat a griddle or large cast-iron skillet over high heat and brush with 1 teaspoon of the olive oil. Once hot, place the flatbread in the pan and cook, flipping once, until golden brown, 1½ to 2½ minutes per side. If the dough starts to puff while cooking, gently press it down with a spatula. Let cool on a wire rack for about 5 minutes.

4. Place the flatbread on the prepared baking sheet and brush with the remaining 1 tablespoon olive oil.

5. Evenly distribute the mozzarella on top of the flatbread. Bake until the crust crisps and cheese melts, 10 minutes. Carefully remove from the oven and let cool on the rack for 5 minutes.

6. Evenly sprinkle the arugula over the top of the flatbread. Tear the prosciutto into long strips and place on top of the arugula. Drizzle with the balsamic glaze. Cut into even rectangles and serve promptly.

7. Store in the refrigerator in an airtight container for up to 3 days.

Makes 4 to 6 servings

Homemade Loaded Fries

PREP: *90 minutes*   **COOK**: *45 minutes*   **COOL**: *none*

HOMEMADE FRIES

2 pounds russet potatoes

1 tablespoon freshly cracked black pepper

1 tablespoon garlic powder

1 tablespoon onion salt

1 tablespoon paprika

1 tablespoon dried parsley

1 teaspoon sugar

1 teaspoon kosher salt

4 cups canola oil

CHEESE SAUCE

1 tablespoon unsalted butter

1 tablespoon all-purpose flour

1 cup whole milk

8 ounces Cheddar cheese, shredded (about 2 cups)

¼ cup ranch dressing (page 130 or store-bought)

3 slices bacon, cooked and chopped

1 tablespoon chopped chives

1. To make the fries: Fill a large bowl with ice-cold water. Place a wire rack on top of a baking sheet lined with paper towels.

2. Peel the potatoes, then cut them into ½-inch sticks, and place in the cold water for 30 minutes. Remove the soaked potatoes and pat dry using paper towels.

3. In a small bowl, stir together the pepper, garlic powder, onion salt, paprika, parsley, sugar, and salt. Set aside.

4. Pour the oil into a large Dutch oven. Heat the oil over medium-high heat until it reaches 335°F on a deep-fry thermometer. Using a spider or slotted spoon, carefully place a small amount of potatoes at a time in the oil and cook, stirring occasionally and gently, until the fries are pale and just cooked through, 5 to 7 minutes. Carefully remove the fries from the oil and place on the prepared rack. Repeat until all fries have been parcooked. Set the oil aside.

5. To make the cheese sauce: In a small saucepan, melt the butter over medium heat. Add the flour and cook, whisking constantly, until a paste forms and smells nutty, 30 seconds. Slowly add the milk, whisking constantly, until smooth. Raise the heat to medium-high, bring to a vigorous simmer, then reduce the heat to low and cook, whisking often, until thickened slightly, about 2 minutes. Remove from the heat and gradually whisk in the Cheddar until smooth. Stir in 1½ teaspoons of the fry seasoning. Cover to keep warm.

6. Heat the oil again over medium-high heat until it reaches 365°F to 375°F on a deep-fry thermometer. Using a spider or slotted spoon, carefully place a small amount of parcooked potatoes at a time in the oil and cook, stirring occasionally, until the potatoes are deep golden brown and crisp, 2 to 3 minutes. Carefully remove the fries from the oil and transfer to the prepared rack to drain. Sprinkle the fry seasoning over the hot fries. Repeat until all fries are finished, maintaining oil temperature between batches. Place all the fries into a large bowl and toss, adding a little more seasoning to fully coat all the fries.

7. If necessary, reheat the cheese sauce on low heat, whisking constantly, until just warm—do not simmer. To assemble, evenly layer the fries on a large plate or platter, drizzling the cheese sauce in between each layer. Drizzle the top layer with the cheese sauce, ranch dressing, chopped bacon, and chives. Serve the remaining cheese sauce on the side.

Makes 4 servings

Roasted Red Pepper Hummus

WITH PITA BREAD

PREP: *1 hour*　　**COOK:** *50 minutes*　　**COOL:** *none*

I've found that when I make hummus, there's a good chance I already have a handful of snacks perfect for dipping—carrots, cucumbers, celery, crackers. Almost anything works. During summer months, I like to serve hummus as a refreshing appetizer before dinner, especially if we are eating outside. If I have a little extra time, I'll also bake a batch of homemade pita bread. Both the bread and the hummus store well, which makes for easy prep and a healthy ready-made snack for the week.

PITA BREAD

1½ cups all-purpose flour

1 teaspoon kosher salt

1 teaspoon baking powder

1 teaspoon sugar

1 cup plus 2 tablespoons plain whole-milk Greek yogurt

ROASTED RED PEPPER HUMMUS

One 15.5-ounce can chickpeas, drained and rinsed

1 cup olive oil, plus more for garnish

One 16-ounce jar roasted red peppers, drained

½ cup tahini

¼ cup fresh lemon juice

5 garlic cloves, minced

1 teaspoon freshly cracked black pepper

1 teaspoon kosher salt

1. To make the pita bread: In a medium bowl, whisk together the flour, salt, baking powder, and sugar. Add in the Greek yogurt and stir using a wooden spoon. When stirring becomes difficult, use your hands to knead the dough until all the ingredients are combined and a dough ball has formed. Cover and set aside to rest for 30 minutes.

2. Portion the dough into 8 equal pieces. Pat each piece into a circle about ⅛ inch thick.

3. In a medium nonstick skillet over medium heat, place one dough circle at a time and cook, flipping once, 2 to 3 minutes per side. When the dough puffs up as it cooks, gently press it down to release the air. Repeat until all pita bread has been cooked.

4. To make the hummus: In a food processor, combine the chickpeas and olive oil and process for 1 minute. Turn off the food processor and scrape down the sides and bottom with a spatula. Add the roasted red peppers, tahini, lemon juice, garlic, pepper, and salt and process for another minute. Scrape the sides and bottom once more and pulse a few more times to make sure everything has been well mixed.

5. Transfer the hummus to a bowl and serve with a drizzle of olive oil over the top and cut pitas on the side.

6. Store the pitas in a sealed bag at room temperature for up to 2 days. Store the hummus in an airtight container in the refrigerator for up to 5 days.

Makes 6 servings

Summer Rolls with Peanut Sauce

PREP: *40 minutes*　　**COOK:** *none*　　**COOL:** *none*

When we make spring rolls, we set up an assembly line in the kitchen. That way, as soon as the rice paper comes out of the warm water it's ready to fill and roll. If I'm in charge of veggies, I'll always try to sneak in another helping—the extra crunch is always welcome.

SPRING ROLLS

2½ ounces uncooked rice
　vermicelli

Twelve 22-centimeter rice
　paper rounds

¾ cup matchstick-cut carrots

¾ cup lightly packed fresh
　cilantro leaves

12 green-leaf lettuce leaves,
　ribs removed, leaves
　cut into large pieces

PEANUT SAUCE

½ cup hoisin sauce

¼ cup creamy peanut butter

1 tablespoon rice vinegar

2 teaspoons grated fresh
　ginger

1 garlic clove, grated

¼ teaspoon crushed
　red pepper flakes,
　plus more for garnish

1. Cook the vermicelli according to the package directions. Drain and rinse under cold running water. Chill in the refrigerator until ready to use.

2. To make the peanut sauce: In a small bowl, whisk together the hoisin, peanut butter, ¼ cup of water, the rice vinegar, ginger, garlic, and pepper flakes until all ingredients are well combined. Top with another small pinch of the pepper flakes to garnish. Cover and refrigerate until ready to serve.

3. Prepare a stack of damp paper towels. Fill a pie dish or shallow bowl with warm water.

4. To assemble the spring rolls: Working one roll at a time, soak one piece of rice paper in the warm water, rotating the sheet with your hands, until just pliable, 15 seconds, then place it on the damp paper towels. In the center of the softened rice paper, arrange 1 tablespoon of carrots, a few cilantro leaves, 3 tablespoons of cooked noodles, and a lettuce leaf into a compact 4- to 5-inch-wide bundle. Fold the bottom of the rice paper up and over the filling, fold in both sides, then roll into a tight cylinder to seal. Repeat to make 11 more rolls. Serve immediately with the peanut sauce for dipping.

5. Store topped with a damp paper towel in an airtight container in the refrigerator for up to 2 days.

TIP: A half pound of cooked steak, chicken, shrimp, or tofu can be added to these rolls—just place a few pieces on top of the noodles prior to rolling.

Makes 12 rolls

Marinated Shrimp Salad

PREP: *15 minutes*   **COOK:** *none*   **COOL:** *4 hours*

One of the true pleasures of late spring is always the first evening we can dine al fresco. After a long season of being bundled up indoors, nourishing ourselves with heavier soups and stews, this shrimp salad is a welcome change. Simple yet special, it feels like stepping into the lighter ease of the new season. I like that it can be made in advance, which allows plenty of time for prepping other dishes or enjoying time with the family.

¼ cup red wine vinegar

2 tablespoons fresh
   lemon juice

1 tablespoon olive oil

1 teaspoon minced garlic

1 teaspoon ground mustard

1 teaspoon kosher salt

1 teaspoon freshly
   cracked black pepper

2 pounds medium shrimp,
   cooked, peeled,
   and deveined

2 Roma (plum) tomatoes,
   cut into 8 wedges

One 6-ounce can pitted
   whole black olives, drained

½ cup thinly sliced red onion

One 3.5-ounce jar capers,
   drained

1 tablespoon minced
   fresh parsley

1. In a large, shallow container with a lid, whisk together the vinegar, lemon juice, olive oil, garlic, ground mustard, salt, and pepper until well combined.

2. Add the shrimp, tomatoes, olives, onion, capers, and parsley to the marinade and toss well to combine.

3. Cover and marinate in the refrigerator for a minimum of 4 hours or up to overnight. Toss well before serving.

4. Store in an airtight container in the refrigerator for up to 2 days.

TIP: This is great in a lettuce cup as a salad but also nice as an appetizer paired with a garlic toast point.

Makes 4 servings

Bacon-Wrapped Scallops
WITH LEMON-PARSLEY SAUCE

PREP: *30 minutes*   **COOK:** *30 minutes*   **COOL:** *10 minutes*

¼ cup packed light brown sugar

2 teaspoons garlic powder

8 slices thick-cut bacon

8 large scallops

1 tablespoon plus ¼ teaspoon kosher salt

1 tablespoon freshly cracked black pepper

4 tablespoons unsalted butter

1 cup heavy cream

1 tablespoon all-purpose flour

5 garlic cloves, minced

¼ cup dry white wine

1 tablespoon fresh lemon juice

¼ cup plus 2 tablespoons chopped fresh parsley

3 to 4 lemon wedges (optional)

1. Preheat the oven to 400°F. Line a baking sheet with foil. Line a plate with paper towels.

2. In a medium bowl, stir together the brown sugar and garlic powder. Press one side of each slice of bacon into the brown sugar mixture and shake off any excess. Lay the bacon strips brown sugar side up on the prepared baking sheet.

3. Bake for 13 to 15 minutes, until the bacon is cooked but still flexible. Place the cooked bacon on the prepared plate and let cool for 10 minutes.

4. Rinse the scallops and pat dry with a paper towel. Wrap a piece of bacon around the side of each scallop and secure with a toothpick. Sprinkle the tops and bottoms of the scallops with 1 tablespoon salt and 1 tablespoon pepper.

5. In a heavy-bottomed nonstick skillet, melt 2 tablespoons of the butter over medium-high heat. Working in batches to avoid overcrowding the pan, place the scallops into the melted butter. Cook, flipping once, until the tops and bottoms are lightly browned and the inside is opaque, 2 to 3 minutes per side. Place the cooked scallops on a platter and remove the toothpicks. Repeat until all scallops have been cooked.

6. In a small bowl, stir together the cream, flour, and ¼ teaspoon of the salt until the flour is dissolved.

7. In a small saucepan, melt the remaining 2 tablespoons of butter over medium heat. Add the garlic and cook, stirring, until fragrant, about 1 minute. Slowly pour in the white wine and simmer until the wine reduces by about half, about 2 minutes. Add in the cream mixture and the lemon juice, bring to a boil, and cook, stirring occasionally, for about 2 minutes. Reduce the heat to low and simmer the sauce for 2 more minutes to thicken, then stir in ¼ cup of the parsley. Remove from the heat.

8. Serve the scallops with the sauce alongside and with lemon wedges (if using). Garnish with the remaining 2 tablespoons parsley.

Makes 8 scallops

Crispy Salmon Bites

WITH SPICY CAPER RÉMOULADE

PREP: *15 minutes*　**COOK:** *30 minutes*　**COOL:** *none*

It's easy to get behind eating meals that taste good or satisfy a certain craving. For me, that often means a lot of comfort foods and sweets or any dish that celebrates butter. But there's something to be said for taking time to fuel up on meals that make you feel good. So whenever we're craving something simple and light, salmon always comes to mind. But it used to be that I pictured salmon only one way—a typical cut with a very leafy green salad on the side—so this recipe for crispy salmon bites puts the perfect spin on a meal we can all feel good about.

SPICY CAPER RÉMOULADE

1 cup mayonnaise

2 tablespoons fresh lemon juice

2 tablespoons roughly chopped drained capers

1 tablespoon hot sauce

1 teaspoon chopped chives

½ teaspoon freshly cracked black pepper

¼ teaspoon kosher salt

SALMON BITES

2 pounds salmon, skin removed

2 cups panko bread crumbs

1 teaspoon onion powder

1 teaspoon kosher salt

½ teaspoon freshly cracked black pepper

6 tablespoons olive oil

Lemon wedges, for garnish

Chopped fresh parsley, for garnish

1. To make the spicy caper rémoulade: In a small bowl, combine the mayonnaise, lemon juice, capers, hot sauce, chives, pepper, and salt and stir well to combine. Refrigerate for at least 15 minutes.

2. To make the salmon bites: Cut the salmon into bite-size pieces.

3. In a large bowl, stir together the bread crumbs, onion powder, salt, and pepper.

4. In a large skillet, heat 2 tablespoons of the olive oil over medium heat. When it's hot enough, a bread crumb added to the oil will bubble. Line a plate with paper towels.

5. Toss the salmon chunks into the bread crumb mixture, pressing the crumbs so they adhere to all sides.

6. Working in three small batches, fry the salmon bites, flipping once, until golden brown, 1½ to 2 minutes per side. Allow each batch to drain on the prepared plate. Repeat twice more using 2 tablespoons of oil per batch.

7. Place the bites in a serving dish, garnish with lemon wedges and parsley, and serve with the spicy rémoulade and toothpicks.

8. The salmon bites do not store well. The rémoulade can be made ahead and stored in an airtight container in the refrigerator for 2 to 3 days.

Makes 8 servings

Crab Cakes

WITH SPICY CAPER RÉMOULADE

PREP: *20 minutes*   **COOK:** *20 minutes*   **COOL:** *15 minutes*

1 pound fresh lump crabmeat, picked over for shells

½ cup panko bread crumbs

⅓ cup chopped green onions (both white and green parts)

⅓ cup chopped red bell pepper

¼ cup mayonnaise

2 tablespoons stone-ground mustard

1 large egg, lightly beaten

1 teaspoon hot sauce

½ teaspoon Worcestershire sauce

¼ teaspoon kosher salt

¼ teaspoon freshly cracked black pepper

4 tablespoons vegetable oil (for skillet method)

Lemon wedges, for garnish

Minced fresh parsley, for garnish

Spicy Caper Rémoulade (page 105), for serving

1. In a large bowl, combine the crab, panko, green onions, red bell pepper, mayonnaise, mustard, egg, hot sauce, Worcestershire sauce, salt, and black pepper and stir well to combine. Form the mixture into 8 round, flat cakes.

2. To cook the crab cakes in an air fryer, place the cakes in the air fryer at 350°F. If your air fryer is small, cook in two batches so the fryer isn't overcrowded. Cook, flipping halfway through, until the exteriors are crispy and brown, 12 minutes.

3. To cook the crab cakes in a skillet, heat 2 tablespoons of the vegetable oil in a large skillet over medium heat. Place 4 crab cakes in the skillet and cook, flipping once, until lightly golden brown, about 4 minutes per side. Transfer to a paper towel–lined plate. Repeat with the remaining oil and cakes.

4. Place the hot crab cakes in a serving dish, garnish with lemon wedges and fresh parsley, and serve immediately with the chilled rémoulade.

NOTE: For a gluten-free option, replace the panko with an equal amount of almond flour. If using an air fryer, cook for 14 minutes total. Cooking in a skillet should take the same amount of time.

Makes 4 servings

The Art of Pickling

Believe it or not, pickling is a pretty simple process. I kept my distance for years, sure that the time it took would test my patience. But once you break it down, you realize the ingredients are so few and the time, while essential, works its magic without a lot of effort from you. All you'll need is vinegar and your seasonings of choice.

With such a basic process, the finished product seems just a little bit extraordinary. The way the flavor can change with a shift in spice. How the texture of a pickled ingredient can be so surprisingly different from its original form. Setting up for an afternoon of pickling feels to me like sowing what the family will get to reap in just a couple months' time— savoring the best of our harvest for another day, when the fruits of the garden return to the table with a twist. Here, I'm sharing a few of my favorite recipes plus a couple of cheats that expedite the pickling process.

Homemade Kimchi

PREP: *10 minutes*   COOK: *none*   COOL: *14 hours' soaking, 3 to 12 days' fermenting*

Homemade kimchi is one of my favorite Korean staples. I've always wanted to make this but was intimidated to try to match my grandmother's recipe. As it is with most things, when I finally took the time to give it a shot, I found there was a delicious reward waiting on the other side.

1 large head napa cabbage, cored and cut into 1-inch pieces

¾ cup kosher salt

4 garlic cloves

4 tablespoons gochugaru (Korean red pepper flakes)

2 tablespoons soy sauce

1 tablespoon chopped peeled fresh ginger

1 tablespoon fish sauce

1 tablespoon sugar

1 bunch green onions, sliced into 1-inch pieces

One 64-ounce glass jar with a lid, sterilized

1. In a large bowl, combine the cabbage with the salt and water to cover. Stir to combine. Cover with a plate to keep the cabbage submerged. Leave on the counter for 6 hours.

2. In a mini food processor, process the garlic, gochugaru, soy sauce, ginger, fish sauce, and sugar until a paste forms, about 30 seconds, scraping down the sides as needed. Refrigerate while the cabbage soaks.

3. Rinse the wilted cabbage and drain. Place in a large bowl with the garlic mixture and the green onions. Using your hands, massage the paste into the cabbage until well combined.

4. Place the cabbage into the jar. Compress the cabbage, pushing it down into the jar, until full. Seal the lid tightly and set the jar in a dark cabinet at room temperature for 8 hours or up to overnight.

5. Remove the lid and place loose-fitting plastic wrap over the top. Return the jar to a dark cabinet at room temperature to ferment to taste, a minimum of 3 days or up to 12 days. The shorter it ferments, the crunchier it will be; the longer it ferments, the stronger the pickled flavor.

6. When fermented to your liking, place the lid back onto the jar and refrigerate for up to 6 months. Transfer to smaller jars if you prefer.

TIP: This much kimchi makes an accompaniment for 15 or a side dish for 6.

Makes one 64-ounce jar

Spicy Marinated Okra

PREP: *15 minutes*   **COOK:** *5 minutes*   **COOL:** *14 days*

When I began experimenting with pickling, Chip and the kids were unsure if they were going to like what was in all the mason jars stacking up in the pantry. Spicy pickled okra was what I used to get them hooked. Sometimes I serve this recipe as an unexpected side for a burger or a nice, tangy addition to an afternoon charcuterie board.

2 quart-size glass jars with lids, sterilized

2 ounces fresh dill sprigs

6 garlic cloves, smashed

2 bay leaves

2 teaspoons black peppercorns

2 teaspoons yellow mustard seeds

2 teaspoons fennel seeds

2 teaspoons crushed red pepper flakes

15 ounces fresh okra

2½ cups white vinegar

4½ tablespoons kosher salt

¼ cup sugar

1. Between the two jars, equally divide the dill, garlic, bay leaves, peppercorns, mustard seeds, fennel seeds, and pepper flakes.

2. Do not trim the okra—keep the stems on. Slice the okra in half lengthwise. Equally divide the okra between the jars.

3. To make the brine: In a small saucepan, bring the vinegar, 2½ cups of water, the salt, and sugar to a boil over medium-high heat. Boil, stirring occasionally, to allow the sugar to dissolve completely, 2 minutes.

4. Pour the brine into the jars, filling ¼ inch from the top of each jar. Cover with the lids and let cool on the counter for 30 minutes.

5. Refrigerate the jars for at least 2 weeks before serving. (The longer they pickle, the better they are.) Keep the finished pickles in the fridge.

6. Store in the refrigerator for up to 2 months.

TIP: Great for a quick snack or to add a kick to a charcuterie board or a burger.

Makes two 32-ounce jars

Larkin's Pickled Asparagus

PREP: *10 minutes*   **COOK:** *15 minutes*   **COOL:** *36 hours*

1 cup sugar

¼ cup pickling salt
(or ½ cup kosher salt)

1½ teaspoons pickling spice,
cloves removed

½ teaspoon cream of tartar

2½ cups white vinegar

4 pounds asparagus, trimmed

Four 16-ounce glass jars
with lids, sterilized

8 garlic cloves, smashed

2 teaspoons mustard seeds

2 teaspoons dillseed
(or dried dill)

½ teaspoon crushed
red pepper flakes

1. To make the brine: In a large pot, combine 5 cups of water, the sugar, salt, pickling spice, and cream of tartar and bring to a boil over high heat. Boil for 5 minutes.

2. Remove the brine from the heat and add the vinegar. Let cool on the countertop for 24 hours.

3. Strain the brine, discarding the mixed pickling spice.

4. To make the asparagus: Cut the asparagus to fit just short of the neck of the jars, saving the trimmings for another use.

5. In a large bowl, make an ice bath with half ice and half cold water.

6. In a large pan, bring 2 inches of salted water to a boil over medium-high heat. Add the asparagus and cook until bright green and crisp, 1 to 2 minutes. Using tongs, carefully remove the asparagus from the pan and place directly into the ice bath to cool. Remove the cooled asparagus from the ice bath and place on paper towels to dry.

7. Pack the asparagus tightly into the glass jars. Equally divide the garlic, mustard seeds, dillseeds, and pepper flakes between the jars. Pour in the strained brine, filling ¼ inch from the top of each jar. Cover tightly with the lids.

8. Fill a large pot with enough water to cover the jars vertically. Set the jars aside and bring the water to a boil over high heat. Using canning tongs or heatproof gloves, carefully lower the jars into the boiling water and boil gently for 5 minutes.

9. Place a clean, dry kitchen towel on the countertop. Using canning tongs or heatproof gloves, carefully remove the jars from the water and place them gently on the towel. Let rest on the countertop for at least 12 hours.

10. Store unopened jars in a cool, dark place for up to 6 months. Store opened jars in the refrigerator.

Makes four 16-ounce jars

Grandma Willard's Quick Pickles

PREP: *25 minutes*   **COOK:** *10 minutes*   **COOL:** *10 minutes plus 4 days*

1 gallon whole kosher
  dill pickles with brine

4 pounds sugar

4 garlic cloves, smashed

¼ cup Tabasco sauce

4 quart-size glass jars
  with lids, sterilized

1. Slice the pickles ¼ inch thick and place them in a large pot. Add the brine, sugar, garlic, and Tabasco sauce and stir to combine. Bring to a boil over medium-high heat, stirring occasionally, until the sugar has dissolved, about 10 minutes. Remove the pot from the heat and allow the pickles to cool for 10 minutes in the pot.

2. Carefully divide the pickles equally among the jars. Pour in the brine mixture, filling ¼ inch from the top of each jar (discard excess brine). Cover with the lids and let cool on the counter. The heat from the pickles will naturally seal the jars as they cool.

3. Refrigerate the jars, gently shaking them once a day, for 3 to 4 days, to allow the flavors to meld together.

4. Store in the refrigerator for up to 1 year.

Makes four 32-ounce jars

Quick Candied Jalapeños

PREP: *5 minutes*   **COOK:** *none*   **COOL:** *2 days*

Four 15.5-ounce jars
  sliced pickled jalapeños

3 cups sugar

Two 16-ounce glass jars
  with lids, sterilized

1. Drain the jalapeños, discarding the brine. In a large container with a leakproof lid, combine the jalapeños and the sugar and stir to combine. Cover and refrigerate, stirring the mixture twice a day for 2 days.

2. After 2 days, divide the jalapeños equally between the jars. Cover with the accumulated syrup. Cover with the lids and store in the refrigerator until ready to serve.

3. Store in the refrigerator for up to 1 month.

Makes two 16-ounce jars

Jo's Cherry Burrata

PREP: *10 minutes*   **COOK:** *none*   **COOL:** *none*

One of my close friends absolutely loves cherries. One year, a group of us decided we would all make cherry-based dishes for her birthday dinner. I was in charge of the appetizer (and at the time, wished I'd been luckier and assigned to dessert). But I'm happy to say that this fruit-forward twist on burrata—served with a crusty French bread—ended up being a crowd favorite.

3 cups tart cherries, halved
    and pitted

1 tablespoon store-bought
    balsamic glaze, plus
    extra for serving
    (optional, see Tip)

1 tablespoon finely
    grated lemon zest

8 ounces burrata cheese

Flaky salt (such as Maldon)

Freshly cracked black pepper

Fresh herbs, such as mint
    or lemon thyme,
    chopped or torn (optional)

French bread (page 13),
    for serving

1. In a medium bowl, toss the cherries with the balsamic glaze and half of the lemon zest. Set aside.

2. When ready to serve, place the burrata in the center of a serving dish and split it open. Spoon the balsamic cherries around the cheese.

3. Top with a pinch of the flaky salt, some pepper, the remaining lemon zest, and some herbs (if using). Drizzle with a small amount of balsamic glaze, if desired. Serve with toasted French bread.

4. Store in an airtight container in the refrigerator for up to 3 days.

TIP: If cherries are out of season, use 16 ounces frozen cherries that have been thawed, rinsed, and patted dry with a paper towel. If you're unable to find burrata, use fresh mozzarella cheese.

Makes 4 servings

Dried Fig & Honey Cheeseball

PREP: *20 minutes*   **COOK:** *none*   **COOL:** *2 hours*

I love a good cheeseball—and this particular combination of flavors makes this recipe a favorite of mine during the holidays. I'll typically make a batch at the beginning of December so that when guests drop by I can easily pull together some crackers for serving. I've found that having something special on standby can turn a quick visit into a memory that stands out in the season.

8 ounces cream cheese, at room temperature

1½ cups finely chopped toasted pecans

1 cup chopped dried figs

1 tablespoon honey

1 teaspoon chopped fresh rosemary

1 teaspoon chopped chives

½ teaspoon minced garlic

½ teaspoon kosher salt

½ teaspoon freshly cracked black pepper

Crackers or fresh sourdough bread, for serving

1. In a medium bowl, stir together the cream cheese, half of the pecans, the figs, honey, rosemary, chives, garlic, salt, and pepper until combined.

2. On a plate, spread out the remaining pecans.

3. Using your hands, form the cheese mixture into a ball and roll it in the pecans to fully coat the outside.

4. Cover the cheese ball with plastic wrap and refrigerate for 2 hours.

5. When ready to serve, remove the plastic wrap and place it on a plate. Serve whole or cut in quarters, with crackers or bread.

6. Store in plastic wrap in the refrigerator for up to 3 days.

Makes 8 to 10 servings

Texas Caviar

PREP: *15 minutes*   **COOK:** *none*   **COOL:** *1 hour*

The name "Texas caviar" will always make me laugh, but there is a certain truth to it. Whenever I serve this dip, people treat it as though it's something very special. It can flex, too, as an easy side to a Mexican meal like enchiladas, or at the end of a taco bar. It also works great as a stand-alone dinner with a simple addition of grilled chicken.

Two 15.5-ounce cans black-eyed peas, drained and rinsed

One 15.5-ounce can chickpeas, drained and rinsed

½ cup diced tomato

½ cup roughly chopped jarred jalapeño slices

¼ cup diced red bell pepper

¼ cup diced green onions (white part only)

2 tablespoons fresh lime juice

2 tablespoons olive oil

1 teaspoon kosher salt

½ teaspoon freshly cracked black pepper

¾ cup diced avocado

¼ cup chopped fresh cilantro

Corn chips or griddled corn tortillas, for serving

Lime wedges, for serving

1. In a large nonmetal bowl, combine the black-eyed peas, chickpeas, tomato, jalapeño, red pepper, green onions, lime juice, oil, salt, and black pepper and stir gently. Cover and refrigerate for 1 hour.

2. Place the dip in a serving dish and top with the avocado and cilantro. Serve with corn chips or griddled tortillas and lime wedges.

3. Store without the avocado in an airtight container in the refrigerator for 2 to 3 days. Add the avocado right before serving.

Makes 8 to 10 servings

Jalapeño Popper Dip

PREP: *10 minutes*   **COOK:** *25 minutes*   **COOL:** *none*

4 slices thick-cut bacon, chopped

8 ounces cream cheese, at room temperature

1 to 2 jalapeños, seeded, finely chopped

1 teaspoon freshly cracked black pepper

½ teaspoon garlic powder

½ teaspoon paprika

1 cup shredded sharp Cheddar cheese (about 4 ounces)

1 thinly sliced jalapeño, for garnish

Tortilla chips (below), corn chips, and/or your favorite vegetable, for serving

1. Preheat the oven to 375°F. Line a plate with paper towels.

2. In a small skillet, cook the bacon over medium-high heat, stirring often, until crisp, about 7 minutes. Transfer to the prepared plate to drain and discard the drippings.

3. In a medium bowl, stir together the cream cheese, chopped jalapeños, pepper, garlic powder, and paprika. Fold in the Cheddar and cooked bacon.

4. Spoon the mixture into a 1-quart baking dish or a small (6-inch) cast-iron skillet.

5. Bake, uncovered, until the cheese is melted, 15 minutes. Garnish with the jalapeño slices and serve hot with the tortilla chips on the side.

6. Store in an airtight container in the refrigerator for 3 days.

TIP: This dip can be made through step 3 and refrigerated, then baked 15 minutes before your guests arrive.

Makes 4 to 6 servings

Fried Tortilla Chips

PREP: *5 minutes*   **COOK:** *20 minutes*   **COOL:** *5 minutes*

Twelve 6-inch flour or corn tortillas

Vegetable oil, for deep-frying

Kosher salt

1. Preheat the oven to 325°F. Using two baking sheets so there are no overlaps, lay the tortillas out in a single layer. Bake for about 5 minutes. Pour about 2 inches oil into a large high-sided cast-iron skillet or Dutch oven. Have ready a baking sheet with paper towels to use for draining. Heat the oil over medium-high heat until it reaches 350°F on a deep-fry thermometer.

2. Cut each baked tortilla into 6 equal wedges. Carefully add enough tortilla wedges to the skillet to cover the bottom. Fry the tortillas until golden brown and crispy, 1 to 1½ minutes per side. With a spider or slotted spoon, carefully remove the chips and place on the prepared baking sheet. Immediately sprinkle salt over the chips and let cool for 3 to 5 minutes. Repeat with the remaining tortillas.

3. Store in a sealed bag for up to 2 days.

Makes 4 servings

Tailgate Dip

PREP: *10 minutes*   **COOK:** *20 minutes*   **COOL:** *none*

This is one of those no-fail dips that is delicious any time of day, and in any season. When I feel like changing things up, it's fun to serve this recipe in hollowed-out jalapeños with cheese baked on top. Turning them into poppers gives them a slightly fancier feel.

1 tablespoon olive oil

½ cup diced yellow onion

1 garlic clove, minced

1 jalapeño, chopped

1 pound ground beef

¼ cup ketchup

1 tablespoon chili powder

½ teaspoon Worcestershire
   sauce

½ teaspoon hot sauce

½ teaspoon paprika

½ teaspoon onion powder

½ teaspoon garlic powder

½ teaspoon kosher salt

½ teaspoon freshly cracked
   black pepper

1 cup shredded sharp Cheddar
   cheese (about 4 ounces)

1 teaspoon chopped chives

Corn chip scoops or tortilla
   chips, for serving

1. In a medium skillet, heat the oil over medium-high heat, then add the onion and cook, stirring occasionally, until soft, about 4 minutes. Add the garlic and jalapeño and cook for 3 minutes. Add the ground beef to the skillet and cook, breaking it up into small pieces, until it is no longer pink, 6 to 8 minutes.

2. Add the ketchup, chili powder, Worcestershire sauce, hot sauce, paprika, onion powder, garlic powder, salt, and pepper and stir well to combine. Reduce the heat to low and cook for 5 minutes.

3. If tailgating, sprinkle the Cheddar on top of the meat mixture and cook on low until the cheese melts, about 5 minutes; alternatively, if at home, broil until the cheese is bubbly and slightly browned, about 3 minutes. Top with chives and serve hot with chips.

4. Store in an airtight container in the refrigerator for 3 to 5 days.

Makes 6 servings

Cold Artichoke Dip

PREP: *15 minutes* **COOK:** *none* **COOL:** *2 hours*

Sometimes it's hard to keep from digging into a dish before it's served. Chip can have even less patience than me! If I'm cooking in the kitchen, often he's hovering, waiting for the first moment he can sneak a quick bite. With this dip, we have learned we really have to hold back because the chill time truly makes a difference. Two hours allow the flavors time to come together, giving the dip the depth in flavor that makes it so delicious.

2 cups shredded Parmesan (about 8 ounces)

One 12-ounce jar quartered marinated artichokes, drained and roughly chopped

⅓ cup plain Greek yogurt

⅓ cup sour cream

1 tablespoon finely sliced chives

1 teaspoon fresh lemon juice

1 teaspoon minced garlic

1 teaspoon dried dill

¼ teaspoon garlic salt

Red bell pepper slices, cucumber slices, and Rosemary Seasoned Crackers (page 131), for serving

1. In a medium bowl, add the Parmesan, artichokes, yogurt, sour cream, chives, lemon juice, garlic, dill, and garlic salt and stir until well combined. Cover the bowl with plastic wrap and chill for 2 hours before serving.

2. Serve with red pepper strips or scoop onto cucumber slices and crackers.

3. Store in an airtight container in the refrigerator for 3 to 5 days.

Makes 4 to 6 servings

BLT Dip

PREP: *10 minutes*   **COOK:** *none*   **COOL:** *1 hour*

Think about the best BLT you've ever had. This recipe takes all the flavors from that classic sandwich, then brings them together in a dip that can be made year-round. I love to whip this up and bring it along anywhere a typical BLT sandwich couldn't go—such as a quick picnic or a longer day on the lake. It pairs perfectly with a big bag of potato chips, and when I have a little more time, I'll go ahead and make a batch of homemade potato chips (page 129).

8 slices bacon, cooked until crispy and chopped

2 cups halved cherry tomatoes

½ cup sour cream

¼ cup mayonnaise

2 tablespoons cream cheese, at room temperature

1 tablespoon roughly chopped fresh parsley

1 tablespoon roughly chopped chives

1 tablespoon roughly chopped fresh dill

½ teaspoon freshly cracked black pepper

½ teaspoon kosher salt

Potato chips, for serving

1. In a medium bowl, add three-quarters of the bacon, the tomatoes, sour cream, mayonnaise, cream cheese, parsley, chives, dill, pepper, and salt and stir until well combined.

2. Refrigerate for 1 hour to let the flavors bloom.

3. Garnish with the remaining bacon. Serve with potato chips.

Makes 4 servings

Potato Chips

PREP: *40 minutes*   **COOK**: *35 minutes*   **COOL**: *none*

The classics will always be my favorites. And in a world that has a thousand potato chips, finding the one standard recipe for light, airy chips that crisp up just right feels like a victory indeed. It took a few batches to find the correct amount of salt for our family, so consider experimenting to find the right seasoning for your tastes. Remember that the thinner you slice the potato, the crispier the finished chips will be.

2 tablespoons kosher salt

2 pounds russet potatoes, scrubbed

1 teaspoon garlic powder

1 teaspoon freshly cracked black pepper

1 teaspoon onion salt

1 teaspoon paprika

¼ teaspoon sugar

Vegetable oil, for deep-frying

2 tablespoons chopped fresh parsley

Flaky salt (such as Maldon)

Homemade Ranch Dip (page 130), for serving

1. Fill a large bowl with water and add the kosher salt.

2. Using a knife or a mandoline, slice the potatoes very thin, about ¹⁄₁₆ inch thick. Place the sliced potatoes into the bowl and let soak for at least 30 minutes.

3. Drain the potatoes, then place them on paper towels and pat dry.

4. In a small bowl, stir together the garlic powder, pepper, onion salt, paprika, and sugar and set aside.

5. Pour 2 inches of oil into a large stockpot or Dutch oven. Have ready a plate lined with paper towels to use for draining. Heat the oil over medium-high heat until it reaches 350°F to 365°F on a deep-fry thermometer.

6. Working in small batches, carefully place some potato slices into the hot oil and cook, stirring frequently, until they turn a deep golden color, 1 to 2 minutes. Using a spider or slotted spoon, carefully remove the chips from the oil and place on the prepared plate. Immediately sprinkle the chips with the seasoning. Repeat with the remaining potato slices, allowing the oil to return to 350°F to 365°F in between batches.

7. To serve, place the chips in a large bowl and top with chopped parsley and flaky salt. Serve with ranch dip.

8. Store leftovers in an airtight container for up to 2 days.

Makes 4 to 6 servings

Homemade Ranch Dip

PREP: *15 minutes*   **COOK:** *none*   **COOL:** *2 hours*

Most salad dressings do just what you would expect—they go on top of a salad. In Texas, ranch is anything but a typical dressing. Here, we use it as a dip for fries, and even for pizza. If you're curious to try ranch in new ways, I recommend beginning with our Homemade Loaded Fries (page 95).

¾ cup mayonnaise

¾ cup sour cream

1 tablespoon chopped fresh dill

1 tablespoon chopped fresh parsley

1 tablespoon chopped chives

1 tablespoon garlic powder

1 tablespoon onion powder

2 teaspoons fresh lemon juice

1 teaspoon freshly cracked black pepper

½ teaspoon kosher salt

½ teaspoon Worcestershire sauce

1 tablespoon cayenne pepper (optional)

Potato chips and/or cut raw vegetables, for serving

1. In a medium bowl, combine the mayonnaise, sour cream, dill, parsley, chives, garlic powder, onion powder, lemon juice, black pepper, salt, and Worcestershire sauce. Stir until well combined. Cover the bowl with plastic wrap and chill for 2 hours before serving.

2. Store in an airtight container in the refrigerator for up to 1 week.

NOTE: To make ranch dressing, add buttermilk, a tablespoon at a time, until you get the consistency you want.

TIP: For spicy ranch add 1 tablespoon cayenne pepper.

Makes 2 cups

Rosemary Seasoned Crackers

PREP: *20 minutes*   **COOK:** *20 minutes*   **COOL:** *15 minutes*

Whenever you serve a dip and tell your guests you made the crackers, there's always a moment where you see them wondering if they heard you right. Granted, making the crackers is an extra step that can be a little time-intensive, but that moment makes the work worth it. That's when you see your guests really understanding that you went the extra mile for them, turning what could have been ordinary into something much more memorable.

1½ cups all-purpose flour, plus more for kneading

¼ cup finely shredded Parmesan cheese (about 1 ounce)

3 tablespoons olive oil

2 tablespoons chopped fresh rosemary or another herb

1½ teaspoons kosher salt

1 teaspoon sugar

½ teaspoon garlic powder

½ teaspoon paprika

½ cup cold water

2 tablespoons flaky salt (such as Maldon)

1. Preheat the oven to 400°F. Line two baking sheets with parchment paper.

2. In a food processor, combine the flour, Parmesan, olive oil, rosemary, salt, sugar, garlic powder, and paprika. Pulse until the ingredients are mixed together. With the processor running, slowly pour in the cold water until a dough starts to form, 10 seconds.

3. Transfer the dough to a lightly floured surface. Knead until it just comes together and is thoroughly blended (overworking the dough will create a tough, chewy cracker). Divide the dough in half.

4. On a lightly floured surface, using a rolling pin, roll one of the dough balls into a sheet ⅛ inch thick. Transfer the dough to a prepared baking sheet. Pat the surface of the dough with a damp paper towel, then sprinkle with 1 tablespoon of the flaky salt. Using a pizza cutter or sharp knife, cut the dough into 1 × 1-inch squares. Transfer the dough squares to a prepared baking sheet. Using a fork, poke each square twice to keep the cracker from puffing up in the oven. Repeat with the second dough ball and remaining salt.

5. Bake until the edges of the crackers are a deep golden brown, 15 to 18 minutes. Let cool on the pan for 15 minutes.

6. Store in an airtight container for up to 1 week.

Makes 6 servings

CHAPTER FOUR

Soups & Salads

LETTING FOODS FLOURISH

IN NEW WAYS, CRISP AND FRESH,

BRIGHT AND FULL OF FLAVOR

Enchilada Soup

PREP: *10 minutes*   **COOK:** *30 minutes*   **COOL:** *none*

Enchiladas always sound good to me, but some days there simply isn't time to roll an entire pan of them. This soup has all the flavors of that beloved Tex-Mex meal with a lot less work. My favorite way to serve this soup is alongside a bar of toppings. People get to choose to add whatever they're craving— fresh avocado, crispy tortilla strips, or shredded Cheddar cheese. Typically, I'll also serve guacamole on the side with homemade tortilla chips (page 121).

2 tablespoons unsalted butter

1 cup diced white onion

½ cup diced celery

3 garlic cloves, minced

⅓ cup all-purpose flour

6 cups chicken stock (page 145 or store-bought)

One 10-ounce can red enchilada sauce

1 cup diced fire-roasted tomatoes

One 4-ounce can diced green chiles

½ cup vegetable oil

Six 6-inch flour tortillas, cut into ¼-inch strips

Kosher salt

2 cups cooked, shredded chicken breast

One 15-ounce can whole kernel corn, drained

One 15.5-ounce can black beans, drained and rinsed

1 cup cooked rice

Freshly cracked black pepper

1½ cups shredded Monterey Jack cheese (about 6 ounces)

2 large avocados, diced

1. In a large soup pot, melt the butter over medium heat. Add the onion and celery and cook, stirring occasionally, until the onion is tender and translucent, about 5 minutes. Stir in the garlic and cook until fragrant, about 1 minute. Add the flour and cook, stirring constantly, for 2 minutes.

2. While stirring, slowly pour in the chicken stock. Add the enchilada sauce, tomatoes, and green chiles. Bring to a boil, then reduce the heat to medium-low and simmer for 15 minutes.

3. While the soup simmers, prepare the fried tortilla strips: Pour the vegetable oil into a medium skillet and heat over medium-high heat. Line a plate with paper towels.

4. Working in batches, fry the tortilla strips, stirring often, until golden on both sides, about 2 minutes. Place the tortilla strips on the prepared plate to drain and sprinkle lightly with salt.

5. Add the chicken, corn, beans, rice, and salt and pepper to taste to the pot and stir to combine. Simmer until heated through, about 3 minutes.

6. Serve in bowls, topped with fried tortilla strips, shredded cheese, and avocado.

7. Store in an airtight container in the refrigerator for 3 to 5 days.

Makes 6 to 8 servings

Crew's Spaghetti & Meatballs

PREP: *30 minutes*   **COOK:** *40 minutes*   **COOL:** *none*

I grew up eating the processed spaghetti and meatballs that came in a can, and the truth is that sometimes I still find myself craving the meal. It just takes me straight back to the basics of childhood. I created this recipe to see if Crew might take to them the same way. Some of my favorite recent meals are when he and I have been sitting around with our bowls of O's. Whether or not he remembers the meals, they are ones I know I won't forget.

SOUP

1 tablespoon unsalted butter

¼ cup diced yellow onion

2¾ cups chicken stock
   (page 145 or store-bought)

One 15-ounce can tomato sauce

6 tablespoons tomato paste

1 cup anellini (ring) pasta,
   cooked

MEATBALLS

1½ cups panko bread crumbs

1 cup whole milk

½ pound ground beef (92% lean)

½ pound ground pork

½ cup diced yellow onion

⅓ cup shredded Parmesan
   cheese (about 2½ ounces)

1 large egg

2 garlic cloves, minced

2 tablespoons chopped
   fresh basil, plus additional
   for garnish (optional)

2 teaspoons kosher salt

1 teaspoon freshly
   cracked black pepper

1 teaspoon Italian seasoning

2 tablespoons olive oil

1. To make the soup: In a Dutch oven, melt the butter over medium-high heat, then add the onion and cook, stirring occasionally, until fragrant, 3 minutes. Add the chicken stock, tomato sauce, and tomato paste to the pot and stir to combine. Bring to a boil, then reduce the heat to medium-low and simmer for 20 minutes.

2. To make the meatballs: In a large bowl, stir together the panko and milk until well combined. Let sit for 4 to 7 minutes, so the panko can absorb the milk.

3. Add the beef, pork, onion, Parmesan, egg, garlic, basil, salt, pepper, and Italian seasoning to the panko mixture. Using your hands, mix until all the ingredients are evenly distributed.

4. Using your hands, roll the meat mixture into ¼- to ½-inch balls. Line a plate with paper towels.

5. In a large cast-iron skillet, heat the oil over medium heat. Add half of the meatballs to the pan and cook, turning occasionally to sear on all sides, until dark brown and crusty. Place on the prepared plate to drain. Repeat with the remaining meatballs.

6. Add the seared meatballs to the pot and simmer until the meatballs are cooked through, 10 to 15 minutes. Add the cooked pasta and stir well to combine. Garnish with basil, if you like, and serve.

7. Store in an airtight container in the refrigerator for up to 2 days.

Makes 6 to 8 servings

Chicken Pho

PREP: *30 minutes*   **COOK:** *50 minutes*   **COOL:** *none*

Pho wasn't a dish you could easily find in Waco until the last few years, so serving it to friends always felt like revealing a best-kept secret. If you can't find rice noodles at your grocery store, you can always substitute ramen in a pinch. The finished product won't be traditional pho, but you will still receive all the warmth and restoration a bowl of pho can give.

6 whole cloves

2 cardamom pods

One 4-inch cinnamon stick

1 star anise pod

2 teaspoons coriander seeds

½ teaspoon fennel seeds

1 tablespoon canola oil

1 white onion, halved

One 2-inch piece ginger,
   peeled and thickly sliced

1 garlic clove, peeled

4 cups chicken stock
   (page 145 or store-bought)

2 tablespoons fish sauce

1 tablespoon light brown sugar

½ teaspoon kosher salt

1 bay leaf

9 ounces thin rice noodles
   such as Caravelle

3 cups cooked,
   shredded chicken

2 cups mung bean sprouts

½ cup thinly sliced red onion

1 jalapeño, sliced

Thai basil, chopped, for garnish

Cilantro leaves, for garnish

2 limes, cut into wedges,
   for garnish

Hoisin sauce (optional)

Sriracha (optional)

1. Preheat the oven to 400°F.

2. On a baking sheet, combine the cloves, cardamom, cinnamon stick, star anise, coriander seeds, and fennel seeds. Bake for 10 minutes, then put on a plate to cool.

3. In a large stockpot, heat the canola oil on medium-high heat until shimmering. Add the white onion, ginger, and garlic, spreading out so as not to crowd the pot, and sear until blackened, 2 to 3 minutes per side. Add the chicken stock, 2 cups of water, the fish sauce, brown sugar, salt, bay leaf, and toasted spices and bring to a boil. Reduce the heat to low and simmer, covered, for 30 minutes.

4. Meanwhile, prepare the noodles according to the package instructions, drain, and set aside.

5. With a fine-mesh sieve set over a large bowl, strain the broth, discarding the spices and aromatics. Return the strained broth to the stockpot and add the shredded chicken. Bring to a boil.

6. To serve, add the noodles to individual bowls and ladle on the hot chicken and broth. Top with sprouts, red onion, jalapeño, basil, and cilantro. Serve immediately with a lime wedge on the side, adding hoisin and sriracha to taste (if using).

7. Store broth and chicken in an airtight container in the refrigerator for up to 3 days. Store noodles and toppings separately in the refrigerator.

Makes 4 servings

Cream of Chicken Soup (top),
Cream of Mushroom Soup (bottom)

Cream of Chicken Soup

PREP: *15 minutes*   **COOK:** *8 minutes*   **COOL:** *6 hours or overnight*

Perhaps because I grew up with these soups as staples, making them from scratch now brings me so much delight. There is so much more to the process—a discovery, a learning, and then the satisfaction of being able to share what you've made around the table with people you can't wait to feed. Of course, I still keep a couple of cans on hand in the pantry—the canned version of anything can be a lifesaver in a pinch. When I have the time, I like to dive into these recipes. Each is a reminder of how much good there is to savor in everyday items we might otherwise take for granted.

1 cup chicken stock
  (page 145 or store-bought)

1 tablespoon unsalted butter

¼ teaspoon onion powder

⅛ teaspoon garlic powder

¼ teaspoon celery seed

¼ teaspoon dried parsley

¼ teaspoon dried thyme

¼ teaspoon kosher salt

¼ cup heavy cream

¼ cup whole milk

¼ cup all-purpose flour

1. In a medium pot, bring the chicken stock and butter to a boil. Stir in the onion powder, garlic powder, celery seed, parsley, thyme, and salt and boil for 1 minute to bloom the spices.

2. Meanwhile, in a medium bowl, whisk together the cream, milk, and flour until smooth.

3. While whisking constantly, pour the milk mixture into the boiling stock. Boil for 1 minute, continuing to whisk, until the mixture thickens. Immediately remove from the heat and let cool completely.

4. Use in casseroles and soups in place of a can of condensed cream of chicken soup.

5. Store in an airtight container in the refrigerator for 3 to 5 days, or freeze in zip-top sandwich bags for up to 3 months.

Makes 1½ cups

Cream of Mushroom Soup

PREP: *15 minutes*   COOK: *35 minutes*   COOL: *none*

I grew up thinking of cream of mushroom soup as an ingredient to cook with. I liked how it added to the taste of casseroles, and other dishes where my mom used it, but there was something about how it glopped out of the can in one big lump that kept me from considering it as a soup to eat on its own. With this recipe, that perception changed. The rich flavor that comes out when you make it from scratch turned it into a soup I look forward to serving in the winter. But whether it's going into a casserole or straight into a bowl, if you have the time, I think this recipe makes a difference you can taste.

6 tablespoons unsalted butter

1 medium yellow onion, diced

5 garlic cloves, minced

1 pound mushrooms, sliced

1 tablespoon chopped
   fresh thyme

½ cup all-purpose flour

½ cup dry white wine

4 cups chicken stock
   (opposite or store-bought)

1 teaspoon freshly
   cracked black pepper

½ teaspoon kosher salt

1 cup heavy cream

2 teaspoons chopped
   fresh thyme, for garnish

2 teaspoons chopped
   fresh parsley, for garnish

1. In a large soup pot, melt the butter over medium-high heat. Add the onion and garlic and cook, stirring occasionally, until the onion softens, about 3 minutes. Add the mushrooms and thyme and cook until the mushrooms have softened, 5 to 8 minutes.

2. Add the flour to the pot and cook, stirring constantly, until it coats the vegetables and turns light brown, 1 to 2 minutes. Add the wine and stir, scraping the bottom of the pot, until there are no lumps. Stirring constantly, slowly pour in the chicken stock, pepper, and salt. Bring the soup to a boil and boil for about 1 minute.

3. Reduce the heat to medium-low and stir in the cream. Simmer, stirring occasionally, for 20 minutes.

4. Portion the soup into bowls and sprinkle with thyme and parsley to garnish.

5. Store in an airtight container in the refrigerator for up to 5 days.

Makes 4 to 6 servings

Homemade Chicken Stock

PREP: *15 minutes*   **COOK:** *8 hours*   **COOL:** *30 minutes to overnight*

An easy way to gather vegetables for this recipe is to keep a baggie in the freezer and whenever you have leftover vegetables you can just toss them in. That way, as soon as you cook a recipe that leaves you with chicken bones, you have what you need to make the stock—you can just put it all in a large pot on the stove and let it simmer. I always try to make as much of this stock as possible so that I can freeze at least half the batch. There is satisfaction in using every last bit of food you can, and knowing that nothing is going to waste.

Two 2-pound cooked chicken carcasses (see Note)

4 cups raw vegetable trimmings (see Tip)

¼ cup apple cider vinegar

1 teaspoon kosher salt

Herb bundle (see Note)

12 cups filtered water

1. Add the chicken carcasses, vegetable trimmings, vinegar, salt, and herb bundle to a large Dutch oven or stockpot and top with the filtered water.

2. Bring to a boil over medium-high heat, then reduce the heat to low, cover, and simmer for 4 to 8 hours.

3. Line a strainer with cheesecloth and set over a large bowl. Strain the liquid, discarding the solids. Let the stock cool for 30 minutes. If you like, refrigerate the cooled stock overnight. The next morning remove the white solidified fat collected at the top of the liquid.

4. Store in an airtight container in the refrigerator for 2 to 3 days, or freeze for 4 to 6 weeks (leave 2 inches at the top of the container for the stock to expand when it freezes).

NOTE: The carcass of a roasted chicken is ideal for this. Used to flavor stocks and stews, an herb bundle (also known as a bouquet garni) consists of fresh herbs tied together with twine. You can use whatever herbs you like; I often use sage, dill, thyme, and rosemary.

TIP: Store vegetable trimmings—such as onions, celery, and carrots— all month long in a baggie in the freezer, then pull them out when it's time to make chicken stock.

Makes 8 cups

Roasted Red Pepper Gouda Soup

PREP: *10 minutes*   **COOK:** *40 minutes*   **COOL:** *none*

This twist on the classic tomato soup packs a punch with the combination of red pepper and Gouda. I often pair it with a panini for lunch or serve it as a first course to a more elaborate dinner. While I love a lot about this soup, the fact that the serving size allows me to use the smallest bowls in my cupboard really sweetens the deal. I'm a bit of a collector, and I have an entire shelf in my kitchen dedicated to small antique bowls that are too cute to walk away from but that I rarely have a use for. I'm always glad when the weather calls for this hearty soup, giving me a delicious reason to pull out the collection.

3 tablespoons olive oil

4 medium vine tomatoes, cored and quartered

2 garlic cloves, peeled and smashed

½ teaspoon freshly cracked black pepper

¼ teaspoon kosher salt

One 12-ounce jar roasted red peppers, drained and roughly chopped

1½ cups chicken stock (page 145 or store-bought)

8 ounces smoked Gouda, shredded (about 2 cups)

Fresh parsley leaves, for garnish (optional)

Freshly cracked black pepper, for garnish (optional)

1. In a medium soup pot, heat the olive oil over medium heat. Add the tomatoes, smashed garlic, black pepper, and salt to the pot. Cook, stirring often, until the tomatoes break down, 15 minutes. Add the roasted red peppers and cook another 10 minutes.

2. Add the chicken stock and bring to a boil. Reduce the heat to medium-low and simmer for 5 minutes.

3. Remove the pot from the heat and use an immersion blender to carefully blend the soup until smooth. (Alternatively, use a blender, but do so in small batches and with caution, as the contents will be hot.)

4. Add the Gouda to the soup and cook, stirring often, over medium-low until the cheese melts into the soup, 5 to 10 minutes.

5. If you like, blend the soup again for a super-smooth texture or leave it slightly rustic with bits of Gouda throughout.

6. Garnish with fresh parsley and cracked black pepper (if using).

7. Store in an airtight container in the refrigerator for 3 to 5 days.

Makes 2 to 4 servings

Greek Lemon Chicken Soup

PREP: *15 minutes*   **COOK:** *45 minutes*   **COOL:** *none*

Chicken noodle soup is such a classic comfort food, but I love the fresh spin this variation offers—all the same comfort you expect from the traditional but with a brighter flavor. Tempering the eggs adds a richness, so you still get the feeling of it being creamy without having to use heavy cream. That makes me feel especially good about serving it to anyone who could use the restorative power of homemade soup.

1 tablespoon unsalted butter

1 cup diced white onion

½ cup chopped carrots

½ cup diced celery

6 cups chicken stock
(page 145 or store-bought)

¼ cup fresh lemon juice

3 large egg yolks

2 cups cooked, shredded
chicken breast

1½ cups cooked orzo
or Israeli couscous

½ teaspoon kosher salt

¼ teaspoon ground
white pepper

½ cup crumbled feta,
for garnish

¼ cup minced fresh parsley,
for garnish

Lemon wedges, for garnish

1. In a large soup pot, melt the butter over medium heat. Add the onion, carrots, and celery and cook, stirring occasionally, until tender, about 6 minutes.

2. Add the chicken stock and lemon juice, bring to a boil over medium-high heat, then reduce the heat to medium-low and simmer for 30 minutes.

3. In a medium bowl, whisk the egg yolks until lighter in color. While whisking constantly, slowly ladle 2 cups of the hot broth, one at a time, into the yolks. (If the broth is poured in too quickly, the eggs will curdle and will no longer be usable.)

4. Add the yolk mixture, chicken, orzo, salt, and pepper to the pot. Stir to combine and simmer on medium-low until heated through, 5 minutes.

5. Serve immediately, topped with crumbled feta and minced parsley and garnished with a lemon wedge per serving.

6. Store in an airtight container in the refrigerator for 3 to 5 days. When reheating, add more chicken stock, as the orzo may have absorbed much of the broth.

Makes 6 servings

Arugula and Dried Cherry Salad

PREP: *45 minutes to overnight*   **COOK**: *none*   **COOL**: *none*

This salad strikes that sweet spot between simple and elevated. It's all the more enjoyable because it surprises people with unexpected flavors. Arugula is a peppery green, so combining it with cherries gives this recipe a nice blend of sweet and spice. Since the prep work for the cherries can happen the night before, this side is a favorite of mine whenever I'm hosting. I like to pair it with whitefish or grilled chicken, but really, it's delicious on the side of anything.

½ cup apple cider vinegar

4 ounces dried tart cherries

5 ounces baby arugula

½ cup chopped toasted almonds

4 ounces crumbled Gorgonzola cheese (about 1 cup)

¼ cup olive oil

1 teaspoon Dijon mustard

½ teaspoon crushed red pepper flakes

1 small garlic clove, grated

¼ teaspoon kosher salt

¼ teaspoon freshly cracked black pepper

1. Add the apple cider vinegar and ½ cup of water to a small bowl with a lid and stir in the cherries. Cover and let sit at room temperature for 6 hours or up to overnight. Alternatively, microwave the mixture for 1 minute and let stand at room temperature for 30 minutes. The cherries will plump slightly and soak up some of the vinegar mixture.

2. When ready to make the salad, add the arugula, almonds, and Gorgonzola to a large bowl.

3. Drain the vinegar mixture from the cherries into a small jar with a lid, reserving the cherries. To the jar, add the olive oil, 1 tablespoon of water, the mustard, pepper flakes, garlic, salt, and pepper. Shake well.

4. Add half the dressing to the salad, toss well, and taste. Add more dressing if desired. Top with the cherries and serve.

Makes 4 to 5 servings

Cobb Salad

PREP: *20 minutes*   **COOK:** *none*   **COOL:** *none*

HOUSE VINAIGRETTE

1 cup white balsamic vinegar

⅓ cup honey

1 tablespoon Dijon mustard

1 teaspoon freshly
   cracked black pepper

¼ teaspoon kosher salt

1 garlic clove

1 cup extra virgin olive oil

2 tablespoons minced chives

DEVILED EGGS

6 hard-boiled eggs

¼ cup mayonnaise

1 teaspoon white vinegar

1 teaspoon Dijon mustard

¼ teaspoon kosher salt

¼ teaspoon freshly
   cracked black pepper

Paprika, for garnish

SALAD

1 pound spring mix

1 pound bacon, cooked and chopped

1 large tomato, diced

1 medium red onion, thinly sliced

1 avocado, diced

1¼ cups croutons

¾ cup crumbled blue cheese
   (about 3 ounces)

1. To make the house vinaigrette: In a blender, combine the vinegar, honey, mustard, pepper, salt, and garlic and blend until smooth. With the blender running on low, slowly add in the olive oil and blend until emulsified. Stir in the chives and set aside.

2. To make the deviled eggs: Cut the hard-boiled eggs in half lengthwise and carefully separate the yolks and whites. In a medium bowl, combine the egg yolks, mayonnaise, vinegar, mustard, salt, and pepper and mix, using the back of the spoon to break up the yolks, until smooth. Spoon the yolk mixture into the egg white halves and top each with a small pinch of paprika.

3. To make the salad: Place the spring mix in a large bowl and toss with 1 cup of the vinaigrette.

4. Top the tossed greens with the bacon, tomato, onion, avocado, croutons, and blue cheese, then the deviled eggs. Drizzle with additional vinaigrette to taste and serve immediately.

5. Store leftover vinaigrette in an airtight container in the refrigerator for up to 1 week.

Makes 6 servings

Antipasto Salad

PREP: *25 minutes*   **COOK:** *none*   **COOL:** *none*

An antipasto salad is meant to be enjoyed, quite literally "before the meal," and I love to use this recipe as an introduction for what's to come in the courses that follow. It also works well for lunch, since the mix of meats, cheeses, and greens makes it pretty hearty—something that can stand alone.

SUN-DRIED TOMATO VINAIGRETTE

⅓ cup olive oil

¼ cup sun-dried tomatoes packed in olive oil, drained

¼ cup shredded Parmesan cheese (about 2 ounces)

2 tablespoons fresh lemon juice

1 tablespoon apple cider vinegar

1 teaspoon freshly cracked black pepper

¼ teaspoon kosher salt

SALAD

1 pound salami (whole, not sliced)

4 ounces Parmesan cheese (whole, not grated)

5 ounces arugula

1 cup halved cherry tomatoes

Kosher salt and freshly cracked black pepper

1. To make the vinaigrette: In a mini food processor, combine the olive oil, sun-dried tomatoes, Parmesan, lemon juice, vinegar, pepper, and salt. Pulse until well combined and smooth, about 30 seconds.

2. To make the salad: Chop the salami into 1-inch chunks. Slice each chunk into 4 slices, then cut each slice into 4 matchsticks. Repeat with the Parmesan.

3. In a large bowl, combine the arugula, salami, Parmesan, and tomatoes. Toss with your desired amount of vinaigrette until thoroughly coated. Top with salt and pepper to taste.

4. Store the elements in separate airtight containers in the refrigerator for up to 2 days.

Makes 4 servings

Wedge Salad

WITH BLUE CHEESE DRESSING

PREP: *5 minutes*   **COOK:** *none*   **COOL:** *none*

A dish that looks fancy but is secretly simple will always have a place on my table. Wedge salads in general are great at pulling this off—and fortunately, everyone in our family enjoys them. I like to slice the iceberg wedges beforehand, then serve the toppings family-style so everyone can tailor their own. The kids and I like to dress our salad with ranch, but Chip always prefers blue cheese. Since this is one of Chip's favorite salads, that classic take is what I've shared here.

5 ounces blue cheese, crumbled

¼ cup sour cream

2 tablespoons whole-milk buttermilk

2 tablespoons sliced chives

½ teaspoon freshly cracked black pepper

¼ heaped teaspoon kosher salt

1 garlic clove, minced

1 head iceberg lettuce

4 slices bacon, cooked until crispy and chopped

½ cup diced tomatoes

1. In a small bowl, combine half of the crumbled blue cheese, the sour cream, buttermilk, 1 tablespoon of the chives, the pepper, salt, and garlic and stir to combine.

2. Core the lettuce and cut into four wedges.

3. Place the wedges on individual plates for serving. To allow all toppings to stick, top the wedges first with the dressing, then garnish with the bacon, tomatoes, remaining half of the blue cheese crumbles, and remaining tablespoon of chives.

4. Store unassembled in separate airtight containers in the refrigerator for up to 2 days.

TIP: To prepare this salad family style, set out all the toppings with the undressed wedges, so each person can top theirs to taste.

Makes 4 servings

Butternut Squash Salad

PREP: *15 minutes*   **COOK:** *30 minutes*   **COOL:** *25 minutes*

This salad is a favorite of mine once the sunnier days of summer are behind us. The butternut squash immediately feels like fall and curbs my appetite for foods that lean into comfort. At first, these thick squashes can be intimidating vegetables to work with. I've found that popping one in the microwave for just 15 or 30 seconds softens it just enough to lessen the task of peeling and slicing.

SALAD

2 tablespoons olive oil

1 teaspoon kosher salt

1 teaspoon freshly cracked black pepper

One 3-pound butternut squash, peeled and cut into ½-inch cubes (about 6 cups)

1 tablespoon agave

12 ounces baby spinach

½ cup dried cranberries

¼ cup toasted pepitas

CHEESE CRISPS

½ cup finely shredded Parmesan cheese (about 2 ounces)

DRESSING

¼ cup olive oil

2 tablespoons white balsamic vinegar

2 teaspoons fresh lemon juice

2 teaspoons honey

1 teaspoon Dijon mustard

Kosher salt and freshly cracked black pepper

1. To make the salad: Preheat the oven to 450°F. Line a baking sheet with foil.

2. In a large bowl, stir together the olive oil, salt, and pepper. Add the butternut squash and toss until the squash is completely coated. Evenly spread the squash onto the prepared pan.

3. Roast until tender and lightly browned, 20 minutes. Carefully remove the pan from the oven and drizzle the agave over the squash. Toss to coat. Let cool for about 15 minutes.

4. To make the cheese crisps: Line a plate with a paper towel. Working in batches, in a nonstick skillet, spread even circles made of single tablespoons of Parmesan about 1 inch apart. Place the pan over medium heat and cook until the cheese is melted and golden brown, 2 to 3 minutes. Flip and cook until the other side turns golden brown, about 2 more minutes. Transfer to the prepared plate and let cool for 10 minutes. Repeat with the remaining cheese.

5. In a large bowl, combine the spinach, cranberries, pepitas, and cooled butternut squash.

6. To make the dressing: In a small bowl, whisk together the olive oil, vinegar, lemon juice, honey, mustard, and a pinch of salt and pepper until well combined. Pour over the salad and toss to combine. Serve immediately, topped with the Parmesan crisps.

Makes 4 servings

Apple Pear Salad

PREP: *50 minutes*   **COOK:** *1 hour 5 minutes*   **COOL:** *35 minutes*

BROWN SUGAR PECANS

1 cup pecans

¼ cup packed light brown sugar

1 tablespoon plus 1 teaspoon unsalted butter

Kosher salt

SPICY ROASTED CHICKPEAS

One 29-ounce can chickpeas, drained and rinsed

2 tablespoons olive oil

2 teaspoons garlic powder

1 teaspoon chili powder

1 teaspoon kosher salt

½ teaspoon ground cumin

½ teaspoon cayenne pepper

SALAD

4 slices bacon

4 ounces crumbled feta cheese (about 1 cup)

5 ounces baby spring mix

1 medium pear, cored and thinly sliced

1 medium apple, cored and thinly sliced

½ cup dried cranberries

HONEY MUSTARD VINAIGRETTE

½ cup olive oil

3 tablespoons red wine vinegar

2 tablespoons honey

2 garlic cloves, grated

4 teaspoons yellow mustard

1 teaspoon freshly cracked black pepper

½ teaspoon kosher salt

1. To make the brown sugar pecans: In a nonstick skillet, stir together the pecans, brown sugar, and butter. Cook over medium-high heat until the pecans are coated in sugar and the butter has melted. Continue cooking, stirring constantly, until the sugar begins to caramelize, about 4 minutes. Carefully transfer the pecans to a piece of parchment paper and sprinkle with a pinch of salt. Let cool.

2. To make the chickpeas: Preheat the oven to 400°F. Line a baking sheet with foil and a plate with paper towels.

3. Place the chickpeas on the lined plate and top with another paper towel. Dry the chickpeas thoroughly by gently rubbing and rolling them. (If the skins start to come off, just remove them and discard.) In a medium bowl, add the dry chickpeas, olive oil, garlic powder, chili powder, salt, cumin, and cayenne and toss to coat.

4. Place the chickpeas on the prepared baking sheet. Roast for 40 minutes, stirring halfway through. Set aside. Leave the oven on.

5. To make the salad: Line a baking sheet with parchment paper and a plate with paper towels. Lay the bacon on the prepared baking sheet. Bake until crispy, 18 to 20 minutes. Carefully transfer the bacon to the second lined plate to soak up any excess grease. Let cool for about 15 minutes, then chop into ¼-inch pieces.

6. In a large bowl, toss together the chopped bacon, feta, spring mix, pear, apple, cranberries, and ½ cup of the roasted chickpeas (save the rest for another use).

7. To make the honey mustard vinaigrette: In a mason jar, combine the oil, vinegar, honey, garlic, mustard, pepper, and salt. Cover and shake the jar for about 15 seconds to emulsify. Drizzle the vinaigrette over the salad and toss to coat. Top with the cooled pecans and serve.

TIP: When pears are out of season, substitute strawberries, blueberries, or blackberries.

Makes 4 servings

CHAPTER FIVE

Side Dishes

FINE DETAILS, SHIFTS IN

FLAVOR, EVERY MEAL

AND MOMENT CAN BECOME

WHAT WE MAKE OF IT

Fried Okra

PREP: *1 hour 5 minutes*   **COOK:** *10 minutes*   **COOL:** *5 minutes*

Fried okra is one of Chip's favorite foods, and as we've experimented with it over the years, we've become particular about two things: the batter should be lighter in color so we can see all the delicious seasonings, and the okra shouldn't be slimy. I've found that letting it dry after slicing ensures it doesn't retain any water. This recipe is a staple that I serve with fried chicken and mashed potatoes, and I love to watch everyone make their way to the kitchen when I start tossing okra into the frying pan.

1 pound okra, trimmed

Vegetable oil, for deep-frying

½ cup all-purpose flour

1 tablespoon Cajun seasoning

1½ tablespoons garlic salt

1½ teaspoons freshly cracked black pepper

3 large eggs

1½ cups panko bread crumbs

¼ cup grated Parmesan cheese (about 1 ounce), plus more for sprinkling

Kosher salt

1. Slice the okra crosswise into ½-inch pieces. Stack a few paper towels on top of each other and arrange the sliced okra in a single layer. Let the okra air-dry for about 30 minutes.

2. Pour about ¾-inch oil into a 12-inch cast-iron skillet. Have ready a large baking sheet lined with paper towels to use for draining. Heat the oil over medium-high heat until it reaches 350°F on a deep-fry thermometer.

3. In a medium shallow bowl, stir together the flour, Cajun seasoning, garlic salt, and pepper until well combined. In a second medium shallow bowl, whisk together the eggs until well blended, about 30 seconds. In a third medium shallow bowl, combine the bread crumbs and Parmesan.

4. Working in batches, coat the okra in the flour mixture, shaking off any excess flour. Next, dip the okra in the egg mixture, shaking off any excess liquid. Finally, toss the okra in the bread crumb mixture, making sure it is fully coated. Place the breaded okra on a separate baking sheet.

5. Using a spider or slotted spoon, carefully add a small amount of the okra to the hot oil. Fry in batches, stirring occasionally, until the okra is deep golden brown and crispy, 2 to 4 minutes. Place the fried okra on the prepared baking sheet to drain. Sprinkle with Parmesan and kosher salt to taste. Repeat with the remaining okra. Let cool for 3 to 5 minutes before serving. Serve immediately.

Makes 4 servings

Italian Pasta Salad

PREP: *1 hour 15 minutes*   **COOK:** *10 minutes*   **COOL:** *none*

I love a good potluck dinner. Anticipating what people might bring and hearing the stories behind the dishes they chose make sharing a meal together so fun. This pasta salad is perfect for the occasion. It pairs well with basically anything and can stay fresh for as long as people linger. It's also a great take-along choice for a picnic.

ITALIAN DRESSING

⅔ cup olive oil

¼ cup red wine vinegar

2 tablespoons fresh lemon juice

2 teaspoons kosher salt

1 teaspoon garlic powder

1 teaspoon dried oregano

1 teaspoon dried basil

1 teaspoon freshly
   cracked black pepper

½ teaspoon onion powder

½ teaspoon crushed
   red pepper flakes

PASTA SALAD

1 pound rotini

1 tablespoon olive oil

1 pound salami, thinly
   sliced and chopped

4 ounces white Cheddar cheese,
   chopped (about 1 cup)

1 cup pitted and halved
   black olives

1 cup halved cherry tomatoes

1 green bell pepper,
   cored and chopped

1 yellow bell pepper,
   cored and chopped

1. To make the dressing: In a small bowl, whisk together the olive oil, vinegar, lemon juice, salt, garlic powder, oregano, basil, pepper, onion powder, and pepper flakes. Cover and let sit at room temperature for at least an hour to meld the flavors.

2. To make the pasta salad: Bring a large pot of generously salted water to a boil. Cook the rotini until al dente. Drain, then rinse the pasta with cool water and drain again. In a large bowl, toss the pasta with the olive oil.

3. Add the salami, Cheddar, olives, tomatoes, and peppers to the pasta in the bowl and toss with the dressing until evenly coated.

4. Store in an airtight container in the refrigerator for up to 1 week.

Makes 6 servings

Brown Butter Mashed Potatoes

PREP: *20 minutes*   **COOK:** *40 minutes*   **COOL:** *none*

Sliced, roasted, mashed, baked, or used as a boat to hold the good stuff, the potato never exhausts my interest in dreaming up different ways to eat it. This recipe is my latest take on mashed potatoes and one I really enjoy on fancier occasions when we are serving steak. The Gruyère gives this dish a richness that complements the creamy texture of the potato oh so deliciously.

8 tablespoons (1 stick) unsalted butter

6 garlic cloves, peeled

3 pounds Yukon Gold potatoes

3 teaspoons kosher salt

1½ cups shredded Gruyère cheese (about 6 ounces)

⅓ cup heavy cream

¼ cup chicken stock (page 145 or store-bought)

1 teaspoon freshly cracked black pepper

1 teaspoon garlic powder

1 tablespoon chopped chives

1. In a medium skillet, add the butter and whole garlic cloves and cook over medium heat, stirring often, until the butter turns light brown and smells nutty, 5 to 8 minutes. Pour the mixture into a small bowl.

2. In a large pot, add the potatoes, 2 teaspoons of the salt, and enough water to cover by 1 inch. Remove the garlic cloves from the butter mixture and add them to the pot. Bring to a boil over high heat, then reduce the heat to low and simmer until the potatoes are fork-tender, 25 to 30 minutes. Drain and place the potatoes and garlic back in the pot.

3. Over low heat, add the browned butter, Gruyère, cream, chicken stock, remaining 1 teaspoon salt, pepper, and garlic powder to the pot. Using a potato masher, gently mash the ingredients together until they are thoroughly combined, the cheese has melted, and the potatoes are creamy, 1 to 2 minutes.

4. Top the potatoes with chives and serve immediately.

5. Store in the refrigerator in an airtight container for up to 5 days.

Makes 4 to 6 servings

Brussels Sprout Gruyère Gratin

PREP: *25 minutes*   **COOK:** *40 minutes*   **COOL:** *5 minutes*

It's easy for side dishes to become routine while we give more of our attention and energy to the entrée. But I think it makes a meal more interesting when an unassuming side can steal the show. Every now and then, I like to prepare a dish that feels a little unexpected, like this Brussels sprout gratin. It's full of texture and rich in flavor, and I love to watch it fill the plates around our table as if it were the main event.

5 tablespoons unsalted butter

¾ cup panko bread crumbs

2 tablespoons chopped
    fresh parsley

4 garlic cloves, chopped

2 large shallots, chopped

2 pounds Brussels sprouts,
    trimmed and quartered

1 tablespoon all-purpose flour

1 cup whole milk

1 cup heavy cream

1½ cups finely shredded
    Gruyère cheese, divided
    (about 4 ounces)

1 teaspoon kosher salt

1 teaspoon freshly
    cracked black pepper

2 tablespoons chopped chives,
    for garnish

1. Preheat the oven to 400°F.

2. In a small skillet, melt 1 tablespoon of the butter over medium heat. Add the panko and cook, stirring often, until lightly brown, 3 to 4 minutes. Transfer the panko to a small bowl and stir in the parsley. Set aside. Wipe the pan clean.

3. In the wiped-out skillet, melt 3 tablespoons of the butter over medium heat. Add the garlic and shallots and cook, stirring often, until softened, 2 to 3 minutes.

4. In a 9 × 13-inch baking dish, toss the Brussels sprouts with the shallot mixture until evenly coated. Spread into an even layer and bake, stirring halfway through, until the Brussels sprouts are just tender, 25 to 35 minutes.

5. Meanwhile, make the cheese sauce. In a small saucepan, melt the remaining 1 tablespoon butter over medium heat. Add the flour and cook, whisking constantly, until a paste forms and smells nutty, 30 seconds. Slowly whisk in the milk and ½ cup of the cream. Bring to a simmer over low heat, whisking often, until thickened, about 4 minutes. Remove from the heat and add 1 cup of the shredded Gruyère, stirring until melted, about 1 minute. Stir in the salt and pepper.

6. Remove the Brussels sprouts from the oven. Stir the cheese sauce into the Brussels sprouts. Sprinkle the remaining ½ cup Gruyère on top, then the bread crumb mixture. Bake until the cheese is bubbly around the edges of the pan, 5 to 7 minutes. Let cool for 5 minutes. Garnish with chives and serve.

7. Store in an airtight container in the refrigerator for up to 3 days.

Makes 6 servings

Potato Pancakes

PREP: *20 minutes*   **COOK**: *20 minutes*   **COOL**: *5 minutes*

I love a meal layered with texture. These potato pancakes are always a welcome break in our dinner rotation, because they bring a unique sort of crunch and thickness that feels very satisfying alongside a meat entrée. Typically, I'll try to fry them right before the meal so they're still warm when served.

2 large russet potatoes,
   peeled and grated
   (about 3 cups)

½ white onion, grated
   (about ⅓ cup)

3 tablespoons
   all-purpose flour

1 teaspoon kosher salt

1 teaspoon freshly
   cracked black pepper

½ teaspoon onion powder

½ teaspoon garlic powder

2 large eggs

6 tablespoons vegetable oil

1 cup sour cream,
   for serving (optional)

1 tablespoon chopped chives

1. Place the grated potatoes and onion on a clean kitchen towel. Squeeze, wringing out the water over the sink, until the contents are as dry as possible.

2. In a large bowl, stir together the flour, salt, pepper, onion powder, and garlic powder. Add the eggs and mix well. Add the potatoes and onion and combine well, making sure there are no flour or egg clumps.

3. In a large skillet, heat 3 tablespoons of the oil over medium-high heat. When a very small amount of potato mixture added to the oil bubbles and fries, the oil is hot enough.

4. Scoop and gently pack the potato mixture into a ⅓-cup measuring cup and lightly squeeze out any residual water. Carefully flip the packed potatoes from the measuring cup into the hot skillet to make a pancake. Use the back of the measuring cup to press down on the pancake to spread it a little. Cook, flipping gently once, until lightly browned and crispy, 3 to 5 minutes per side. Drain on a wire rack and let cool for 2 to 3 minutes. Working in batches as needed, repeat with the remaining potato mixture and remaining 3 tablespoons of oil, but do not crowd the skillet.

5. Transfer the pancakes to a plate and serve immediately with sour cream (if using) and chives.

6. Store in an airtight container in the refrigerator for 2 to 3 days.

Makes 3 servings

Mema Pat's Holiday Dressing

PREP: *20 minutes*   **COOK**: *1 hour 25 minutes*   **COOL**: *1 hour 10 minutes*

Mema Pat was the beloved grandmother of a good friend of mine. This recipe of hers always makes me nostalgic when I think about how many hands have also held it, and how many bellies this dish has filled. A lot has changed for cooks in the generations since. In some ways, we can prepare a dish like this faster and easier than those who came before. But I'm grateful for the things that have stayed the same, like being able to create a meaningful meal with my own two hands and put something on the table that makes everyone feel at home.

CORNBREAD

Cooking spray

1 cup all-purpose flour

1 cup plain cornmeal

2 teaspoons baking powder

½ teaspoon baking soda

½ teaspoon kosher salt

2 large eggs

1½ cups whole milk

8 tablespoons (1 stick)
   unsalted butter, melted

1 white onion, diced

6 small celery stalks, diced

DRESSING

8 tablespoons (1 stick)
   unsalted butter

⅓ cup all-purpose flour

1 cup whole milk

2¼ cups chicken stock
   (page 145 or store-bought)

1 teaspoon rubbed sage

1 teaspoon poultry seasoning

1 teaspoon kosher salt

1 teaspoon freshly
   cracked black pepper

2 hard-boiled eggs,
   peeled and chopped

1. To make the cornbread: Preheat the oven to 375°F. Spray an 8½ × 11-inch casserole dish with cooking spray. Lightly spray a 13 × 9-inch baking dish with cooking spray. (See Tip.)

2. In a medium bowl, combine the flour, cornmeal, baking powder, baking soda, and salt. In a separate medium bowl, lightly beat the eggs, then whisk in the milk and melted butter. Add the dry ingredients to the wet ingredients and stir until just combined.

3. Add the onion and celery to the batter. Pour the batter into the prepared 8½ × 11-inch casserole dish and bake until set and slightly brown and crispy on top, 35 to 40 minutes. Let cool to the touch on the counter, about 1 hour.

4. To make the dressing: In a medium saucepan, melt the butter over medium heat. Add the flour and whisk until smooth. While whisking constantly, slowly pour in the milk and ¼ cup of the chicken stock. Add the sage, poultry seasoning, salt, and pepper, and mix well to combine. Cook, whisking, until the dressing begins to thicken, about 1 minute. Remove from the heat.

5. Crumble the cornbread into a large bowl. Add the dressing, hard-boiled eggs, and remaining 2 cups chicken stock and stir to combine. Pour the mixture into the remaining prepared baking dish.

6. Bake until lightly brown and crisp around the edges, 35 to 45 minutes.

7. Store in an airtight container in the refrigerator for 3 to 5 days.

TIP: You can substitute two 6-ounce packages of store-bought cornbread mix for the homemade cornbread. Prepare according to the package directions, adding the celery and onion before baking.

Makes 8 servings

Bacon Butternut Squash

PREP: *15 minutes*   **COOK:** *25 minutes*   **COOL:** *none*

When a busy evening calls for a few shortcuts to get dinner on the table, I like to have a few really good sides that I can make quickly and will pair well with basically anything. The squash here is simple to cook, but I love the little something the bacon adds. A delicious yet quick side like this helps make sure we still get to enjoy a good dinner around the table as a family.

4 slices applewood-smoked bacon, chopped

20 ounces butternut squash, cut into ½-inch pieces (about 4 cups)

¼ cup chopped shallots

1 teaspoon minced garlic

1 teaspoon kosher salt

1 teaspoon freshly cracked black pepper

¾ cup shredded Parmesan cheese (about 3 ounces)

½ cup heavy cream

1 teaspoon fresh thyme leaves

1. In a large skillet, cook the bacon over medium heat, stirring occasionally, until the bacon is crisp and the fat has rendered, 6 to 8 minutes. Transfer to a plate lined with paper towels to drain. Reserve the drippings in the skillet.

2. Add the squash and shallots to the skillet and cook, covered, stirring often, until the squash is tender, 10 to 12 minutes, adding a splash of water to the pan if it gets dry before the squash is cooked. Add the garlic, salt, and pepper and cook, stirring constantly, for 1 more minute.

3. Reduce the heat to low. Add the Parmesan, cream, ½ teaspoon of the thyme, and the bacon, and stir constantly until the cheese melts into the cream, about 1 minute. Remove from the heat and add a splash of water to loosen the sauce, if needed.

4. Spoon into a serving dish and top with the remaining ½ teaspoon thyme.

5. Store in an airtight container in the refrigerator for 3 to 5 days.

Makes 4 servings

Stuffed Sweet Potatoes

PREP: *15 minutes*   **COOK:** *1 hour 15 minutes*   **COOL:** *15 minutes*

It feels like cheating to say my favorite vegetable is a sweet potato, but a single bite of this recipe only reminds me how true that is. If I'm cooking for the kids (or myself!), I'll add a little extra of the marshmallow fluff.

4 large sweet potatoes
  (about 3 pounds in total)

4 tablespoons unsalted butter,
  at room temperature

½ cup packed light brown
  sugar

½ cup marshmallow fluff
  (page 285 or store-bought)

1. Position a rack in the middle of the oven and preheat the oven to 400°F.

2. Prick the potatoes all over with a fork and tightly wrap each potato in foil. Place the potatoes on a large baking sheet and bake until a paring knife slides easily into the center of each potato, 1 hour to 1 hour 15 minutes. Let cool for about 15 minutes, then remove the foil from each potato and discard.

3. Make a lengthwise cut in the top of each potato and, using a kitchen towel, push the ends together to open the potato, making a slot for the fillings.

4. Carefully stir 1 tablespoon of the butter and 2 tablespoons of the brown sugar into the flesh of each potato. Top each potato with 2 tablespoons of the marshmallow fluff.

5. Use a kitchen torch to lightly toast just the top of the marshmallow fluff. Alternatively, place the stuffed potatoes back on the baking sheet and broil on high until the marshmallow is lightly toasted, 1 to 3 minutes.

6. Store in an airtight container in the refrigerator for up to 5 days.

Makes 4 servings

Cast-Iron Spicy Street Corn

PREP: *5 minutes*   **COOK:** *20 minutes*   **COOL:** *none*

My favorite way to eat corn from the garden is straight off the cob. This recipe is a close second, mostly because it works beautifully as a side dish or as a dip. When I serve it as a dip, I put the skillet out with chips and let people eat straight from the pan. If corn isn't in season, frozen works here too.

1 tablespoon unsalted butter

½ cup chopped white onion

1 pound frozen corn kernels

1 tablespoon chili powder

½ teaspoon kosher salt

½ teaspoon freshly
    cracked black pepper

1 cup crumbled cotija cheese
    (about 4 ounces)

3 tablespoons mayonnaise,
    plus more for serving
    (optional)

2 tablespoons fresh lime juice

1 tablespoon fresh cilantro
    leaves

Lime wedges, for serving
    (optional)

1. In a large cast-iron skillet, melt the butter over medium-high heat. Add the onion and cook, stirring occasionally, until tender and starting to brown around the edges, about 5 minutes. Add the corn and cook, stirring occasionally, until the corn also begins to brown around the edges, 15 minutes.

2. Reduce the heat to low. Add the chili powder, salt, and pepper, and stir to coat the corn and onion. Stir in the cotija, mayonnaise, and lime juice until thoroughly combined.

3. Transfer the corn mixture to a serving bowl and sprinkle with cilantro leaves. If you like, add a dollop of mayonnaise and a lime wedge to each serving.

4. Store in an airtight container in the refrigerator for 3 days.

Makes 4 servings

Potato Medley

PREP: *15 minutes*   **COOK:** *1 hour*   **COOL:** *5 minutes*

Sometimes I think we could eat potatoes for a year straight and Chip would never tire of them. He likes his meat and potatoes, and I like to keep dishes feeling fresh and interesting, so that means I'm always on the lookout for dependable yet tasty new takes on this classic dinner dish. This is one I've recently had in rotation quite a bit—it's close enough to a traditional potato dish to pair with briskets, roasts, and steaks. You can also add a fried egg on top and call it breakfast.

1½ pounds baby potatoes, halved

1 medium sweet potato, cut into 1-inch pieces

⅓ cup olive oil

⅓ cup chicken stock (page 145 or store-bought)

Juice of 1 small lemon

2 teaspoons dried rosemary (optional)

1 teaspoon grated garlic

¼ cup chopped yellow onion

1 teaspoon kosher salt

½ teaspoon freshly cracked black pepper

1. Preheat the oven to 425°F. Line a large baking sheet with two sheets of foil, pressing the foil into the corners and up the sides.

2. Place the baby potatoes and sweet potato on the prepared baking sheet and toss with the olive oil, chicken stock, lemon juice, rosemary (if using), and garlic.

3. Bake, uncovered, for 45 minutes. Stir in the onion and sprinkle the potatoes with the salt and pepper, then continue baking until the potatoes are browned in spots, an additional 15 minutes. Let cool for about 5 minutes before serving.

4. Store in an airtight container in the refrigerator for up to 3 days.

Makes 4 servings

CHAPTER SIX

Dinner

ANTICIPATION GIVES WAY TO
SUSTENANCE, FOOD
AND CONVERSATION THAT
CARRY US THROUGH THE
EVENING, LEAVING US FULL IN
MORE WAYS THAN ONE

Mexican Tostadas

PREP: *45 minutes*   **COOK:** *1 hour 5 minutes*   **COOL:** *10 minutes*

REFRIED BEANS

2 tablespoons lard

½ cup diced yellow onion

6 garlic cloves, minced

1 teaspoon ground cumin

1 teaspoon chili powder

Two 15.5-ounce cans pinto beans, drained and rinsed

1 cup chicken stock (page 145 or store-bought)

2 teaspoons fresh lime juice

1 teaspoon kosher salt

½ teaspoon freshly cracked black pepper

TOSTADAS

Canola oil, for deep-frying

10 corn tortillas

1 pound ground beef

½ cup diced yellow onion

1 garlic clove, minced

2 tablespoons chili powder

1 teaspoon garlic powder

1 teaspoon kosher salt

½ teaspoon ground cumin

¼ teaspoon crushed red pepper flakes

2 cups shredded iceberg lettuce

1 tomato, diced

8 ounces Cheddar cheese, shredded (about 2 cups)

4 avocados, sliced

1 cup sour cream

2 tablespoons fresh cilantro, chopped

1. To make the refried beans: In a large cast-iron skillet, heat the lard over medium-high heat. Add the onion and cook, stirring occasionally, until translucent, 4 to 5 minutes. Add the garlic, cumin, and chili powder and cook and stir until fragrant, about 1 minute. Pour the pinto beans and chicken stock into the pan. Bring to a boil, then reduce the heat to simmer and cook, stirring occasionally, for 10 minutes.

2. Remove the skillet from the heat and use an immersion blender to carefully puree the beans until smooth. (Alternatively, use a blender, but do so in small batches and with caution as the contents will be hot.)

3. Place the pureed beans into a medium bowl and stir in the lime juice, salt, and pepper until well combined.

4. To make the tostadas: Pour 1 inch of oil into a Dutch oven. Have ready a baking sheet lined with paper towels to use for draining. Heat the oil over medium-high heat until it reaches 325°F on a deep-fry thermometer.

5. Using tongs, place one tortilla flat in the oil and fry, flipping once, until golden brown, about 90 seconds per side. Place on the prepared baking sheet and sprinkle with a pinch of salt. Repeat until all the tortillas have been fried. Set aside to cool.

6. Wipe the pan clean. Over medium heat, add the beef, onion, and garlic and cook, breaking up the beef into small pieces, until the meat is no longer pink, 6 to 8 minutes. Drain the grease from the meat. Stir in ½ cup of water, the chili powder, garlic powder, salt, cumin, and pepper flakes and bring the mixture to a boil. Reduce the heat and simmer, stirring occasionally, until the water has evaporated, about 10 minutes.

7. To assemble, spread a layer of beans on the top of the tostadas, then spoon a layer of seasoned beef on top of the beans. Evenly divide the lettuce, tomato, Cheddar, avocado, sour cream, and cilantro among the tostadas.

8. Store unassembled in separate airtight containers in the refrigerator for up to 3 days.

TIP: To serve the refried beans as a side dish, top with ¼ cup cotija cheese and sprinkle with 1 teaspoon chopped cilantro, if you like.

Makes 5 servings

Spinach Enchiladas

PREP: *20 minutes*   **COOK:** *45 minutes*   **COOL:** *10 minutes*

Cooking spray

2 tablespoons olive oil

1 cup diced white onion

1 teaspoon minced garlic

20 ounces baby spinach

2 tablespoons unsalted butter

2 tablespoons all-purpose flour

1½ cups chicken stock (page 145 or store-bought)

1½ cups heavy whipping cream

½ teaspoon kosher salt

½ teaspoon garlic powder

½ teaspoon freshly cracked black pepper

16 ounces shredded Monterey Jack cheese (about 4 cups)

1 cup vegetable oil

Twelve 6-inch flour tortillas

1 teaspoon chopped cilantro, for garnish (optional)

Sour cream, for serving

Sliced avocado, for serving

1. Preheat the oven to 375°F. Line a baking sheet with paper towels. Spray a 9 × 13-inch baking dish or pan with cooking spray.

2. In a large, deep sauté pan, heat the olive oil over medium-high heat for 1 minute. Add the onion and cook, stirring occasionally, until translucent and slightly browned, 4 minutes. Add the garlic and cook until fragrant, 1 minute. Add three-fourths of the spinach and cook until wilted, 3 minutes. Transfer to a medium bowl and set aside.

3. Lower the heat to medium and add the butter to the pan. Once it has melted, add the flour and cook, whisking constantly, for 1 minute. Slowly whisk in the chicken stock until smooth. Bring the sauce to a simmer, whisking often, until thickened, 2 minutes. Add the remaining spinach to the pan and stir until wilted, 2 minutes.

4. Add the cream, salt, garlic powder, pepper, and half of the Monterey Jack cheese. Cook, stirring constantly, until the cheese is just melted and the sauce is thickened, 90 seconds. Remove from the heat.

5. Pour the vegetable oil into a medium skillet. Heat the oil over medium-high heat until it reaches 325°F on a deep-fry thermometer. Add one tortilla to the oil at a time and cook, flipping once carefully with tongs, until slightly brown, 30 seconds per side. Set the fried tortillas on the prepared baking sheet to drain completely.

6. To assemble the enchiladas: Working with one tortilla at a time, place 3 to 4 tablespoons of the spinach mixture and 1½ teaspoons of the Monterey Jack into the center of the tortilla. Roll up tightly. Place the tortilla seam side down into the prepared baking dish. Repeat with the remaining tortillas.

7. Pour the sauce over the top of the tortillas. Sprinkle with the remaining cheese (a little less than ⅔ cup).

8. Bake until bubbly and slightly brown on top, 15 minutes. Let cool for 10 minutes, then top with chopped cilantro (if using) and serve with sour cream and avocado.

9. Store in an airtight container in the refrigerator for 3 to 5 days. You can also store assembled but not yet baked in an airtight container in the freezer for 4 weeks; when ready to serve, thaw in the refrigerator, then bake at 350°F for 15 minutes.

Makes 6 to 12 servings

Chicken Taquitos

SERVED AT
THE TACO TRUCK
WACO . TX

PREP: *45 minutes*　　**COOK:** *45 minutes*　　**COOL:** *1 hour 25 minutes*

SALSA VERDE

2 ripe avocados

2 tomatillos, quartered

1 small green tomato, quartered

1 serrano pepper,
　　stemmed and halved

2 garlic cloves

¼ cup fresh cilantro leaves

¼ cup chopped yellow onion

1 tablespoon fresh lime juice

1½ teaspoons kosher salt

CHICKEN TAQUITOS

Cooking spray

1½ pounds boneless, skinless
　　chicken breasts (about 3)

1½ teaspoons kosher salt

1½ teaspoons freshly
　　cracked black pepper

1 teaspoon ground cumin

½ teaspoon garlic powder

½ teaspoon paprika

¼ teaspoon chili powder

¼ teaspoon crushed
　　red pepper flakes

¼ teaspoon onion powder

2 ounces cream cheese,
　　at room temperature

Juice of 1 lime
　　(about 2 tablespoons)

20 small corn tortillas

8 ounces Colby Jack cheese,
　　shredded (about 2 cups)

4 tablespoons (½ stick)
　　salted butter, melted

1. To make the salsa verde: In a blender, combine the avocados, tomatillos, green tomato, serrano, garlic, cilantro, onion, lime juice, salt, and 1 cup of water and puree until smooth, 2 to 3 minutes. Transfer the salsa to an airtight container and chill for at least 1 hour, or until ready to serve.

2. To make the chicken taquitos: Preheat the oven to 425°F. Spray a 9 × 13-inch baking dish or half sheet pan with cooking spray. Line a baking sheet with parchment paper.

3. Put the chicken in the prepared baking dish and evenly season with 1 teaspoon each of the salt and pepper.

4. Bake until the chicken reaches an internal temperature of 165°F, 18 to 25 minutes. Let rest for 15 minutes. Leave the oven on.

5. In a small bowl, stir together the remaining ½ teaspoon each salt and pepper, the cumin, garlic powder, paprika, chili powder, pepper flakes, and onion powder.

6. Place the chicken in a medium bowl and shred into little pieces using two forks. Add the spice mixture, cream cheese, and lime juice, and stir until the chicken is well coated and the cream cheese is incorporated.

7. Wrap the corn tortillas in a damp paper towel and microwave for 20 to 30 seconds. Working with one tortilla at a time, place about 2 tablespoons of the chicken mixture and 1 tablespoon of shredded cheese in the center of the tortilla. Fold one side of the tortilla over the chicken and roll to fully enclose the filling. Place a toothpick in the center of the rolled tortilla to keep it closed. Place the rolled tortilla on the prepared baking sheet. Repeat until all the tortillas have been filled.

8. Brush the melted butter over the top of the rolled tortillas.

9. Bake until golden brown and crispy, 15 to 18 minutes. Let cool for 10 minutes, then remove the toothpicks and serve with the salsa verde.

10. Store taquitos in an airtight container in the refrigerator for up to 3 days. Store salsa verde in an airtight container in the refrigerator for up to 5 days.

Makes 20 taquitos

Pastitsio

PREP: *25 minutes* **COOK:** *1 hour 50 minutes* **COOL:** *20 minutes*

2 tablespoons olive oil

1 large red onion, grated

2 garlic cloves, minced

1 pound ground beef
(92% lean)

¾ cup dry red wine

One 14.5-ounce
can petite diced
tomatoes

2 tablespoons tomato
paste

3½ teaspoons
kosher salt

1 teaspoon freshly
cracked black pepper

2 bay leaves

One 3-inch cinnamon
stick

1 pinch ground cloves

1 pound penne or ziti

2 large eggs, separated

4 ounces feta cheese
(about 1 cup)

8 tablespoons (1 stick)
unsalted butter

½ cup all-purpose flour

4 cups heavy cream

1 cup grated
Parmesan cheese
(about 4 ounces)

1 pinch ground nutmeg

1. Preheat the oven to 350°F.

2. In a large skillet, heat the olive oil over medium-high heat. Add the onion and cook, stirring occasionally, until tender and translucent, 3 to 4 minutes. Add the garlic and cook until fragrant, 1 more minute. Add the ground beef and cook, breaking it up into small pieces, until browned, about 5 minutes.

3. Stir in the red wine, tomatoes, tomato paste, 2 teaspoons of the salt, and ½ teaspoon of the pepper. Bring the mixture to a boil and reduce the heat to medium and cook, stirring occasionally, until the liquid reduces by half, 5 to 7 minutes.

4. Add the bay leaves, cinnamon stick, and ground cloves to the skillet. Reduce the heat to medium-low, cover, and simmer, stirring occasionally, for 30 minutes.

5. Meanwhile, bring a large pot of generously salted water to a boil. Cook the penne until al dente, then drain and let cool for 5 minutes. In a large bowl, beat the egg whites until loosened. Add the penne and the feta and toss together. Set aside.

6. In a large saucepan, melt the butter over medium heat. Add the flour and cook, whisking constantly, until a paste forms and starts to smell nutty, 2 minutes. Gradually add the cream, whisking constantly, until well combined. Add ½ cup of the Parmesan and continue to whisk. Cook until the sauce is bubbling and thick, about 6 minutes, then remove the pan from the heat.

7. While whisking constantly, add the egg yolks to the cream sauce and continue whisking until the sauce cools a bit and is smooth and creamy. Add the remaining 1½ teaspoons salt, ½ teaspoon pepper, and the nutmeg and stir well to combine.

8. To assemble, spoon the penne mixture evenly into an 11 × 14-inch baking dish. Remove the bay leaves and cinnamon stick from the meat mixture. Evenly spoon the meat mixture over the penne and smooth until level. Pour the cream sauce over the meat mixture, completely covering the meat and penne. Top with the remaining ½ cup Parmesan.

9. Bake until the top is golden brown and slightly springy to the touch, like an egg custard, 40 to 45 minutes.

10. Let cool for 20 minutes before serving.

11. Store in an airtight container in the refrigerator for 3 to 5 days.

TIP: You can assemble this ahead of time, refrigerate, and bake the following day.

Makes 8 to 10 servings

Chicken Gyros

WITH TZATZIKI

PREP: *30 minutes*   **COOK:** *25 minutes*   **COOL:** *5 minutes*

On this gyro, the tzatziki is really the star of the show. A few simple ingredients come together to create a bold flavor. Most people like the tzatziki drizzled on top, but I will usually keep a little bowl next to my plate so that I can spoon more on top of the gyro as I go. For me, it's a good thing you can't have too much of.

1 medium cucumber

1 cup plain Greek yogurt

¼ cup plus 1 tablespoon olive oil

3 tablespoons fresh lemon juice

3 teaspoons minced garlic

2½ teaspoons kosher salt

2½ teaspoons freshly cracked black pepper

1 teaspoon chopped fresh dill

Cooking spray

2 pounds boneless, skinless chicken breasts (about 4)

Grated zest of 1 large lemon

8 pita breads (page 97 or store-bought)

1 cup halved cherry tomatoes

1. Using a food processor or a cheese grater, shred the cucumber. Place the shredded cucumber in a paper towel and gently squeeze to release any excess liquid.

2. To make the tzatziki sauce: In a medium bowl, stir together ½ cup of the shredded cucumber (reserve the rest), the yogurt, 1 tablespoon of the olive oil, the lemon juice, 1 teaspoon of the minced garlic, 1 teaspoon of the salt, 1 teaspoon of the pepper, and the dill until well combined. Refrigerate until ready to serve.

3. Preheat the oven to 425°F.

4. Spray a 13 × 9-inch baking dish with cooking spray. Arrange the chicken in one layer, pour the remaining ¼ cup olive oil over the top, then season the chicken all over with the remaining 1½ teaspoons salt and 1½ teaspoons pepper. Sprinkle with the remaining 2 teaspoons minced garlic and the lemon zest.

5. Bake until the chicken reaches an internal temperature of 165°F, about 18 minutes. Let rest in the baking dish for 5 minutes. Wrap the pita bread in foil and place in the turned-off oven to warm up, about 5 minutes.

6. Slice the chicken into ¼-inch strips.

7. To assemble the gyros: Place the pita breads on separate pieces of parchment paper or foil, then top each with ½ cup sliced chicken, 2 tablespoons tzatziki sauce, about 6 cherry tomato halves, and 2 tablespoons of reserved shredded cucumber. Roll the gyro, then wrap the bottom half securely with the parchment or foil to keep the gyro together while eating.

8. Store unassembled in separate airtight containers in the refrigerator for up to 3 days.

Makes 4 servings

Spanakopita

PREP: *20 minutes*   **COOK:** *1 hour*   **COOL:** *10 minutes*

My good friend Becki comes from a long line of Greek cooks and restaurant owners. After playing with her family's spanakopita recipe for a long time, Becki was gracious enough to lend it to me. After one bite, I knew it was something worth sharing here.

1 pound frozen chopped spinach, thawed

3 cups chopped fresh parsley (3 to 4 bunches)

12 ounces feta cheese, crumbled (about 3 cups)

4 large eggs

1 white onion, minced

2 tablespoons minced fresh dill

3 garlic cloves, minced

1 teaspoon kosher salt

1 teaspoon freshly cracked black pepper

½ cup olive oil plus 2 tablespoons

8 ounces phyllo dough, thawed

1. Preheat the oven to 325°F.

2. Using a kitchen towel, wring the water out of the spinach until it is as dry as possible.

3. In a large bowl, combine the spinach, parsley, feta, eggs, onion, dill, garlic, salt, pepper, and 2 tablespoons of the olive oil, stirring until completely combined.

4. Using some of the remaining ½ cup olive oil, brush the bottom and sides of a 9 × 13-inch baking dish with a thin coating of oil. Place two sheets of phyllo dough in the center of the dish, allowing it to come up the sides. Brush the top of the dough completely with olive oil but do not saturate it. Continue placing and brushing sheets of dough two at a time, until 16 sheets are down. Reserve the remaining sheets.

5. Spoon the spinach mixture on top of the sheets in the pan and spread evenly. Top the spinach mixture with two more sheets of dough and brush with olive oil. Continue placing and brushing sheets of dough two at a time until all phyllo sheets are used.

6. Brush the top layer of dough with olive oil and fold the sides down and inward. Brush the folded edges well with olive oil. Sprinkle a few drops of water on the top layer.

7. Bake until the top is crisp and golden brown, 1 hour.

8. Carefully remove the baking dish from the oven and let rest until cool to the touch, about 10 minutes. Cut into squares or triangles, and serve warm.

9. Store in an airtight container in the refrigerator for 3 to 5 days.

Makes 12 servings

Spinach Manicotti

PREP: *25 minutes*   **COOK:** *50 minutes*   **COOL:** *15 minutes*

This is one of my favorite meals to make ahead. Once it's prepped, I can forget about it in the refrigerator until I'm ready to put it in the oven. The cheesy insides of the manicotti are the best part—and what seem to make this delicious dish disappear fast.

1 tablespoon olive oil

2 teaspoons minced garlic

3 cups fresh spinach

1 teaspoon kosher salt,
    plus more for
    the pasta water

8 ounces manicotti

15 ounces whole-milk
    ricotta cheese

2½ cups shredded part-skim
    mozzarella cheese
    (about 10 ounces)

1½ cups shredded Parmesan
    (about 6 ounces)

2 large eggs

1 tablespoon freshly
    cracked black pepper

3 cups Jo's Marinara Sauce
    (page 207 or store-bought)

2 tablespoons chopped
    fresh parsley, for garnish

1. In a medium skillet, heat the olive oil and garlic over medium-high heat, stirring constantly, until fragrant, about 1 minute. Add the spinach and stir occasionally, until the spinach wilts and is deep green, 3 to 5 minutes. Transfer the spinach to a cutting board to cool for about 5 minutes. Roughly chop the spinach.

2. Bring a large pot of generously salted water to a boil. Cook the manicotti for 8 minutes, then drain and let cool slightly.

3. Preheat the oven to 350°F.

4. In a medium bowl, stir together the ricotta, 2 cups of the shredded mozzarella, 1 cup of the shredded Parmesan, the eggs, pepper, remaining teaspoon of salt, and the chopped spinach until well combined. Place the spinach mixture in a gallon-size zip-top plastic bag.

5. Evenly spread approximately 1 cup of the marinara around the bottom of a 9 × 13-inch casserole dish. Cut off a corner of the bag, a little smaller than the opening of the manicotti. Using the cut bag like a pastry bag, evenly fill each manicotti shell with the filling. Arrange the filled manicotti in a single layer in the casserole dish.

6. Pour the rest of the marinara evenly over the top of the manicotti. Sprinkle evenly with the remaining ½ cup each Parmesan and mozzarella.

7. Cover the dish with foil and bake for 20 minutes. Carefully remove the foil and bake, uncovered, for another 15 minutes. Let cool for about 10 minutes.

8. Sprinkle with parsley and serve.

9. Store in an airtight container in the refrigerator for up to 5 days.

Makes 4 to 6 servings

Buffalo Chicken Sliders

PREP: *55 minutes*   **COOK:** *25 minutes*   **COOL:** *1 hour*

I love a good chicken wing. These sliders deliver that same taste, and, as a bonus, they are a lot easier to eat than a messy plate of wings.

SLAW

¼ cup mayonnaise

¼ cup sour cream

2 tablespoons fresh lemon juice

1 garlic clove, minced

¼ teaspoon kosher salt

1 cup shredded celery

1 cup shredded carrots

SPREAD

½ cup mayonnaise

¼ cup hot sauce

2 tablespoons barbecue sauce

1 tablespoon yellow mustard

1 teaspoon freshly cracked black pepper

CHICKEN

½ cup hot sauce

6 tablespoons unsalted butter, melted

1 teaspoon white vinegar

1 teaspoon Worcestershire sauce

1 pound boneless, skinless chicken breasts (about 2)

2¼ cups all-purpose flour

¾ cup whole-milk buttermilk

1 large egg

1. To make the slaw: In a medium bowl, whisk together the mayonnaise, sour cream, lemon juice, garlic, and salt until well combined. Fold in the celery and carrots. Cover and refrigerate for at least 1 hour.

2. To make the spread: In a small bowl, whisk together the mayonnaise, hot sauce, barbecue sauce, mustard, and pepper. Cover and refrigerate until ready to assemble the sliders.

3. To make the chicken: In a medium bowl, whisk together the hot sauce, 4 tablespoons of the melted butter, the vinegar, and Worcestershire sauce. Cover and set aside.

4. Using a sharp knife, cut each chicken breast horizontally through the thickest part to create 2 thin separate pieces. Cut each piece in half, to better fit the buns.

5. Set out 3 shallow bowls. In the first bowl, add ¾ cup of the flour. In the second bowl, whisk together the buttermilk, egg, 1 teaspoon of the garlic powder, and the black pepper. In the third bowl, whisk together the remaining 1½ cups flour, the cayenne, cornstarch, onion powder, salt, paprika, and remaining 1 tablespoon garlic powder.

6. Preheat the oven to 350°F. Pour 1½ to 2 inches of oil into a high-sided cast-iron skillet. Have ready a baking sheet lined with paper towels to use for draining. Heat the oil over medium heat until it reaches 350°F on a deep-fry thermometer.

7. Working with one piece of chicken at a time, dredge the chicken in the plain flour, shaking the excess flour off. Then dip it in the egg mixture to coat completely, then coat in the seasoned flour.

CONTINUED FROM PAGE 205

1 tablespoon plus
   1 teaspoon garlic powder

1 teaspoon freshly
   cracked black pepper

1½ tablespoons cayenne
   pepper

1 tablespoon cornstarch

1 tablespoon onion powder

1 tablespoon kosher salt

1 tablespoon paprika

Vegetable oil, for deep-frying

8 brioche slider buns

1 teaspoon black sesame seeds

1 teaspoon white sesame seeds

8. Carefully place 4 coated pieces of chicken into the hot oil. Cook, flipping once, until deep golden brown and the internal temperature is at least 165°F, about 3 minutes per side. Place the cooked chicken on the prepared baking sheet. Repeat with the remaining chicken. Dip the cooked chicken in the hot sauce and butter mixture, coating it completely, and set aside.

9. Place the buns on a baking sheet. Brush the remaining 2 tablespoons melted butter on the tops of the buns and sprinkle with the sesame seeds. Bake until the seeds adhere to the top of the buns and the buns have warmed through, 7 to 8 minutes.

10. To build the sliders, open the buns and spread about 1 tablespoon of the spread on the bottom bun. Next, place the sauced chicken, then a couple of tablespoons of the slaw, then the top bun. Serve immediately.

11. Store components in separate airtight containers in the refrigerator for up to 2 days.

TIP: Drizzle the chicken with ranch dressing (page 130) or place a dollop of it on your plate to dip the slider in.

Makes 4 servings

Jo's Marinara Sauce

PREP: *15 minutes*   **COOK:** *under 40 minutes*   **COOL:** *none*

1 tablespoon olive oil

⅓ cup diced red onion
(about ½ small)

2 garlic cloves, minced

1 teaspoon kosher salt,
plus more to taste

1 teaspoon freshly ground
black pepper, plus more
to taste

One 28-ounce can crushed
tomatoes

One 6-ounce can tomato
paste

3 bay leaves

2 tablespoons chopped
fresh basil

1 tablespoon chopped
fresh parsley

1 teaspoon dried oregano

1. In a large pot, heat the olive oil over medium heat. Add the onion and sauté until translucent and browning, 8 to 10 minutes.

2. Add the garlic, salt, and pepper and cook for 1 minute, stirring occasionally. Add the tomatoes, tomato paste, and 2 cups water. Stir well to combine. Stir in the bay leaves, basil, parsley, and oregano. Reduce the heat to low and simmer, stirring occasionally, until thick, 20 to 30 minutes.

3. Remove and discard the bay leaves. Season the sauce with salt and pepper to taste.

4. Serve immediately, or let cool and store in an airtight container in the fridge for up to 3 days or in the freezer for up to 1 month.

TIP: Extra marinara can be served as a dipping sauce for Truffle Butter Rolls (page 17) or stored in an airtight container and frozen for up to 3 months.

Makes about 5 cups

Meatball Subs

WITH JO'S MARINARA

PREP: *40 minutes*   **COOK:** *1 hour 30 minutes*   **COOL:** *none*

No one in my house complains when meatball subs are on the menu. Over the years, this meal has become such a family favorite that we eat it about once a month. It's delicious as is, but I've also found myself making just the meatballs and serving them with the marinara sauce on top of spaghetti. This recipe is perfect for a potluck or a meal drop at a friend's, too, as you can transport the marinara sauce in a mason jar for easy serving.

1¾ cups panko bread crumbs

⅔ cup whole milk

1 pound ground beef (92% lean)

1 pound ground pork

1 cup shredded Parmesan cheese (about 4 ounces)

¼ cup minced yellow onion

1 large egg

2 garlic cloves, minced

2 tablespoons chopped fresh basil, plus more for serving

2 tablespoons chopped fresh parsley

1 tablespoon chopped fresh oregano

1½ teaspoons freshly cracked black pepper

¾ teaspoon garlic salt

¾ teaspoon kosher salt

3 tablespoons olive oil

1 recipe Jo's Marinara Sauce (page 207) or 5 cups marinara sauce

8 hoagie buns

⅔ cup mayonnaise

16 slices provolone cheese

1. In a large bowl, stir together the bread crumbs and milk. Let sit for about 5 minutes.

2. Add the beef, pork, Parmesan, onion, egg, garlic, basil, parsley, oregano, pepper, garlic salt, and salt to the bowl. Using your hands, gently mix all components until well combined.

3. Roll the meat mixture into twenty-four 1½-inch (about 2-ounce) balls and place on a plate.

4. In a 14-inch cast-iron skillet, heat 1½ tablespoons of the olive oil over medium-high heat. Add half of the meatballs and cook, flipping once, until browned on two sides, about 2 minutes per side. Transfer to a clean plate. Repeat with the remaining meatballs and oil.

5. In a large high-sided pan, bring the sauce to a simmer over high heat. Nestle the meatballs in the sauce in an even layer and simmer gently, uncovered, until an instant-read thermometer inserted into the middle of a meatball registers at least 165°F, about 30 minutes.

6. Meanwhile, in the last 10 minutes of cook time, slice the hoagie buns in half and coat each side with 2 teaspoons of mayonnaise. Working in batches as necessary, in a large skillet, place the buns facedown and toast over medium-high heat until golden brown, about 2 to 3 minutes. Repeat until all the buns are toasted.

7. Place 2 slices of provolone on each toasted hoagie bottom. Place 3 meatballs on the cheese and pour a little of the marinara over the top. Garnish with additional chopped basil and top with the other half of the hoagie.

8. Store in an airtight container in the refrigerator for 3 days or freeze for up to 3 months.

Makes 8 sandwiches

Baked Ziti

WITH BOLOGNESE SAUCE

PREP: *25 minutes*   **COOK:** *2 hours*   **COOL:** *10 minutes*

2 tablespoons olive oil

1 tablespoon unsalted butter

1¼ cups finely chopped
   yellow onion

2 teaspoons minced garlic

3 ounces pancetta, diced

1 pound ground beef
   (92% lean)

4 tablespoons tomato paste

1 cup chicken stock
   (page 145 or store-bought)

1 cup dry white wine

1 bay leaf

1 teaspoon kosher salt

1 teaspoon freshly
   cracked black pepper

1 teaspoon garlic powder

⅛ teaspoon grated nutmeg

1 pound ziti

Cooking spray

2 cups heavy cream

½ cup grated Parmesan
   cheese (about 2 ounces)

1 tablespoon chopped
   fresh parsley

1 cup shredded Parmesan
   cheese (about 4 ounces)

8 ounces low-moisture
   mozzarella cheese,
   shredded (about 2 cups)

2 tablespoons chopped
   fresh basil

1. In a medium stockpot, heat the oil and butter over medium heat for 2 minutes. Add the onion and cook, stirring occasionally, for 5 minutes, then add the garlic and cook and stir for 2 more minutes. Add the pancetta and cook for 2 minutes. Add the ground beef and cook, breaking it up into small pieces, until browned and fully cooked, 4 to 5 minutes. Stir in the tomato paste and cook for 2 minutes.

2. Add the stock, wine, bay leaf, salt, pepper, garlic powder, and nutmeg to the meat mixture and scrape the bottom of the pot with a wooden spoon to release any browned bits. Partially cover the pot, reduce the heat, and simmer, stirring occasionally, for 30 minutes.

3. Meanwhile, bring a large pot of generously salted water to a boil. Cook the ziti until al dente. Drain, reserving 1 cup pasta cooking water. Set the ziti aside.

4. When the sauce has simmered for 30 minutes, add the reserved pasta cooking water and cook for another 30 minutes.

5. Preheat the oven to 375°F. Spray a 9 ×13-inch baking dish with cooking spray.

6. Add the cream, grated Parmesan, and parsley to the sauce. Increase the heat to medium and bring to a simmer, stirring constantly, until the mixture thickens slightly, 6 to 7 minutes. Remove from the heat.

7. Add the cooked, drained ziti to the sauce along with the shredded Parmesan and 1 cup of the shredded mozzarella. Stir to combine.

8. Transfer the ziti mixture to the prepared baking dish and sprinkle the remaining cup of shredded mozzarella on top.

9. Cover the baking dish with foil and bake for 20 minutes. Carefully remove the foil and continue baking until the cheese has completely melted, an additional 10 minutes.

10. Let cool for about 10 minutes, then sprinkle with basil and serve.

11. Store in an airtight container in the refrigerator for 3 to 5 days.

Makes 6 to 8 servings

White Chicken Alfredo Lasagna

PREP: *20 minutes*   **COOK:** *1 hour 25 minutes*   **COOL:** *10 minutes*

My daughter Ella loves white sauce with pasta. Besides chicken, it's her favorite way to top pizza and pasta. This recipe was an experiment in combining her two favorite toppings in a classic lasagna—and I love the way it turned out. Thankfully Ella did, too.

Cooking spray

16 lasagna noodles
(approximately 1½ pounds)

1 tablespoon olive oil

3 tablespoons unsalted butter

1 cup chopped shallots

1 teaspoon minced garlic

4 cups heavy cream

1 cup whole milk

1½ cups shredded Parmesan
cheese (about 6 ounces)

1 teaspoon crushed red
pepper flakes

1 teaspoon kosher salt

1 teaspoon freshly
cracked black pepper

8 ounces cream cheese,
cut into 6 pieces

4 cups baby spinach

2 cups cooked shredded
chicken

Fresh chives or parsley,
for garnish (optional)

1. Preheat the oven to 375°F. Spray a 9 × 13-inch baking dish with cooking spray.

2. Bring a large pot of generously salted water to a boil. Cook the noodles until a bit firmer than al dente. Drain, then toss with the olive oil so they do not stick together.

3. In a medium skillet, melt the butter over medium heat. Add the shallots and cook, stirring occasionally, until tender, 5 minutes. Add the garlic and cook and stir until fragrant, 1 minute. Stir in the cream and milk and bring to a simmer, then reduce the heat to maintain a simmer. Add 1 cup of the Parmesan, the pepper flakes, salt, and black pepper and cook, stirring constantly, until the cheese is completely melted and smooth, 3 to 5 minutes. Add the cream cheese and cook, stirring occasionally, until smooth, another 3 minutes. Remove from the heat and set aside.

4. Spread ½ cup of sauce on the bottom of the dish. Arrange four noodles on top of the sauce. Top the noodles with 1 cup of the spinach, ½ cup of the shredded chicken, 1½ cups of the sauce, and 2 tablespoons of the Parmesan. Repeat three more times to create a total of four layers starting with the noodles and ending with Parmesan.

5. Cover the baking dish with foil and bake for 40 minutes. Carefully remove the foil and continue baking until lightly browned and bubbly, an additional 15 to 20 minutes. Let cool for 10 minutes.

6. Serve garnished with fresh chives or parsley (if using).

7. Store in an airtight container in the refrigerator for 3 to 5 days.

Makes 6 to 8 servings

Pink Baked Ziti

PREP: *15 minutes*   **COOK:** *1 hour 45 minutes*   **COOL:** *10 minutes*

My girls love pink sauce and they love ziti—so this recipe is their absolutely favorite combination of pasta. I have to say, it's become a favorite of mine, too!

1 pound ziti

1 tablespoon unsalted butter

1½ teaspoons olive oil

¾ cup chopped onion

4 garlic cloves, peeled

1½ pounds Roma (plum) tomatoes, cored and quartered (about 7)

6 fresh basil leaves

1 teaspoon kosher salt

½ teaspoon onion powder

½ teaspoon freshly cracked black pepper

½ cup heavy cream

4 ounces fresh mozzarella cheese, torn into 1-inch pieces

½ cup grated Parmesan cheese (about 2 ounces)

2 tablespoons torn fresh basil, for garnish

1. Bring a large pot of generously salted water to a boil. Cook the ziti until just shy of al dente according to the package directions.

2. In a medium pot, heat the butter and olive oil over medium-high heat until the butter melts. Add the onion and cook, stirring occasionally, until the onion is soft and translucent, 6 minutes. Add the whole garlic cloves and cook for 3 more minutes. Stir in the tomatoes, basil leaves, salt, onion powder, and pepper. Reduce the heat to medium-low and simmer for 50 minutes, stirring occasionally.

3. Preheat the oven to 350°F.

4. Remove the pot from the heat and, using an immersion blender, pulse the sauce in 10-second intervals until smooth. While blending, slowly pour in the cream. (Alternatively, use a blender, but do so in small batches and with caution as the contents will be hot.)

5. Return the sauce to the pot, if needed, and bring to a slow simmer over medium heat, then remove from the heat.

6. In a 7 × 11-inch baking dish, stir the ziti with the sauce until well coated. Nestle the mozzarella into the ziti, then sprinkle evenly with the Parmesan.

7. Cover the baking dish with foil and bake until the cheese is melted and the ziti is hot throughout, 30 minutes. Let cool for 10 minutes.

8. Garnish with the torn fresh basil and serve.

9. Store in an airtight container in the refrigerator for 3 to 5 days or freeze for up to 6 weeks. Thaw frozen ziti in the fridge or heat over low heat.

Makes 4 servings

Japchae

PREP: *30 minutes*   **COOK:** *30 minutes*   **COOL:** *15 minutes*

NOODLE SAUCE

3 tablespoons soy sauce

1 tablespoon sesame oil

1 tablespoon sugar

1½ teaspoons sesame seeds

1 teaspoon minced garlic

1 teaspoon freshly
   cracked black pepper

RIB EYE MARINADE

1 tablespoon soy sauce

1 teaspoon mirin

1 teaspoon minced garlic

½ teaspoon sugar

½ teaspoon sesame seeds

1½ pounds rib eye steak,
   cut into thin slices

JAPCHAE

4 tablespoons plus
   ½ teaspoon sesame oil

2 cups fresh spinach

1 teaspoon minced garlic

1 teaspoon freshly
   cracked black pepper

1½ teaspoons sesame seeds

¼ teaspoon kosher salt

7 ounces sweet potato
   noodles

1 yellow onion, diced

½ cup matchstick-cut carrots

6 shiitake mushrooms,
   thinly sliced

1. To make the noodle sauce: In a medium bowl, whisk together the soy sauce, sesame oil, sugar, sesame seeds, garlic, pepper, and 1 tablespoon of water until well combined. Set aside.

2. To marinate the rib eye: In a medium bowl, whisk together the soy sauce, mirin, garlic, sugar, and sesame seeds until well combined. Add the sliced rib eye. Mix well to ensure that the rib eye is completely coated. Cover and refrigerate for at least 15 minutes.

3. To make the japchae: In a large skillet, heat ½ teaspoon of the sesame oil over medium heat, then add the spinach and garlic. Cook, stirring occasionally, until the spinach is wilted, 2 minutes. Remove from the heat and stir in the pepper, ½ teaspoon of the sesame seeds, and the salt. Transfer to a plate and set aside. Wipe the pan clean.

4. In a medium saucepan, bring 5 cups of water to a boil. Add the noodles and cook, stirring frequently to prevent clumping, until tender, 10 to 15 minutes.

5. Meanwhile, in the wiped-out skillet, heat 1 tablespoon of the sesame oil over medium heat. Add the onion and cook, stirring occasionally, until tender, 3 to 5 minutes. Transfer to the plate with the spinach and set aside.

6. In the same pan, heat another tablespoon of sesame oil over medium heat. Add the carrots and mushrooms and cook until tender and soft, 5 to 7 minutes. Transfer to the plate with the onion and set aside.

7. Drain but do not rinse the noodles. Add them to the pan along with another tablespoon of the sesame oil and toss. Transfer the noodles to the bowl with the noodle sauce and mix together.

8. In the same pan, heat the remaining 1 tablespoon sesame oil over high heat. Add the marinated rib eye with its marinade and cook, stirring often, until there is less than 1 tablespoon of liquid left in the pan, 4 to 6 minutes.

9. Transfer the vegetables and cooked rib eye to the bowl of noodles and mix together, using tongs.

10. Transfer to a serving dish and sprinkle with the remaining 1 teaspoon sesame seeds. Japchae can be served hot, room temperature, or cold.

11. Store in an airtight container in the refrigerator for up to 3 days.

Makes 2 to 4 servings

Bibimbap

PREP: *1 hour*   **COOK:** *25 minutes*   **COOL:** *none*

1 cup matchstick-cut carrots

3¼ teaspoons kosher salt

1 cup matchstick-cut
   daikon radish

2 tablespoons plus
   ½ teaspoon sesame oil

2 cups fresh spinach

2½ teaspoons minced garlic

½ teaspoon sesame seeds

¼ teaspoon freshly
   cracked black pepper

12 ounces rib eye steak,
   cut into thin slices

½ yellow onion, diced

½ cup chopped green onions

¼ cup soy sauce

1 tablespoon gochujang

1 tablespoon chili powder

1 cup sliced shiitake
   mushrooms

2 cups cooked short-grain rice

1 cup bean sprouts, rinsed

¼ cup Homemade Kimchi
   (page 110 or store-bought)

1 large egg (optional)

Sriracha, for serving

1. In a small bowl, toss together the carrots and 1 teaspoon of the salt. In a separate small bowl, toss together the radish and another 1 teaspoon of salt. Set both side for 10 to 15 minutes.

2. In a medium skillet, heat ½ teaspoon of the sesame oil over medium heat. Add the spinach and 1 teaspoon of the garlic and cook, stirring occasionally, until the spinach is wilted, 2 minutes. Remove the pan from the heat and stir in ¼ teaspoon of the salt, the sesame seeds, and black pepper. Transfer to a small bowl and set aside. Wipe the pan clean.

3. In a medium bowl, add the sliced rib eye, yellow onion, ¼ cup of the green onions, the soy sauce, gochujang, and remaining 1½ teaspoons garlic and stir well to combine. Heat the wiped-out skillet over medium heat. Add the beef mixture and cook until the meat reaches the desired doneness, 3 to 5 minutes for medium-well. Transfer to a clean bowl and set aside. Wipe the pan clean again.

4. Drain the carrots and set them aside. Using your hands, drain and squeeze the radish to remove any excess water. Place back in the bowl and toss with the chili powder until well combined.

5. In the wiped-out pan, heat 1 tablespoon of the sesame oil over medium heat. Add the mushrooms and cook, stirring occasionally, until soft but not mushy, 3 to 5 minutes. Remove from the heat and stir in the remaining 1 teaspoon salt.

6. Brush the inside cavity of a stone dolsot, 10-inch cast-iron skillet, or wok with the remaining 1 tablespoon sesame oil. Place the rice in the bottom of the vessel. In distinct sections around the inside edge, place the carrots, radish, spinach, mushrooms, rib eye, bean sprouts, remaining ¼ cup green onions, and the kimchi. Crack an egg in the center, if desired.

7. Place the vessel on the stove on low heat and let cook for 3 minutes—do not stir. Increase the heat to medium-high and cook until the rice on the bottom of the dish is toasted, 5 to 7 minutes—again, do not stir.

8. Carefully remove from the heat. Stir everything together (with chopsticks, if you have them) and serve immediately with sriracha.

Makes 2 servings

Chicken Fried Rice

PREP: *25 minutes*   COOK: *40 minutes*   COOL: *30 minutes*

Chicken fried rice always takes me back to a time in college when I lived in New York. I was interning and didn't have a lot of money, so most nights I would stop at this little Chinese restaurant around the corner from my apartment and order a side of chicken fried rice. It came in a small white takeout box. That memory is such a part of this dish, even today it's hard to separate the two. I wouldn't want to though—I actually prefer the nostalgia and familiarity of the flavors. Even though I'm not usually a peas and carrots kind of girl, this is the one dish where I am always happy to find them.

1 cup jasmine rice

1 tablespoon vegetable oil

2 tablespoons sesame oil

2 chicken breasts, cut into ½-inch pieces (about 1 pound)

1 tablespoon soy sauce

1 teaspoon kosher salt

1 teaspoon freshly cracked black pepper

¾ cup fresh or frozen green peas

¾ cup diced carrots

¼ cup diced yellow onion

5 garlic cloves, minced

2 large eggs

¼ cup hoisin sauce

1 teaspoon grated fresh ginger

3 tablespoons thinly sliced green onions, for garnish

1. In a medium bowl, combine the rice with cool water to cover. Agitate the rice and pour out the cloudy water, repeating until the water runs clear. Drain in a fine-mesh sieve.

2. In a large saucepan, bring 2 cups of water to a boil. Add the rice, return to a boil, then reduce the heat to low, cover, and let simmer for 12 minutes. Remove the pan from the heat and set aside, covered, for 5 to 10 minutes. Spread the rice onto a baking sheet and let cool to room temperature.

3. In a 14-inch wok or nonstick skillet, heat the vegetable oil and 1 tablespoon of the sesame oil over medium-high heat. Add the chicken, soy sauce, salt, and pepper. Cook, stirring constantly, until the chicken is dark golden brown, 10 to 12 minutes. Using a slotted spoon, transfer the chicken to a medium bowl.

4. Add the remaining 1 tablespoon sesame oil to the wok. Add the peas, carrots, and onion and cook, stirring often, until almost tender, about 4 minutes. Add the garlic and continue cooking, stirring constantly, until the vegetables are crisp-tender and the garlic is fragrant, about 1 more minute. Transfer the vegetables to the bowl with the chicken.

5. Crack the eggs into the wok and cook, stirring constantly, until scrambled, 1 to 2 minutes. Add the chicken, vegetables, cooled rice, hoisin, and ginger to the wok and stir until hot and thoroughly mixed. Serve sprinkled with green onions.

6. Store in an airtight container in the refrigerator for up to 3 days.

TIP: Make the rice a day ahead and place in the refrigerator overnight. This will keep the fried rice from getting mushy.

Makes 4 servings

Mongolian Beef

PREP: *10 minutes*   **COOK:** *30 minutes*   **COOL:** *none*

For years, I wouldn't even try to cook Chinese food at home. Re-creating the same tastes our family loved from takeout felt futile. This Mongolian beef changed that perception for me and boosted my confidence. It's easy to throw together on a weeknight. I just make sure everyone is ready to eat as soon as the dish is ready—it's best served hot!

1 pound flank steak

1 cup cornstarch

6 tablespoons vegetable oil

½ cup chopped green onions, white and green parts separated

1 teaspoon minced garlic

1 teaspoon grated fresh ginger

6 tablespoons low-sodium soy sauce

¼ cup packed light brown sugar

1 tablespoon sesame seeds, for garnish

1. Using a sharp knife, cut the flank steak against the grain into ¼-inch slices. Put the cornstarch in a medium bowl and add the sliced steak. Toss until the steak is well coated, then shake to remove the excess starch. Set the steak aside on a plate.

2. In a medium nonstick skillet, heat 2 tablespoons of the oil over medium-high heat. Add the white parts of the green onions, the garlic, and ginger and cook until fragrant and slightly brown, 1 minute. Add the soy sauce, brown sugar, and 2 tablespoons of water and bring to a boil. Reduce the heat to medium-low and simmer until the sugar is dissolved and the sauce is slightly reduced, 5 minutes.

3. In a large nonstick skillet, heat 2 tablespoons of the oil over medium-high heat. Place half of the steak, cut sides down, in the skillet. Cook, flipping once, for 1 to 2 minutes per side, then transfer to a clean plate. Repeat with the remaining 2 tablespoons oil and steak.

4. Bring the sauce back to a boil over medium-high heat, then add the cooked steak and stir until all the meat is completely coated and the sauce has thickened, 90 seconds.

5. Serve immediately, topped with the green parts of the green onions and the sesame seeds, with rice on the side, if you like.

TIP: Freezing the raw steak for 10 minutes helps firm it up for easier slicing. This dish is excellent tossed with broccoli or fresh green beans, and served with fried or steamed rice.

Makes 2 to 3 servings

Braised Short Ribs

WITH WHITE CHEDDAR MASH AND ASPARAGUS

PREP: *30 minutes*   **COOK:** *2 hours 40 minutes*   **COOL:** *none*

BRAISED SHORT RIBS

4 pounds bone-in beef short ribs

1½ teaspoons kosher salt

½ teaspoon freshly
    cracked black pepper

3 tablespoons olive oil

½ medium white onion,
    sliced ¼ inch thick

2 garlic cloves, minced

2 cups beef stock

1 cup marsala wine

2 tablespoons Worcestershire sauce

2 bay leaves

WHITE CHEDDAR MASH

3½ pounds russet potatoes, peeled
    and chopped into 2-inch pieces

1 teaspoon kosher salt

1 cup heavy cream, warmed

2 garlic cloves, minced

2 tablespoons unsalted butter,
    melted

1½ teaspoons garlic salt

1 teaspoon freshly cracked
    black pepper

1 cup shredded white Cheddar
    cheese (about 4 ounces)

1 tablespoon minced chives

ASPARAGUS

1 pound asparagus, trimmed

1 tablespoon unsalted butter, melted

Kosher salt and freshly cracked
    black pepper

1. To make the short ribs: Preheat the oven to 350°F.

2. Season the short ribs with the salt and pepper. In a large ovenproof skillet, heat the olive oil over medium-high heat. Place the short ribs in the skillet in one layer and sear on all sides until dark brown, about 1 minute per side. Transfer to a plate.

3. Add the onion to the skillet and cook, stirring often, for 2 minutes. Add the garlic and cook, stirring constantly, until fragrant, about 30 seconds.

4. Remove the pan from the heat. Add the beef stock, wine, and Worcestershire to the skillet and stir to incorporate. Add the seared meat, meaty side down, and nestle the bay leaves into the broth. Cover with a lid or foil and bake until tender and falling off the bone, 2 to 2½ hours.

5. To make the white Cheddar mash: In a large pot, add the potatoes, salt, and enough water to cover by 1 inch. Bring to a boil over medium-high heat and cook until fork-tender, 15 to 20 minutes. Drain, then return the potatoes to the pot.

6. Add the cream, garlic, butter, garlic salt, and pepper to the potatoes. Using an electric mixer, beat on medium speed until smooth, about 30 seconds. Stir in the Cheddar and chives until well combined.

7. To make the asparagus: Cut the asparagus into 2- to 3-inch sections.

8. Bring a large saucepan of water to a boil over medium-high heat. Add the asparagus and cook for 2 minutes. Using a slotted spoon, remove the asparagus pieces and place in a medium bowl. Add the butter and salt and pepper to taste and toss to combine.

9. To serve, spoon 1 cup of mashed potatoes into a bowl, top with 1 braised short rib, and ⅓ cup asparagus for each portion. Skim the fat from the sauce, if desired, and spoon some sauce over the meat.

10. Store in an airtight container in the refrigerator for 3 to 5 days. Do not freeze.

TIP: Substitute the Brown Butter Mashed Potatoes (page 171) for these potatoes.

Makes 4 to 6 servings

Coal-Grilled Rib Eye

WITH BEURRE MONTÉ AND RED CHIMICHURRI

PREP: *35 minutes*   **COOK:** *30 minutes*   **COOL:** *1 hour*

Chip reminds me almost every time we have steak that a good cut has all the flavor it needs. There is truth in that, but I still like to play around with sauces that complement the meat and elevate the meal a bit. Here, the beurre monté and red chimichurri work beautifully together.

One 12-ounce jar roasted red peppers, drained

⅓ cup roughly chopped fresh parsley

¼ cup plus 1 tablespoon olive oil

2 tablespoons red wine vinegar

1 tablespoon light brown sugar

1 tablespoon crushed red pepper flakes

8 tablespoons (1 stick) unsalted butter

Two 1-pound, 1½-inch-thick boneless rib eye steaks, at room temperature

2 teaspoons kosher salt, plus more to taste

½ teaspoon freshly cracked black pepper, plus more to taste

1. To make the red chimichurri, in a food processor, combine the roasted red peppers, parsley, ¼ cup of the olive oil, the red wine vinegar, brown sugar, and pepper flakes and pulse, scraping down the sides as needed, until smooth. Transfer the sauce to a bowl and refrigerate for 1 hour before serving.

2. Build a pyramid of charcoal briquettes slightly off-center in a charcoal grill. Light the briquettes; they are ready once the edges are gray, approximately 20 minutes.

3. To make the beurre monté, in a small saucepan, bring 2 tablespoons of water to a boil. Reduce the heat to low and whisk in the butter, 1 tablespoon at a time, until all the butter is incorporated and the mixture is smooth.

4. Rub the steaks with the remaining 1 tablespoon olive oil, then season with the salt and pepper.

5. Place the steaks directly over the briquettes to sear for about 4 minutes on each side, then move them to the cooler side of the grill and cook until an instant-read thermometer reads 115°F (for rare), 4 to 5 minutes per side. For medium to medium-well, the thermometer should read 130°F to 140°F, 6 to 7 minutes per side on the cooler part of the grill. (The meat will continue cooking for a few minutes while resting.) Transfer the steaks to a cutting board and let rest for 10 to 15 minutes before slicing at an angle into ½-inch slices.

6. To serve, spoon the beurre monté onto a plate, place the sliced steak on the sauce, then top with the red chimichurri and additional salt and pepper to taste.

7. Store in an airtight container in the refrigerator for up to 2 days.

Makes 4 servings

Steak & Herb Chimichurri

PREP: *35 minutes*   **COOK:** *20 minutes*   **COOL:** *2 hours 45 minutes*

Steak night is a regular occurrence at our house. When the kids were younger, I quickly learned it was easiest to slice steak before serving. But even now that all the kids, with the exception of Crew, are far beyond the age where they need help cutting their meat, I still prefer to serve steak sliced. I've found that it's easier for people to serve themselves the amount of meat they want and, quite simply, it makes for a prettier presentation. In this recipe, though, the chimichurri sauce is the star.

2 tablespoons Worcestershire sauce

1 tablespoon plus 1 teaspoon kosher salt

1 tablespoon freshly cracked black pepper

Two 12-ounce, 1-inch-thick New York strip steaks, at room temperature

3 cups fresh parsley leaves (from 2 large bunches)

1 cup cilantro leaves (from 1 bunch)

1 garlic clove

¼ cup olive oil

1 tablespoon rice vinegar

¼ teaspoon crushed red pepper flakes

1. In a zip-top plastic bag, combine the Worcestershire, 1 tablespoon of the salt, and the pepper. Add the steaks, seal the bag, and gently massage the bag to coat the meat. Marinate in the refrigerator for 2 hours. Let the meat sit at room temperature for about 30 minutes before grilling.

2. To make the chimichurri sauce: In a food processor, combine the parsley, cilantro, garlic, olive oil, vinegar, remaining 1 teaspoon salt, and the pepper flakes and pulse, scraping down the sides as needed, until the herbs are finely chopped and the sauce has a salsa-like consistency, 8 to 10 pulses. Put the sauce in a bowl and refrigerate for 1 hour before serving.

3. Build a pyramid of charcoal briquettes slightly off-center in a charcoal grill. Light the briquettes; they are ready once the edges are gray, approximately 20 minutes.

4. Place the steaks directly over the briquettes to sear for about 2 minutes on each side, then move them to the cooler side of the grill, cover, and cook until an instant-read thermometer reads 115°F (for rare), 3 minutes per side. For medium to medium-well, the thermometer should read 130°F to 140°F, 4 to 6 minutes per side on the cooler part of the grill. (The meat will continue cooking for a few minutes while resting.) Transfer the steaks to a cutting board and let rest for 10 to 15 minutes before slicing at an angle into ½-inch slices.

5. Serve the sliced steak topped with chimichurri.

6. Store in an airtight container in the refrigerator for up to 2 days.

Makes 2 servings

Beef Tenderloin

WITH MUSHROOM TARRAGON SAUCE

PREP: *20 minutes*   **COOK:** *1 hour*   **COOL:** *15 minutes*

½ cup plus 1 tablespoon olive oil

5 pounds beef tenderloin, at room temperature

1 tablespoon kosher salt

1 tablespoon freshly cracked black pepper

4 tablespoons (½ stick) unsalted butter

1 shallot, minced

1 garlic clove, minced

8 ounces baby bella mushrooms, thinly sliced

2 tablespoons all-purpose flour

½ tablespoon beef bouillon granules

1 cup hot water

½ cup dry red wine

1 teaspoon chopped fresh tarragon

1. Heat a convection oven or outdoor grill to 375°F.

2. On a baking sheet, massage ½ cup of the olive oil onto the beef, coating it completely. Sprinkle evenly with the salt and pepper and rub to coat completely.

3. Place the beef on the baking sheet in the oven or directly on the grill. Cook, flipping once, until the thickest part of the tenderloin reads 115°F to 120°F on an instant-read thermometer (for rare), 13 to 15 minutes per side. For medium to medium-well, the thermometer should read 135°F to 140°F, approximately 15 to 20 minutes per side. Let rest for 15 minutes before slicing.

4. Meanwhile, in a small sauté pan, melt 2 tablespoons of the butter over medium heat. Add the shallot to the pan and cook, stirring often, for 2 minutes. Add the garlic and cook, stirring constantly, 1 more minute. Add the mushrooms to the pan and cook until tender, 3 to 4 minutes. Transfer the mushroom mixture to a bowl.

5. To the same sauté pan over medium heat, melt the remaining 2 tablespoons butter with the remaining tablespoon olive oil. Add the flour and cook, whisking until smooth and starting to bubble, 1 minute.

6. In a small bowl, stir together the bouillon and hot water until dissolved.

7. Add the bouillon mixture to the flour mixture and whisk to combine. Add the wine and stir to combine. Add the mushroom mixture and ½ teaspoon of the tarragon and reduce the heat to low, cooking until thickened, about 5 minutes.

8. Spoon the sauce over the rested, sliced beef. Garnish with the remaining ½ teaspoon fresh tarragon.

9. Store in an airtight container in the refrigerator for 3 to 5 days.

Makes 10 servings

Smash Burgers

PREP: *15 minutes*   **COOK:** *30 minutes*   **COOL:** *none*

SMASH SAUCE

1 cup ketchup

2 tablespoons mayonnaise

2 tablespoons dill relish

1 tablespoon yellow mustard

1 tablespoon sliced
   green onions

½ teaspoon freshly
   cracked black pepper

¼ teaspoon kosher salt

SMASH BURGERS

3 pounds ground beef
   (80% lean)

3 tablespoons grated
   white onion

3 tablespoons
   Worcestershire sauce

3 tablespoons ketchup

¾ teaspoon freshly
   cracked black pepper

¾ teaspoon kosher salt

Vegetable oil, for greasing

2 onions, thinly sliced
   (optional)

2 poblano peppers,
   sliced (optional)

16 slices American cheese

8 teaspoons mayonnaise

8 brioche burger buns

8 green-leaf lettuce leaves

8 thick slices tomato

1. To make the smash sauce: In a small bowl, stir together the ketchup, mayonnaise, relish, mustard, green onions, pepper, and salt and mix until well combined. Cover and refrigerate until ready to serve.

2. To make the smash burgers: In a large bowl, using your hands, mix the ground beef, grated onion, Worcestershire, ketchup, pepper, and salt until combined. Divide the meat into 16 equal portions, then roll into balls.

3. Heat a griddle to 375°F or a cast-iron skillet over medium-high heat and brush it with oil.

4. Place a ball of meat on the hot griddle, then quickly and carefully place a piece of parchment paper directly over the top of the meat. Using a burger press or the bottom side of a saucepan, press the meat firmly onto the griddle to create a patty. Continue pressing patties until the griddle is full. (If using, add the sliced onions and sliced poblano peppers to the griddle as the burgers cook, stirring them frequently until they are golden brown and tender, 4 to 5 minutes.)

5. Cook the patties for 2 minutes. Flip and top each patty with one slice of cheese. Cook until the meat is cooked and cheese is melted, another 2 minutes. Repeat until all the patties have been cooked.

6. Spread ½ teaspoon of mayonnaise on the cut side of each bun and place them facedown on the griddle until toasted, 2 to 3 minutes. Remove and set aside.

7. To assemble the burgers, spread a generous portion of burger sauce over the top and bottom bun. Stack 2 meat patties on the bottom half of the bun. Top with a portion of cooked peppers and onions (if using), then a piece of lettuce and a slice of tomato. Spread a generous portion of burger sauce over the top bun and place it on top.

8. Store the sauce in an airtight container in the refrigerator for up to 5 days. The other components do not store well.

Makes 8 servings

Chili Pie

PREP: *15 minutes*   **COOK**: *35 minutes*   **COOL**: *10 minutes*

Chip prefers a slice of cornbread with his chili. I like cornbread, too, but I've never loved how quickly it gets soggy sitting in the bowl of chili. This recipe offers just the right solution. The textures of the cornbread and chili stay distinct while still giving off that hearty taste we welcome on a cool, fall night.

1 tablespoon unsalted butter

1 cup diced white onion

1 teaspoon minced garlic

1 pound ground beef

3 ounces tomato paste
(half of a 6-ounce can)

One 14.5-ounce can petite
diced tomatoes, drained

1 tablespoon chili powder

1 teaspoon onion powder

1½ teaspoons kosher salt

1 teaspoon freshly
cracked black pepper

1 large egg

1 cup yellow cornmeal

1 cup all-purpose flour

1 cup whole milk

¼ cup vegetable oil

1 tablespoon baking powder

One 15-ounce can
ranch-style beans,
drained and rinsed

2 cups shredded Cheddar
cheese (about 8 ounces)

1 cup sour cream,
for garnish (optional)

1 tablespoon minced chives,
for garnish (optional)

1. Preheat the oven to 400°F.

2. In a medium skillet, melt the butter over medium heat. Add the onion and cook, stirring often, until tender, about 5 minutes. Add the garlic and cook, stirring constantly, until fragrant, 1 more minute. Add the ground beef and cook, breaking it up into small pieces, until browned, 4 to 5 minutes. Drain the fat.

3. Add the tomato paste and cook, stirring, for 2 minutes. Add the canned tomatoes, chili powder, onion powder, 1 teaspoon of the salt, and pepper and stir to combine. Remove from the heat and set aside while preparing the cornbread topping.

4. To make the cornbread topping: In a medium bowl, lightly beat the egg. Add the cornmeal, flour, milk, oil, baking powder, and the remaining ½ teaspoon salt to the bowl. Stir until just combined, leaving some lumps in the batter.

5. In a 9 × 13-inch baking dish, add the meat mixture and spread evenly. Top with the beans, then 1 cup of the Cheddar. Top with the cornbread mixture and smooth into an even layer that doesn't quite reach the edges, allowing the meat mixture to show.

6. Bake, uncovered, until the top is set and slightly browned, 15 to 20 minutes.

7. Let cool for 10 minutes before serving. Top each serving with a sprinkle of the remaining cup of Cheddar, plus sour cream and chives (if using).

8. Store in an airtight container in the refrigerator for 3 to 5 days.

TIP: Add in 1 teaspoon crushed red pepper flakes in step 3 to make this a spicy chili pie.

Makes 8 servings

Beef Bourguignon

PREP: *30 minutes*   **COOK:** *5 hours*   **COOL:** *none*

When we started broadcasting reruns of Julia Child's cooking show on Magnolia Network, I spent an entire weekend curled up on our sofa binge-watching every episode with my girls. I never realized how many of our generation's most-loved recipes actually began in her kitchen. Beef bourguignon is one food that I can't think about without Julia's original, definitive recipe coming to mind. I learned to cook beef bourguignon with that recipe, then made changes to suit our family's taste. Every year, at the first signs of winter, there's a good chance this is the dish you'll find simmering on our stove.

4 tablespoons extra-virgin olive oil

½ pound bacon, chopped

3 pounds chuck roast,
  cut into 1½-inch chunks

2 medium carrots, peeled
  and cut into 1-inch pieces

1 large white onion, sliced

1 teaspoon kosher salt

¾ teaspoon freshly
  ground black pepper

3 tablespoons all-purpose flour

One 750 mL bottle dry red wine

4 cups beef stock

2 tablespoons tomato paste

4 garlic cloves, smashed

2 bay leaves

½ teaspoon fresh thyme leaves

4 tablespoons (½ stick) unsalted
  butter

30 small frozen pearl onions, thawed

1 herb bundle, including 6 fresh
  parsley sprigs, 3 fresh thyme
  sprigs, and 1 bay leaf (see Note,
  page 145)

1 pound white mushrooms,
  trimmed and quartered

Brown Butter Mashed Potatoes
  (page 171) or cheese grits,
  for serving

1. Preheat the oven to 450°F.

2. In a large Dutch oven, heat 2 tablespoons of the olive oil over medium-high heat. Add the bacon and cook, stirring occasionally, until it starts to brown, 5 to 7 minutes. Remove the bacon and set aside, reserving the drippings in the Dutch oven.

3. Dry the beef with paper towels. Increase the heat to medium-high. Working in batches to avoid overcrowding the pan, add the meat to the Dutch oven and sear until browned on all sides, about 6 minutes per batch. Set the meat aside with the bacon.

4. Reduce the heat to medium. Using the fat in the Dutch oven, cook the carrots and onion until softened and lightly browned, about 7 minutes. Drain any remaining fat from the pan, retaining the carrots and onion.

5. Return the bacon and beef to the Dutch oven and season with ½ teaspoon each of the salt and pepper. Toss to evenly distribute. Add the flour and toss to evenly coat. Transfer the Dutch oven, uncovered, to the preheated oven for 5 minutes.

6. Carefully remove the pot from the oven, toss all the ingredients again, and place back in the oven, uncovered, for an additional 5 minutes. Carefully remove the pot from the oven and reduce the heat to 325°F.

7. Stir the wine, 3 cups of the beef broth, the tomato paste, garlic, bay leaves, and thyme into the beef mixture. Bring the pot to a gentle simmer over medium-low heat and cook, scraping the bottom of the pot with a wooden spoon to release any browned bits, until just simmering. Cover and place in the oven. Cook until the beef can be pierced easily with a fork, 3 to 4 hours.

CONTINUED

CONTINUED FROM PAGE 237

8. During the last hour of cooking, in a medium skillet, melt 2 tablespoons of the butter with 1 tablespoon of the olive oil over medium heat. Add the pearl onions to the pan and cook, stirring occasionally, until browned, 8 to 10 minutes. Add the remaining 1 cup beef broth, remaining ¼ teaspoon each of salt and pepper, and the herb bundle. Reduce the heat to low and simmer the onions in the liquid until the liquid has evaporated and the onions are tender, about 20 minutes. Using tongs, remove the onions from the pan and set aside. Discard the herb bundle and wipe out the skillet.

9. In the wiped-out skillet, melt the remaining 2 tablespoons butter with the remaining 1 tablespoon oil over medium heat. Add the mushrooms and cook, stirring occasionally, until lightly browned, 5 to 7 minutes. Remove the pan from the heat and set aside.

10. Place a colander over a large pot. Carefully remove the Dutch oven from the oven and pour the contents into the colander so the sauce is transferred to the pot. Discard the bay leaves. Put the contents of the strainer, plus the pearl onions and mushrooms, back into the Dutch oven and cover with the lid.

11. Simmer the sauce, skimming off the fat, over medium heat until the sauce coats the back of a spoon, 5 to 15 minutes.

12. Pour the reduced sauce over the beef mixture in the Dutch oven and simmer together for 5 to 7 minutes.

13. Serve over mashed potatoes.

14. Store in an airtight container in the refrigerator for up to 5 days.

Makes 6 servings

Grilled Portobellos

PREP: *10 minutes*   **COOK:** *10 minutes*   **COOL:** *none*

I'm not always in the mood for red meat. So these portobellos are always a nice substitute when I'm craving a burger or steak sandwich.

4 large portobello mushrooms

2 tablespoons olive oil

2 tablespoons balsamic vinegar

2 teaspoons freshly cracked black pepper

1 teaspoon soy sauce

1 teaspoon finely minced garlic

1 teaspoon kosher salt

1 teaspoon fresh lemon juice

2 tablespoons store-bought balsamic glaze, for garnish

2 teaspoons chopped fresh parsley, for garnish

1. Preheat a grill or grill pan over medium-high heat (400°F to 450°F).

2. Using a damp paper towel, gently wipe the top of each mushroom to remove any dirt. Twist the stem to remove and discard. Using a small spoon, scrape off and remove the gills on the underside of the mushrooms. Place the clean mushrooms upside down on a baking sheet.

3. In a small bowl, whisk together the olive oil, balsamic vinegar, pepper, soy sauce, garlic, and salt. Using a pastry brush, brush half the marinade on the underside of the mushrooms.

4. Place the mushrooms marinated side down onto the hot grill or grill pan, then brush the other side of each mushroom with the remaining marinade. Grill the mushrooms, flipping once, until tender, about 5 minutes per side. Place the cooked mushrooms on a platter and drizzle with the lemon juice. Garnish with the balsamic glaze and parsley.

5. Store in an airtight container in the refrigerator for up to 2 days.

Makes 4 servings

Pineapple Baked Ham

PREP: *10 minutes*　　**COOK:** *2 hours*　　**COOL:** *10 minutes*

I begin every cookbook project the same way, flipping through my collections of recipes I've loved over the years. Cookbooks from the '70s are my favorite to look through—so many microwaves and so many toothpicks! Cooking methods have changed a lot over the years, but I love seeing familiar flavors in those books that have lasted through the generations since. This holiday ham recipe, for instance, feels like it could have been pulled from the pages of a retro cookbook, in the best way. It's a classic ham that's great for entertaining, and simple enough that you can make it the morning of. But it's also traditional in a timeless sort of way, blurring the lines between past and the present—which is always my favorite way to celebrate a holiday.

1 cup packed light brown sugar

1 tablespoon stone-ground mustard

1 teaspoon freshly cracked black pepper

½ teaspoon kosher salt

One 10-pound bone-in fully cooked ham (not spiral sliced)

1 fresh pineapple, peeled, cored, and sliced into rings

Thyme sprigs, for garnish

1. Preheat the oven to 300°F.

2. In a small bowl, stir together the brown sugar, mustard, pepper, and salt until well combined.

3. Score the ham, making crosshatches through just the skin and fat. In a roasting pan, place the ham cut side down. Rub with the brown sugar mixture, pressing it into the crosshatches of the ham.

4. Using toothpicks, take one pineapple ring and secure it to the ham. Repeat, without overlapping, until the pineapple rings cover the sides of the ham. Tent with foil and bake for 1 hour 30 minutes. Remove foil and bake for 30 more minutes.

5. Let rest for 10 minutes. Remove the pineapple rings and reserve. Slice the ham and place it on a platter. Ladle the pan juices over the sliced ham and serve with rolls or as a main dish with the pineapple rings on the side.

6. Store in an airtight container in the refrigerator for 3 to 5 days.

Makes 10 to 12 servings

Pork Chops

WITH APRICOT HONEY CHIPOTLE GLAZE

PREP: *10 minutes*   **COOK:** *1 hour 10 minutes*   **COOL:** *3 hours 10 minutes*

1 cup apricot preserves

½ cup dry white wine

½ cup packed light brown sugar

¼ cup honey

3 tablespoons apple cider vinegar

2 tablespoons Dijon mustard

1 teaspoon kosher salt

½ teaspoon chipotle chile powder

¼ teaspoon ground white pepper

Four 1-inch-thick bone-in frenched pork chops (see Note; approximately 2½ pounds total)

2 tablespoons canola oil

1. To make the marinade: In a blender, add the apricot preserves, wine, brown sugar, honey, vinegar, mustard, salt, chile powder, and white pepper and blend on high for 1 minute.

2. Place the pork chops in a gallon-size zip-top plastic bag and pour the marinade over them. Seal the bag tightly and gently mix so that the pork chops are thoroughly coated. Refrigerate for at least 3 hours.

3. When ready to cook, preheat the oven to 275°F. Line a baking sheet with foil.

4. Remove the pork chops from the marinade, reserving the marinade, and set them on the prepared baking sheet. Using a paper towel, gently pat the excess marinade from the pork chops. Let rest at room temperature while you make the glaze.

5. In a small saucepan, add the reserved marinade and bring it to a boil. Reduce the heat to a simmer and cook, uncovered, for 15 minutes, stirring occasionally, until the glaze coats the back of a spoon. Let cool to room temperature.

6. In a large cast-iron skillet, heat the oil over medium-high heat. When the oil begins to smoke, add the pork chops. Quickly sear the chops for 1 minute per side, then sear the edges.

7. Place the seared chops back on the foil-lined sheet. Using a basting brush, apply a thin coat of glaze all over the pork chops.

8. Bake until the internal temperature reaches 145°F, 40 to 45 minutes, carefully basting the pork chops every 8 to 10 minutes while they cook. Let rest on a plate for 10 minutes.

9. While the chops rest, in a small saucepan over medium-high heat, simmer the glaze until it thickens to the consistency of honey. Plate the rested pork chops and pour the thickened glaze on top.

10. Store wrapped pork chops in the refrigerator for up to 3 days; reheat on low heat in the oven to retain juiciness. Store the glaze in an airtight container in the refrigerator for up to 1 week.

NOTE: A frenched chop has the meat and fat scraped off the end of the bone so the bone is exposed.

Makes 4 servings

Lobster Rolls

PREP: *20 minutes*   **COOK:** *20 minutes*   **COOL:** *10 minutes*

Lobster rolls will forever remind me of our honeymoon. We flew to New York City for a few days, then rented a car and hit the road toward Maine. It was on this trip that I had my first-ever lobster roll. I can still remember the taste of that lobster paired with a buttered bun. Simple, fresh, and just delicious.

Four 4-ounce raw lobster tails

8 tablespoons (1 stick) unsalted butter, at room temperature

4 New England–style split-top hot dog buns

¼ cup chopped fresh tarragon

¼ cup chopped fresh parsley

3 tablespoons chopped chives

1 lemon, quartered

1. Bring a large pot of generously salted water to a boil. Add the lobster tails to the pot and cook until the shells are red and meat is light pink, about 8 minutes. Using tongs, remove the lobster tails and place in a bowl of water and ice to cool.

2. Place a cooled lobster tail on its side on a cutting board. Using both hands, carefully press down on the tail until it cracks. Using kitchen scissors, cut up the center of the underside of the shell, avoiding the meat. Using your thumbs, pry open the shell and remove the meat in one whole piece. Rinse the meat and remove any veins, then pat dry with paper towels. Using your hands, tear the lobster meat into 1-inch pieces and set aside. Repeat with the other lobster tails.

3. Spread a teaspoon of the butter onto the outside of each bun. In a skillet over medium-low heat, arrange the buns butter side down and lightly toast, flipping once, until the outer sides are light brown, 5 minutes. Set aside.

4. In a small saucepan, melt the remaining butter over medium-low heat. Add the tarragon and parsley and cook for 1 to 2 minutes. Add the lobster to the pan and toss with the butter and herbs until hot, 2 minutes.

5. Using tongs, carefully remove the lobster meat from the pan and divide it evenly among the buns. Drizzle the remaining herb butter over the rolls. Top with chives and serve promptly with lemon wedges.

Makes 2 to 4 servings

Lobster Mac & Cheese

PREP: *20 minutes*   **COOK:** *15 minutes*   **COOL:** *none*

Our classic mac and cheese is in our first cookbook—and even though there have been plenty of times I've served it as the main meal, it's designed to be more of a side dish. This lobster mac and cheese is a different story. Lobster feels special, and adding a protein turns the dish into a heartier, more complete dinner. Typically, when I think of one-pot meals, more casual foods come to mind. I love that this lobster mac and cheese can still offer ease and feel elevated.

1 pound large elbow macaroni

4 ounces cooked lobster meat or two 6-ounce raw lobster tails (fresh, not frozen)

2 tablespoons unsalted butter

½ teaspoon minced garlic

1 cup heavy cream

1 cup shredded Cheddar cheese (about 4 ounces)

1 cup grated Parmesan cheese (about 4 ounces)

1 cup shredded Gruyère cheese (about 4 ounces)

1 teaspoon freshly cracked black pepper

1 teaspoon garlic powder

1 tablespoon chopped chives

Kosher salt

1. Bring a large pot of generously salted water to a boil. Cook the macaroni until al dente according to the package directions. Prior to draining the macaroni, reserve ⅓ cup of the cooking water. If you are using lobster tails, add them to the pot while the macaroni is boiling and cook until the shell is red and meat is light pink, about 8 minutes. Using tongs, remove the lobster tails and place in a bowl of water and ice to cool while the macaroni finishes cooking.

2. Place a cooled lobster tail on its side on a cutting board. Using both hands, carefully press down on the tail until it cracks. Using kitchen scissors, cut up the center of the underside of the shell, avoiding the meat. Using your thumbs, pry open the shell and remove the meat in one whole piece. Rinse the meat and remove any veins, then pat dry with paper towels. Using your hands, tear the lobster meat into bite-size pieces and set aside. Repeat with the other lobster tail.

3. In a medium saucepan, melt the butter over medium heat. Add the garlic and cook, stirring constantly, for 1 minute. Add the cream, the cheeses, pepper, garlic powder, and reserved pasta water and stir until the cheeses melt, about 2 minutes. When the mixture boils, immediately remove the pan from the heat.

4. In a large bowl, combine the sauce and macaroni and stir to coat. Add the lobster meat and gently stir to combine. Top with chives and salt to taste and serve immediately.

Makes 4 to 6 servings

Garlic Shrimp

OVER PARMESAN RISOTTO

PREP: *10 minutes*   **COOK:** *50 minutes*   **COOL:** *none*

I might be alone in this, but one of the things I enjoy most about risotto is how long it takes to properly cook. There's no shortcut. There's no walking away from the stove with your fingers crossed, hoping it comes out okay. The recipe requires that you stand there and be present the entire time, stirring and staying aware of its progress. It's almost meditative for me, how some dishes require you to be fully absorbed in the process. With risotto, the effort is rewarded with a delicious bowl of warm, creamy rice.

PARMESAN RISOTTO

6 cups chicken stock,
   plus more if needed
   (page 145 or store-bought)

2 tablespoons unsalted butter

½ yellow onion, chopped

2 cups arborio rice

1 cup dry white wine

1 cup grated Parmesan cheese
   (about 4 ounces)

2 tablespoons chopped
   fresh parsley

2 teaspoons kosher salt

1 teaspoon freshly
   cracked black pepper

GARLIC SHRIMP

6 tablespoons unsalted butter

6 garlic cloves, minced

1 pound shrimp, shelled
   and deveined

2 teaspoons kosher salt

1 teaspoon freshly
   cracked black pepper

1. To make the risotto: In a medium saucepan, heat the chicken stock over medium heat until simmering.

2. In a Dutch oven, melt the butter over medium heat. Add the onion and cook, stirring often, until tender and translucent, 5 to 7 minutes.

3. Add the rice and stir to coat evenly in the butter. Cook, stirring constantly, to lightly toast the rice, 2 to 3 minutes. Add the wine and continue stirring until the rice absorbs the wine. Add 1 cup of the chicken stock and stir until absorbed. Repeat, adding a cup of stock at a time and stirring, until the rice is tender, about 30 minutes in total. (If all the liquid is absorbed but the rice is not yet tender, add another ¼ to ½ cup of chicken stock at a time and continue cooking.)

4. Stir in the Parmesan, parsley, salt, and pepper until incorporated. Reduce the heat to low to keep the risotto warm while you cook the shrimp.

5. To make the garlic shrimp: In a medium skillet, melt the butter over medium heat. Add the garlic and cook for 2 to 3 minutes. Add the shrimp, salt, and pepper and stir to coat the shrimp in the garlic and butter. Cook until the shrimp are just pink, 3 to 5 minutes.

6. Spoon the risotto into individual serving bowls and top with the shrimp. Serve promptly.

7. Store in an airtight container for up to 3 days. When reheating the risotto, add ¼ cup of either dry white wine or chicken stock and cook over low heat for 5 to 7 minutes.

Makes 4 servings

Pan-Fried Cod

WITH GREENS AND BACON

PREP: *30 minutes*   **COOK:** *30 minutes*   **COOL:** *none*

4 slices thick-cut bacon, cut into 1-inch pieces

2 pounds cod fillets, cut into 6 pieces

1 teaspoon kosher salt

1 teaspoon freshly cracked black pepper

1 cup all-purpose flour

1 teaspoon garlic salt

¼ cup grapeseed oil

2 bunches Swiss chard, trimmed, stems and leaves separated

3 garlic cloves, minced

¼ teaspoon ground coriander

¼ teaspoon crushed red pepper flakes

2 lemons, quartered

1. Preheat the oven to 400°F. Line a small bowl with paper towels.

2. In a large skillet, cook the bacon over medium heat until crispy, about 7 minutes. Using a slotted spoon, transfer the bacon to the prepared bowl. Reserve 2 to 3 tablespoons of the bacon grease and the fond (browned bits) in the pan, discarding the rest. Remove the pan from the heat.

3. Season the cod on both sides with the salt and pepper.

4. In a shallow bowl, stir together the flour and garlic salt. Place one cod fillet into the flour to coat, then shake off the excess and place on a plate. Repeat with the remaining fillets.

5. In a large cast-iron skillet (not the pan used for the bacon), heat the oil over medium-high heat. Add the cod and sear on one side until lightly brown, about 5 minutes, then flip over. Transfer the cast-iron skillet to the oven and bake until the fish flakes easily with a fork or an instant-read thermometer registers 145°F, 4 to 6 minutes.

6. While the fish bakes, cut the chard stems into ½-inch pieces. Cut the leaves into 1½-inch-thick strips. Heat the skillet with the bacon grease over medium-high heat. Add the chard stems and garlic and cook, stirring often, until the stems are crisp-tender, 3 to 5 minutes. Add the chard leaves, coriander, and pepper flakes and cook until the leaves are wilted, 3 to 5 minutes.

7. Plate the cod and greens together. Garnish with the cooked bacon and the lemons.

8. Store in an airtight container in the refrigerator for up to 2 days.

Makes 6 servings

Seafood Paella

PREP: *30 minutes*   **COOK:** *45 minutes*   **COOL:** *1 hour*

SAFFRON AIOLI

¼ teaspoon saffron threads

2 tablespoons hot water

2 garlic cloves, minced

2 large egg yolks

2 teaspoons white wine vinegar

1 teaspoon kosher salt

¾ cup olive oil

SEAFOOD PAELLA

¼ cup olive oil

1 yellow onion, diced

½ red bell pepper, diced

½ green bell pepper, diced

6 garlic cloves, minced

½ green onion, chopped

4 Roma (plum) tomatoes, diced

2 bay leaves

1 teaspoon kosher salt

1 teaspoon freshly cracked black pepper

¾ teaspoon saffron threads

½ teaspoon smoked paprika

¼ cup dry white wine

3 boneless, skinless chicken thighs,
    cut into chunks (about 12 ounces)

2 cups Calasparra or arborio rice

⅓ cup chopped fresh parsley

4 cups chicken stock, plus more if
    needed (page 145 or store-bought)

1 pound littleneck clams, scrubbed

½ pound jumbo shrimp, peeled,
    deveined and tail-on

½ pound mussels, scrubbed and
    beards removed

½ cup frozen peas

2 lemons, quartered

1. To make the saffron aioli: In a small bowl, add the saffron to the hot water and let steep for 10 minutes. Remove and discard the saffron.

2. In a blender, add the saffron water, garlic, egg yolks, vinegar, and salt and blend on medium speed until smooth. With the blender running on low, slowly drizzle in the olive oil until the mixture has a mayonnaise-like consistency. Transfer to an airtight container and refrigerate for at least 1 hour or until ready to serve.

3. To make the paella: In a paella pan or a very large cast-iron skillet, heat the oil over medium heat. Add the onion, red and green bell peppers, garlic, and green onion and cook, stirring often, until the onion is translucent, 3 to 5 minutes.

4. Add the tomato, bay leaves, salt, pepper, saffron, and smoked paprika and stir well to combine. Add the wine and scrape the bottom of the pan with a wooden spoon to release any browned bits. Cook until the wine is reduced by half, 5 minutes. Add the chicken, rice, and 1 tablespoon of the parsley and stir to incorporate. Slowly pour in the chicken stock and stir, then spread the rice into an even layer.

5. Without stirring, bring the rice to a boil, then reduce the heat to medium-low. Cover with a lid or foil and cook until the rice is soft and the liquid has been absorbed, 20 to 25 minutes. (If the liquid is absorbed but the rice is not yet tender, add another ¼ to ½ cup of chicken stock and continue cooking.)

6. Add the clams, shrimp, mussels, and peas to the pan and, using a spatula, press the seafood and peas into the rice—do not stir. Cover and continue cooking over medium-low heat until the mussels and clams start to open, another 5 to 7 minutes. Remove from the heat and let rest, covered, until all the mussels and clams have opened, 10 to 15 minutes.

7. Garnish with the lemon wedges and the remaining parsley. Serve hot directly from the pan, with the saffron aioli.

8. Store in an airtight container in the refrigerator for up to 2 days.

Makes 4 to 6 servings

Sun-Dried Tomato–Baked Chicken

PREP: *15 minutes*   **COOK:** *60 minutes*   **COOL:** *30 minutes*

6 large boneless, skinless
   chicken breasts
   (about 3¾ pounds)

3 teaspoons kosher salt

2 teaspoons freshly
   cracked black pepper

2 tablespoons olive oil

2½ cups chicken stock
   (page 145 or store-bought)

One 8.5-ounce jar
   sun-dried tomatoes in oil

1 cup heavy cream

2 tablespoons chopped
   fresh basil leaves

½ teaspoon garlic powder

2 garlic cloves

6 ounces part-skim mozzarella
   cheese, cut into 6 slices

1 pound trottole or radiatore
   pasta

1 pound broccoli crowns,
   cut into bite-size pieces

3 tablespoons grated
   Parmesan, for garnish

1 tablespoon chopped fresh
   parsley, for garnish

1. Preheat the oven to 375°F.

2. Pat the chicken breasts dry with a paper towel. Cut a 2½-inch slit in the side of each chicken breast, being careful not to cut all the way through. Season all sides of the chicken breasts with 2 teaspoons each of the salt and the pepper.

3. In a large skillet, heat the olive oil over medium-high heat. Place three breasts in the skillet and brown, flipping once, 4 minutes per side. The chicken will not be cooked through after browning. Place the browned chicken on a plate and repeat with the remaining chicken.

4. Meanwhile, make the sauce: In a blender, add the chicken stock, sun-dried tomatoes (including the oil), cream, basil, garlic powder, and garlic cloves. Blend until smooth, 1 minute.

5. Carefully stuff each chicken breast with a mozzarella slice so that the chicken encloses it completely.

6. Spread 1 cup of the sauce in the bottom of a 9 × 13-inch baking dish and nestle the stuffed chicken breasts into the sauce in a single layer. Cover with 1 cup of the sauce. Reserve the remaining sauce.

7. Bake the chicken, uncovered, for 40 minutes.

8. Remove the chicken from the oven and let rest at room temperature for 30 minutes.

9. Bring a large pot of generously salted water to a boil. Cook the pasta according to the package directions, adding the broccoli during the last 4 minutes of cooking. The pasta should be al dente and broccoli tender and bright green. Drain the pasta and broccoli in a colander, then place in a large bowl.

10. Reheat and ladle the remaining sauce and remaining 1 teaspoon salt over the pasta and broccoli and toss to coat.

11. For each serving, top a serving of pasta and broccoli with a chicken breast and garnish with fresh Parmesan and parsley. Serve immediately.

12. Store in an airtight container in the refrigerator for 3 to 5 days. Does not freeze well.

Makes 6 servings

Chicken Cordon Bleu

PREP: *15 minutes*   **COOK**: *30 minutes*   **COOL**: *5 minutes*

My favorite memory associated with this dish is the hospital dinner Chip and I shared together after I gave birth to Drake. It became a tradition—every time I delivered another one of our babies—to celebrate with a meal of chicken cordon bleu. It sometimes feels like those days are a million miles away, but I love that this dish can make them seem like yesterday.

Cooking spray

4 large chicken breasts (about 2½ pounds)

8 thin slices ham (about 4 ounces)

4 thick slices Swiss cheese (about 4 ounces)

2 teaspoons kosher salt

2 teaspoons freshly cracked black pepper

2 tablespoons unsalted butter, melted

⅓ cup panko bread crumbs

1 tablespoon chopped fresh parsley, for garnish

1. Preheat the oven to 375°F. Lightly spray a 9 × 13-inch baking dish with cooking spray.

2. Using a sharp knife, cut the chicken breast horizontally through the thickest part so that it can be hinged open like a book and stuffed. In each chicken breast, place 2 pieces of ham on one side, then cut a slice of Swiss cheese in half and place both pieces on top of the ham. Fold the top half of the chicken over the ham and cheese, enclosing it completely, and secure with 2 wooden toothpicks so the chicken stays closed while baking. Repeat until all chicken breasts have been stuffed.

3. Place the stuffed chicken in the prepared baking dish. Season the top of each breast evenly with the salt and pepper. Pour the melted butter over the top and evenly sprinkle the panko on top of each piece.

4. Bake until the internal temperature reaches 165°F, 22 to 25 minutes. Then broil on low to crisp the bread crumbs and give them a light golden color, 1 to 2 minutes. Remove from the oven and discard the toothpicks. Let cool for 5 minutes, then garnish with the parsley before serving.

5. Store leftovers in an airtight container in the refrigerator for up to 2 days.

Makes 4 servings

CHAPTER SEVEN

Desserts

SWEETNESS THAT SURPRISES,
FLAVORS THAT LINGER, A
REMINDER THAT OUR SENSES
WERE MADE FOR THIS

Peanut Butter Pie
WITH CHOCOLATE CRUST

PREP: *35 minutes*   **COOK:** *15 minutes*   **COOL:** *2 hours 20 minutes*

I've never met a dessert with peanut butter and chocolate I didn't like. And of them all, this pie is one I return to again and again. The crunch of the chocolate cookie crust is the perfect counter to the creamy peanut butter filling. With so many rich ingredients, it might seem as though the whipped cream will make the pie too sweet, but I wholeheartedly recommend including the topping. To me, it has just the right amount of light and airy texture to balance the other components.

CRUST

10 ounces chocolate wafers or Oreo cookies (about 42 wafers or 24 Oreos)

⅓ cup sugar

7 tablespoons unsalted butter, melted

FILLING

1 cup creamy peanut butter

1 cup powdered sugar

4 ounces cream cheese, at room temperature

¼ teaspoon kosher salt

¾ cup heavy cream

1 tablespoon unsalted butter, melted

2 teaspoons pure vanilla extract

ASSEMBLY

1 cup heavy cream

¼ cup powdered sugar

1 teaspoon pure vanilla extract

Crushed peanut brittle, cookie crumble, or nuts, for garnish (optional)

1. To make the crust: Preheat the oven to 350°F.

2. In a food processor, pulse the wafers until they are the consistency of sand. Add the sugar and melted butter and pulse a few more times, until combined.

3. Using your hands, press the wafer mixture into the bottom and up the sides of a 9-inch pie pan.

4. Bake for 12 minutes. Let cool for 20 minutes.

5. To make the filling: In a stand mixer fitted with the whisk attachment, whisk together the peanut butter, powdered sugar, cream cheese, and salt on medium speed. With the mixer on low, add the cream, melted butter, and vanilla and whip until the mixture is smooth and fluffy. Pour the mixture into the baked crust.

6. To assemble: In a stand mixer fitted with the whisk attachment, combine the cream, powdered sugar, and vanilla. Start on low speed, then slowly turn the mixer up to high speed and mix until the cream holds a soft peak when you pull the whisk out of the bowl, about 2 minutes.

7. Spoon the whipped cream on top of the peanut butter filling.

8. Refrigerate for at least 2 hours. Sprinkle with crushed toffee bits, cookie crumble, or nuts if desired. Serve chilled.

9. Store in the refrigerator covered with plastic wrap for up to 3 days.

Makes 6 to 8 servings

Classic Buttermilk Pie

PREP: *20 minutes*   **COOK:** *50 minutes*   **COOL:** *2 hours*

Chip has always loved a good old-fashioned buttermilk pie. It's a tried-and-true classic that is perfect for any occasion. My ideal topping is mixed berries and homemade whipped cream.

1 recipe pie crust (page 67, made through step 2) or 1 store-bought raw pie crust

8 tablespoons (1 stick) unsalted butter, melted

1¼ cups sugar

½ cup whole-milk buttermilk

3 large eggs

3 tablespoons all-purpose flour, plus more for dusting

1 tablespoon freshly grated lemon zest

1 tablespoon fresh lemon juice

1 teaspoon pure vanilla extract

1 teaspoon kosher salt

1. Lightly dust the counter with flour. Using a rolling pin, roll the dough out to an 11½-inch round. Transfer the dough to a 9-inch pie plate and carefully ease it into the edges. Trim the dough to an even ½ inch overhang all around and fold it under itself on top of the rim. Using your fingers, carefully crimp the edges of the pie dough. Refrigerate for 1 hour.

2. Preheat the oven to 350°F.

3. In a medium bowl, whisk together the melted butter and sugar until well incorporated. Add the buttermilk, eggs, flour, lemon zest, lemon juice, vanilla, and salt and whisk thoroughly until the mixture is smooth.

4. Pour the mixture into the prepared chilled pie shell.

5. Bake until the pie has a slight jiggle in the center, 44 to 50 minutes, tenting with foil after 35 minutes if needed to prevent excess browning. The center of the pie might have a pooling of melted butter, but it will settle back into the pie as it cools. Let cool on a wire rack for at least 1 hour.

6. Store in an airtight container in the refrigerator, covered, for up to 5 days.

TIP: Garnish with whipped cream and fresh berries.

Makes 6 to 8 servings

Cherry Pie

WITH STREUSEL

PREP: *25 minutes*   **COOK:** *45 minutes*   **COOL:** *3 hours*

Since I was a kid, cherry pie has always been my favorite. But no one in my house likes it all that much. I was disappointed until I discovered this recipe. Now I've realized that being the only person who likes cherry pie in a house where there's fresh cherry pie isn't a bad thing, because I have the whole pie to myself!

1 recipe pie crust
    (page 67, made through
    step 2) or 1 store-bought
    raw pie crust

8 tablespoons (1 stick)
    unsalted butter

¾ cup all-purpose flour,
    plus more for dusting

½ cup rolled oats

½ cup packed light brown
    sugar

¼ cup sliced almonds

2 teaspoons almond extract

½ teaspoon kosher salt

16 ounces frozen tart cherries

1 cup granulated sugar

¼ cup cornstarch

1. Lightly dust the counter with flour. Using a rolling pin, roll the dough out to an 11½-inch round. Transfer the dough to a 9-inch pie plate and carefully ease it into the edges. Trim the dough to an even ½ inch overhang all around and fold it under itself on top of the rim. Using your fingers, carefully crimp the edges of the pie dough. Refrigerate for 1 hour.

2. To make the streusel topping: In a medium bowl, combine 7 tablespoons of the butter, the flour, oats, brown sugar, almonds, 1 teaspoon of the almond extract, and the salt. Work the ingredients together with a fork until the mixture resembles wet sand. Cover and chill until ready to use.

3. To make the pie filling: In a large skillet, combine the cherries, granulated sugar, cornstarch, remaining 1 tablespoon butter, and remaining 1 teaspoon almond extract over medium-high heat. Cook, stirring occasionally, for 8 minutes. Let cool for 1 hour.

4. Preheat the oven to 375°F.

5. Pour the cherry filling into the chilled pie crust. Top the cherries with the streusel. Bake until the streusel and pie crust are golden brown, 35 minutes. Let cool for 1 hour before serving.

6. Store in the refrigerator, covered, for up to 5 days.

TIP: For a quick assembly, substitute the homemade pie crust with a store-bought 9-inch pie crust.

Makes 6 to 8 servings

Pumpkin Cheesecake

WITH GINGERSNAP CRUST

PREP: *1 hour 15 minutes*   **COOK:** *1 hour 15 minutes*   **COOL:** *6 hours 20 minutes*

The unexpected gingersnap crust paired with hints of pumpkin, then topped with warm caramel sauce is a dream combination. This dish has become a favorite of mine to serve in the fall. When October comes around I always feel like celebrating. For as long as I can remember it's been my favorite month of the year. That might be why this cheesecake has a special place in my heart—every bite tastes like the best parts of the season.

GINGERSNAP CRUST

2 cups gingersnap cookie crumbs

5 tablespoons unsalted butter, melted

CHEESECAKE FILLING

1½ pounds cream cheese, at room temperature

1¼ cups packed light brown sugar

4 large eggs, at room temperature

2 teaspoons pure vanilla extract

One 15-ounce can pumpkin puree

2 tablespoons cornstarch

1½ teaspoons pumpkin spice

½ teaspoon kosher salt

Boiling water, for baking

1. To make the gingersnap crust: Preheat the oven to 350°F. Move the highest oven rack to just below the middle of the oven.

2. In a food processor, pulse the gingersnap cookies until they are a crumb-like consistency and resemble sand. In a medium bowl, stir together 2 cups of the ground cookies and the melted butter. Reserve any remaining gingersnap crumbs to sprinkle on top of the finished cheesecake, or discard.

3. Evenly spread the crumbs in the bottom of a 9 × 3-inch springform pan. Use the bottom of a measuring cup to press the crumbs down into an even, tightly packed layer.

4. Bake the crust for 7 minutes. Let cool.

5. Reduce the oven temperature to 325°F.

6. To make the cheesecake filling: In a stand mixer fitted with the paddle attachment, beat the cream cheese until light and fluffy, about 3 minutes. Turn off the mixer and scrape down the sides of the bowl with a spatula. Add the brown sugar on low speed, then increase the speed to medium-high until the sugar is well combined. Reduce the speed to low and add the eggs, one at a time, mixing well after each addition, then add the vanilla. Scrape down the sides and bottom of the bowl with the spatula. Add the pumpkin puree, cornstarch, pumpkin spice, and salt and mix until well combined, starting on low speed and increasing to medium. Scrape the sides and bottom of the bowl and mix one last time to make sure everything is well incorporated.

7. Wrap the bottom and the sides of the cooled springform pan with foil. Place on a baking sheet with at least a 1-inch lip or a large roasting pan. Pour the filling into the springform pan and gently tap the baking sheet on the counter a couple of times to release any air bubbles.

CONTINUED

CONTINUED FROM PAGE 269

CARAMEL SAUCE

¾ cup granulated sugar

¼ teaspoon cream of tartar

3 tablespoons unsalted butter

¼ cup heavy cream

½ teaspoon kosher salt

Spiced Brown Sugar
  Whipped Cream
  (opposite), for serving

8. Place the pan in the oven and pour ½ inch of boiling water into the baking sheet, making sure not to splash any water into the cheesecake pan. Bake until the cheesecake has a slight 2- to 3-inch jiggle in the center, about 1 hour 5 minutes. Let cool on a wire rack for about an hour. Wrap the cooled cheesecake entirely in foil and place in the freezer for 5 hours or up to overnight to continue setting up.

9. To make the caramel sauce: In a medium heavy-bottomed saucepan, combine the sugar, cream of tartar, and 2 tablespoons of water. Gently stir until the sugar is wet. Turn the heat to medium-high. Using a wooden spoon or heat-resistant spatula, slowly stir to dissolve the sugar, continuing until the mixture boils. Stop stirring and continue boiling until the mixture becomes an amber color, 8 to 10 minutes. Immediately remove the mixture from the heat and carefully stir in the butter until melted. Slowly stir in the cream and salt. Let cool for about 10 minutes.

10. Remove the cheesecake from the freezer and let it rest at room temperature for 1 hour. Run a knife along the inside edge of the pan, then open the pan to release the cheesecake. To serve, cut into slices, then top each with a drizzle of caramel sauce, extra gingersnap crumbs (if using), and a dollop of whipped cream.

11. Store in an airtight container in the refrigerator for up to 5 days.

Makes 8 servings

Four Flavored Whipped Creams

PREP: *10 to 30 minutes*   **COOK:** *none to 10 minutes*   **COOL:** *none to 20 minutes*

PEPPERMINT

1 cup heavy cream, cold

¼ cup powdered sugar

½ teaspoon peppermint
  extract

¼ teaspoon pure vanilla
  extract

PEPPERMINT

In a stand mixer fitted with the whisk attachment, combine the cream, powdered sugar, peppermint extract, and vanilla. Starting with the mixer on low speed and slowly increasing the speed to medium-high, mix until the whipped cream is fluffy and holds its shape, 1 to 2 minutes.

ESPRESSO

¼ cup granulated sugar

2 tablespoons instant
espresso granules

1 teaspoon pure vanilla extract

1 cup heavy cream, cold

2 tablespoons powdered sugar

ESPRESSO

1. In a small saucepan over medium heat, combine the sugar, ¼ cup of water, instant espresso, and vanilla. Bring the mixture to a boil, then continue boiling for about 3 minutes. Remove from the heat and let cool for 20 minutes.

2. In a stand mixer fitted with the whisk attachment, combine the cream and powdered sugar. Starting with the mixer on low speed and slowly increasing the speed to medium-high, mix for about 1 minute. With the mixer running, slowly add the cooled espresso mixture and continue mixing until the whipped cream is fluffy and holds its shape, 1 to 2 more minutes.

SPICED BROWN SUGAR

⅓ cup packed light brown sugar

¼ teaspoon vanilla bean paste

⅛ teaspoon ground cinnamon

1 cup heavy cream, cold

SPICED BROWN SUGAR

1. In a small saucepan, combine the brown sugar, ¼ cup of water, the vanilla bean paste, and cinnamon over medium heat. Bring the mixture to a boil, then continue boiling for about 3 minutes. Remove from the heat and let cool for 20 minutes.

2. In a stand mixer fitted with the whisk attachment, pour in the heavy cream. Starting with the mixer on low speed and slowly increasing the speed to medium-high, mix for about 1 minute. With the mixer running, slowly add the cooled brown sugar mixture and continue mixing until the whipped cream is fluffy and holds its shape, 1 to 2 more minutes.

SALTED CARAMEL

¾ cup sugar

¼ teaspoon cream of tartar

3 tablespoons unsalted butter

1¼ cups heavy cream, cold

½ teaspoon kosher salt

SALTED CARAMEL

1. In a medium heavy-bottomed saucepan, combine the sugar, 2 tablespoons plus 1 teaspoon of water, and the cream of tartar. Gently stir until the sugar is wet. Turn the heat to medium-high. Using a wooden spoon or heat-resistant spatula, slowly stir to dissolve the sugar, continuing until the mixture boils. Stop stirring and continue boiling until the mixture becomes an amber color, 8 to 10 minutes. Immediately take the mixture off the heat and carefully stir in the butter. Once the butter is completely melted, slowly stir in ¼ cup of the cream and the salt. Set aside and let cool for about 20 minutes.

2. In a stand mixer fitted with the whisk attachment, pour in the remaining 1 cup cream. Starting with the mixer on low speed and slowly increasing the speed to medium-high, mix for about 1 minute. With the mixer running, slowly add the cooled caramel sauce and continue mixing until the whipped cream is fluffy and holds its shape, 1 to 2 more minutes.

3. Store in an airtight container in the refrigerator for 5 days.

Each flavor makes 1½ cups

Sopapilla Hand Pies (top),
Strawberry Hand Pies (bottom)

Strawberry Hand Pies

SERVED AT
MAGGIE'S
SWEETS
WACO . TX

PREP: *50 minutes*   **COOK:** *40 minutes*   **COOL:** *2 hours*

One of the challenges I enjoy most in the kitchen is re-creating childhood favorites. We all grew up with boxed toaster tarts—my favorite was always the strawberry filling with icing on top. So the team and I played around with a recipe of my own. Just a bite can take me back to all the goodness of a lazy summer morning as a kid. There's something so special about knowing I can now make those pies from scratch for my own kids anytime—but especially on a lazy summer morning.

DOUGH

2 cups all-purpose flour, plus more for rolling

2 tablespoons sugar

1 teaspoon kosher salt

1 cup (2 sticks) unsalted butter, cold, cubed

2 tablespoons whole milk

1 large egg

STRAWBERRY FILLING

2 cups frozen strawberries, thawed

⅓ cup sugar

2 tablespoons cornstarch

GLAZE

1 large egg

1 tablespoon whole milk

1 cup powdered sugar, sifted

½ teaspoon pure vanilla extract

¼ cup heavy cream

1. To make the dough: In a large bowl, whisk together the flour, sugar, and salt. Scatter in the butter and use a pastry blender or your fingers to cut the butter into the flour until the biggest pieces are the size of small peas.

2. In the center of the flour mixture, make a well, then add the milk and egg to the center of the well. Using a fork, beat the egg and gradually incorporate the flour mixture into the milk mixture. Knead until the dough comes together. Shape the dough into a small rectangle and wrap in plastic wrap. Chill for 1 hour.

3. To make the strawberry filling: In a medium saucepan, combine the strawberries (and any accumulated juice), sugar, and cornstarch. Cook over medium heat, crushing the fruit occasionally with a wooden spoon to break it down, until it comes to a slow boil and the sugar has dissolved, about 6 minutes. Let cool completely, about 1 hour.

4. Place the chilled dough on a lightly floured surface. Using a rolling pin, roll the dough into a rectangle about 12 × 16 inches. Using a pizza cutter, cut the dough into sixteen 3 × 4-inch pieces.

5. To assemble: In a small bowl, beat the egg and milk together to make an egg wash. Using a pastry brush, brush the egg wash mixture onto the edges of 8 pieces of dough.

6. Place a heaping tablespoon of the cooled strawberry mixture onto the center of these 8 pieces of dough. Top each of these with another piece of dough. Use your fingertips to press firmly around each pocket of filling, sealing the dough on all sides. Press the tines of a fork all around the edge of each hand pie.

7. Line a baking sheet with parchment paper. Gently place each hand pie on the prepared baking sheet, about 3 inches apart. Chill the hand pies for 30 minutes.

CONTINUED

CONTINUED FROM PAGE 273

8. Preheat the oven to 350°F.

9. Right before baking, remove the pies from the refrigerator and prick the top of each pie 4 times with a fork to allow the steam to escape when baking.

10. Bake until light golden brown, 30 to 35 minutes. Let cool for 30 minutes.

11. In a small bowl, whisk together the powdered sugar and vanilla to make the glaze, adding the heavy cream, 1 tablespoon at a time, to achieve your desired thickness. Spread the glaze over the tops of the cooled hand pies and serve.

12. Store in an airtight container at room temperature for up to 2 days.

Makes 8 hand pies

Sopapilla Hand Pies

SERVED AT MAGGIE'S SWEETS · WACO · TX

PREP: *30 minutes*   **COOK:** *30 minutes*   **COOL:** *1 hour 45 minutes*

DOUGH

2 cups all-purpose flour, plus more for rolling

2 tablespoons sugar

1 teaspoon kosher salt

1 cup (2 sticks) unsalted butter, cold, cubed

2 tablespoons whole milk

1 large egg

FILLING

8 ounces cream cheese, at room temperature

1 cup sugar

1 teaspoon pure vanilla extract

GLAZE

1 large egg

1 tablespoon whole milk

¼ cup sugar

½ teaspoon ground cinnamon

3 tablespoons unsalted butter, melted

1. To make the dough: In a large bowl, whisk together the flour, sugar, and salt. Scatter in the butter and use a pastry blender or your fingers to cut the butter into the flour until the biggest pieces are the size of small peas.

2. In the center of the flour mixture, make a well, then add the milk and egg to the center of the well. Using a fork, beat the egg and gradually incorporate the flour mixture into the milk mixture. Knead until the dough comes together. Shape the dough into a small rectangle and wrap in plastic wrap. Chill for 1 hour.

3. To make the filling: In a medium bowl, whisk together the cream cheese and sugar until smooth. Add in the vanilla and whisk until combined.

4. Place the chilled dough on a lightly floured surface. Using a rolling pin, roll the dough into a rectangle about 12 × 16 inches. Using a pizza cutter, cut the dough into sixteen 3 × 4-inch pieces.

5. To assemble: In a small bowl, beat the egg and milk together to make an egg wash. Using a pastry brush, brush the egg wash mixture onto the edges of 8 pieces of dough.

6. Place about 1½ tablespoons of the cream cheese mixture onto the center of these 8 pieces of dough. Top each of these with another piece of dough. Use your fingertips to press firmly around each pocket of filling, sealing the dough on all sides. Press the tines of a fork all around the edge of each hand pie.

7. Line a baking sheet with parchment paper. Gently place each hand pie on the prepared baking sheet, about 3 inches apart. Chill the hand pies for 30 minutes.

8. Preheat the oven to 350°F.

9. Right before baking, remove the pies from the refrigerator and prick the top of each 4 times with a fork, to allow the steam to escape when baking.

10. In a small bowl, whisk together the sugar and cinnamon. Brush the tops of the pies with melted butter and sprinkle with the cinnamon sugar.

11. Bake until light golden brown, 25 to 30 minutes. Let cool for 15 minutes.

12. Store in an airtight container in the refrigerator for up to 5 days.

Makes 8 hand pies

Canned Peaches and Crumble

PREP: *45 minutes*　　**COOK:** *35 minutes*　　**COOL:** *2 hours*

The beauty of a crumble is how few ingredients it requires. Add a little heat and you have a topping that gives fruit just the texture it needs to feel like a satisfying dessert. Though crumbles are good in any season and can be especially comforting in fall, I love the crisp contrast of a peach crumble in summer. Served after BBQ or as a dessert for a dinner al fresco, it makes a satisfying finish to the evening.

CANNED PEACHES

1½ cups granulated sugar

3 tablespoons pectin

6 pounds ripe peaches
　(18 to 20)

Six (16-ounce) glass jars
　with lids, sterilized

CRUMBLE

1¼ cups all-purpose flour

½ cup packed light brown
　sugar

½ cup granulated sugar

¼ cup chopped pecans

½ teaspoon ground cinnamon

¼ teaspoon baking powder

⅛ teaspoon kosher salt

8 tablespoons (1 stick)
　unsalted butter, melted

Vanilla ice cream, for serving

1. To make the canned peaches: In a medium pot, bring 6 cups of water to a boil over medium-high heat.

2. In a small bowl, stir together the sugar and pectin. Add the mixture to the boiling water and stir until the sugar and pectin dissolve. Remove the syrup from the heat and set aside.

3. Fill a large pot two-thirds full with water and bring to a boil over high heat. Slice a shallow X through the bottom of each peach. Drop the peaches in the water and cook just until the skin splits, about 4 minutes.

4. While the peaches are blanching, fill a large bowl with ice and water to create an ice bath. Using a slotted spoon, remove the peaches from the boiling water and gently drop them into the ice bath. Let cool for about 5 minutes.

5. Using your hands, carefully peel the peaches, discarding the skins. Cut the peeled peaches into ½-inch wedges. Run your clean fingers along the jars' edges to check for nicks and chips that would impede proper sealing.

6. Tightly pack the peach wedges into the jars, leaving ½-inch headspace. Pour the syrup into the jars, filling ¼ inch from the top of each jar. Put the lids on the jars and close them as tightly as possible.

7. Fill a large pot with enough water to cover the jars vertically. Set the jars aside and bring the water to a boil over high heat. Using canning tongs or heatproof gloves, carefully lower the jars into the boiling water and boil gently, undisturbed, for 20 minutes.

8. Place a clean, dry kitchen towel on the countertop. Using canning tongs or heatproof gloves, carefully remove the jars from the water and place them gently on the towel. Let cool, undisturbed, about 2 hours. Label the jars with the date.

9. To make the crumble: Preheat the oven to 325°F. Line a large baking sheet with parchment paper.

CONTINUED

CONTINUED FROM PAGE 277

10. In a medium bowl, stir together the flour, brown sugar, granulated sugar, pecans, cinnamon, baking powder, and salt. Pour in the melted butter and use a wooden spoon to combine the ingredients until the mixture resembles coarse crumbs.

11. Evenly spread the crumbs on the prepared baking sheet. Bake until the crumble is a light golden brown, 10 to 12 minutes. Let cool for 10 minutes.

12. To serve, place the peaches in individual bowls and top with crumble and ice cream.

13. Store peaches, unopened, at room temperature for up to 12 months. Refrigerate open jars for up to 5 days. Store the crumble in an airtight container in the refrigerator for up to 5 days or in the freezer for up to 1 month.

Makes six 16-ounce jars of peaches, plus 6 servings of crumble

Peach Pie Trifles

PREP: *25 minutes*   **COOK:** *5 minutes*   **COOL:** *1 hour*

Part of the fun in making a trifle is getting to see all the delicious layers come together in such a beautiful display. This recipe is the epitome of summer—juicy fruit at its peak meets light and airy cream filling—making it one of my favorite desserts for a summer gathering. It feels a bit unexpected, too, and isn't that what summer is all about?

GRAHAM CRUST

1½ cups crushed graham
    crackers (about 13 crackers)

⅓ cup toasted and finely
    chopped pecans

1 teaspoon ground cinnamon

⅓ cup sugar

6 tablespoons salted butter,
    melted

FILLING

1 pound cream cheese,
    at room temperature

1 cup powdered sugar

4 teaspoons pure vanilla
    extract

2 pounds canned sliced
    peaches, drained
    and cut into chunks

1 fresh peach, pitted and sliced,
    for serving

6 fresh mint leaves, for garnish

Spiced Brown Sugar Whipped
    Cream (page 271)

1. To make the graham crust: In a large bowl, combine the crushed graham crackers, chopped pecans, cinnamon, and sugar and stir to combine. Stir in the melted butter until evenly incorporated.

2. To make the filling: In a stand mixer fitted with the paddle attachment, beat the cream cheese, powdered sugar, and vanilla, starting on low speed and gradually increasing the speed to medium-high, until the mixture is smooth and creamy, about 1 minute.

3. Sprinkle about ½ cup of the graham mixture into the bottom of each of six 12-ounce glass jars. Add about ½ cup of the cream cheese mixture to each jar. Equally distribute the canned peaches on top of the cream cheese filling, covering it completely. Place the jars into the fridge for at least 1 hour.

4. Evenly spread the spiced brown sugar whipped cream on top of the chilled peach trifles, covering the peaches completely. Add a slice of fresh peach on top of the whipped cream, then garnish with a mint leaf.

5. Store, covered, in the refrigerator for up to 3 days.

Makes 6 servings

Vanilla Bean Panna Cotta

PREP: *15 minutes*   **COOK:** *10 minutes*   **COOL:** *4 hours 30 minutes*

This is a light and versatile dessert that's perfect after a heavy meal. Using the vanilla bean as a base, it's easy to add your preferred flavor on top, with fresh preserves or whatever berries you have on hand. To me, panna cotta is like grown-up pudding. The vanilla bean complements the sweetness of the fruit perfectly, and the heavy cream makes it feel like a substantial dessert but still keeps it light. This recipe is quick to whip up on the spot or it can be made in advance.

1 cup heavy cream

1 cup half-and-half

5 tablespoons sugar

1½ teaspoons vanilla bean paste

2 tablespoons cold water

2 teaspoons unflavored gelatin powder

½ cup raspberry preserves

1 cup fresh blueberries, for serving

Mint sprig, for garnish

1. In a medium saucepan, combine the cream, half-and-half, sugar, and vanilla bean paste over medium heat. Cook, stirring often, until the sugar is dissolved and the mixture is steaming. Remove from the heat.

2. Pour the water into a small bowl and sprinkle the gelatin over the surface. Let stand 2 minutes to bloom the gelatin. Add this mixture to the cream mixture and stir well to dissolve the gelatin. Let cool to room temperature, stirring occasionally, until starting to thicken.

3. Stir the mixture thoroughly again, then divide it evenly (about ½ cup each) into 4 glasses or ramekins. Cover with plastic wrap and refrigerate until set, 4 to 6 hours.

4. Top each panna cotta with 2 tablespoons of raspberry preserves. Serve with blueberries and garnish with mint.

5. Store in the refrigerator, covered in plastic wrap, for up to 3 days.

Makes 4 servings

Sheet Pan S'mores

PREP: *30 minutes*   **COOK:** *25 minutes*   **COOL:** *20 minutes*

CRUST

Nonstick baking spray

1 cup packed light
   brown sugar

8 tablespoons (1 stick)
   unsalted butter,
   melted

⅓ cup honey

1½ teaspoons pure
   vanilla extract

1 cup plus 2 tablespoons
   all-purpose flour

1 cup whole wheat flour

1 teaspoon baking soda

1 teaspoon ground
   cinnamon

½ teaspoon kosher salt

5 tablespoons
   whole milk

S'MORE TOPPING

Eight 1.55-ounce
   Hershey's
   chocolate bars

¾ cup sugar

¾ cup light corn syrup

3 large egg whites

½ teaspoon cream
   of tartar

2 teaspoons pure
   vanilla extract

1. To make the crust: Preheat the oven to 350°F. Spray a quarter sheet pan with nonstick spray.

2. In a large bowl, stir together the brown sugar and melted butter until well combined, then stir in the honey and vanilla. Add both flours, the baking soda, cinnamon, and salt and stir until incorporated. Slowly add the milk, 1 tablespoon at a time, and mix until a dough forms.

3. Using your hands, press the dough into the bottom of the prepared pan, then use a fork to poke small holes throughout the dough.

4. Bake until firm, 15 to 20 minutes.

5. To make the s'more topping: Evenly space the Hershey bars on top of the hot crust. If needed, place the pan back in the oven for 2 minutes to melt the chocolate. Using the back of a spoon, gently spread the warmed chocolate so that it fully covers the crust. Let cool for about 10 minutes on the counter, then place in the freezer for 10 minutes to firm up the chocolate.

6. In a medium heavy-bottomed saucepan, stir together the sugar, corn syrup, and ⅓ cup of water over medium-high heat. Using a wooden spoon or heat-resistant spatula, continue stirring until the mixture starts to boil. Stop stirring and continue boiling until the sugar mixture reaches 240°F on a candy thermometer.

7. Meanwhile, in a stand mixer fitted with the whisk attachment, whip the egg whites until they hold a soft peak when you pull the whisk out of the bowl. Add the cream of tartar, then reduce the speed to the lowest setting and continue whisking while the sugar mixture comes to temperature.

8. With the mixer on medium-high speed, carefully pour the hot sugar mixture down the side of the bowl into the whipped egg whites. Increase the speed to high and allow the mixture to become white and fluffy, about 3 minutes. Reduce the speed to medium-low and add the vanilla, mixing until incorporated, 30 seconds.

9. Take the crust out of the freezer and evenly spread the marshmallow over the top of the chocolate. Using a kitchen torch, toast the marshmallow until it turns a deep golden brown, similar to how a marshmallow would toast over a campfire. (If you don't have a kitchen torch, broil the s'mores, watching continuously, until the marshmallow is deeply golden brown, 1 to 2 minutes.)

10. Cut into squares and serve immediately.

11. Store leftovers in an airtight container at room temperature for up to 3 days.

Makes 12 servings

Orange Mint Mousse and Chocolate Cookies

PREP: *40 minutes*   **COOK:** *20 minutes*   **COOL:** *2 hours*

ORANGE MINT MOUSSE

4 large egg yolks

⅓ cup sugar

2½ cups heavy cream

8 fresh mint leaves, plus more for garnish

1 tablespoon freshly grated orange zest

2 tablespoons fresh orange juice

CHOCOLATE COOKIES

8 tablespoons (1 stick) unsalted butter, at room temperature

½ cup powdered sugar

½ teaspoon kosher salt

1 cup all-purpose flour

¼ cup unsweetened cocoa powder

1 tablespoon whole milk

1 teaspoon pure vanilla extract

8 ounces chocolate candy melts

2 tablespoons freshly grated orange zest

1. To make the orange mint mousse: In a medium bowl, whisk together the egg yolks and sugar until they become a lighter yellow color, about 2 minutes.

2. In a medium saucepan, combine 1 cup of the cream, the mint leaves, orange zest, and orange juice and bring the ingredients to a simmer over medium heat. Temper the egg yolks by adding a small amount of the cream mixture at a time and whisking constantly until all the cream has been added. Return the mixture to the saucepan. Cook, stirring constantly, over medium heat, until the mixture has thickened into a pudding-like consistency, about 5 minutes.

3. Using a fine-mesh sieve over a clean bowl, strain the mixture to remove and discard any lumps, mint leaves, and zest. Place plastic wrap directly on the surface to keep it from forming a "skin" and refrigerate for 2 hours.

4. To make the chocolate cookies: Preheat the oven to 325°F. Line a baking sheet with parchment paper. In a stand mixer fitted with the paddle attachment, combine the butter, powdered sugar, and salt on medium speed for about 2 minutes. Reduce the speed to medium-low and slowly add the flour, cocoa, milk, and vanilla, mixing just until a dough has formed.

5. Place the dough between two pieces of parchment paper and using a rolling pin, roll out the dough ½ inch thick. Using a 2½-inch round cookie cutter, cut out 4 cookies. Place the cookies on the prepared baking sheet at least 2 inches apart.

6. Bake until the edges are set and the cookies no longer look wet, 10 to 12 minutes. Transfer the cookies to a wire rack and let cool for 30 minutes.

7. In a stand mixer fitted with the whisk attachment, whip the remaining 1½ cups cream on medium-high speed until it holds a stiff peak when you pull the whisk out of the bowl, 3 to 4 minutes. Fold the whipped cream into the chilled orange mixture, until it is fully combined. Refrigerate until ready to serve.

8. Melt the chocolate candy melts according to the package directions. Carefully dip three-quarters of each cookie in the melted chocolate, then place the cookies onto a sheet of parchment paper to set. While the chocolate is still wet, sprinkle the orange zest on the chocolate. Let rest until set.

9. To serve, portion the mousse evenly into four 8-ounce glass cups. Garnish with mint and serve with chocolate cookies.

10. Store mousse in an airtight container in the refrigerator for up to 3 days. Store cookies in an airtight container at room temperature for up to 3 days.

Makes 4 servings

Profiteroles

PREP: *35 minutes*   **COOK**: *30 minutes*   **COOL**: *1 hour*

CHOCOLATE GANACHE

1 cup heavy cream

8 ounces semisweet chocolate, finely chopped

CREAM PUFFS

½ cup whole milk

8 tablespoons (1 stick) unsalted butter

2 tablespoons sugar

1 teaspoon kosher salt

1 cup all-purpose flour

4 or 5 large eggs

2 pints vanilla gelato

1. To make the chocolate ganache: In a medium microwave-safe bowl, microwave the cream for 1 minute. Add the chocolate and let stand without stirring for 1 minute. Whisk in the chocolate until smooth. Cover and let sit at room temperature until ready to use.

2. To make the cream puffs: Preheat the oven to 400°F. Line two baking sheets with parchment paper. In a medium saucepan, bring the milk, butter, sugar, salt, and ½ cup of water to a boil. Add the flour and stir constantly for 2 minutes using a wooden spoon.

3. In a stand mixer fitted with the paddle attachment, add the hot dough straight out of the pan and turn the speed to medium-high. Mix until the dough cools slightly and steam is no longer coming out of the bowl, 3 to 5 minutes. Add the eggs one at a time, allowing them to incorporate completely before adding another. After 4 eggs have been added, the dough should be thick, glossy, and smooth. To check, unhook the paddle, stick it into the dough, then slowly pull it out: the dough should fall off the paddle in a V shape. If the dough is too thick, add the fifth egg and mix thoroughly.

4. Put the dough in a large piping bag or zip-top plastic bag. If using a zip-top bag, cut a ½-inch hole at one corner of the bag. Holding the piping bag about 1 inch above the prepared pans, squeeze the bag to create 2-inch-wide by 1-inch-tall domes at least 1 inch apart. Repeat until all the dough has been piped. Wet your finger with water and gently press down any points on the tops of the dough to create a smooth dome.

5. Bake until the cream puffs are puffed and golden, about 20 minutes, then reduce the heat to 300°F without opening the oven, and continue to bake until cooked through, another 6 to 8 minutes. Remove from the oven and let cool for 1 hour.

6. While the cream puffs cool, portion 20 scoops of gelato onto a baking sheet, using a 1½-ounce scoop. Place in freezer until ready to assemble.

7. To assemble: Using a serrated knife, slice each cream puff in half horizontally. Place one premeasured scoop of gelato onto the bottom of each shell and press on the tops. Place each profiterole into an individual serving bowl and drizzle with chocolate ganache. (If the chocolate has hardened, microwave it in 20-second intervals, stirring in between, until pourable again.)

8. Store cream puffs in a sealed bag at room temperature for up to 3 days or in the freezer for up to 2 weeks. Store ganache in an airtight container in the refrigerator for up to 1 week.

Makes 20 profiteroles

Raspberry Lemon Curd Cream Puffs

PREP: *1 hour 15 minutes*   **COOK:** *45 minutes*   **COOL:** *3 hours*

1 cup frozen raspberries, thawed

1 cup granulated sugar

1 tablespoon cornstarch

6 tablespoons unsalted butter

4 large egg yolks

¼ cup fresh lemon juice

2 tablespoons freshly grated lemon zest

Kosher salt

1½ cups heavy cream

Cream Puffs (page 289)

¼ cup powdered sugar, for serving

1. In a small saucepan, stir together the raspberries, ⅓ cup of the granulated sugar, and the cornstarch to make raspberry preserves. Bring the mixture to a boil over high heat and cook, stirring occasionally, for about 5 minutes. Pour the preserves into a medium bowl and let cool.

2. Place the butter in a medium bowl and set aside. In a separate medium heatproof bowl, combine the remaining ⅔ cup sugar and egg yolks, whisking until pale, 3 minutes. Add ¼ cup of the raspberry preserves, the lemon juice, lemon zest, and salt to the egg mixture and whisk to combine. Reserve the remaining raspberry preserves for another use.

3. Make a double boiler by filling a medium saucepan with 1 inch of water and bringing to a simmer. Place the bowl with the egg mixture over the pot so the steam heats the bowl (the bowl should not touch the water). With a spatula, stir the mixture constantly until thickened to the consistency of pudding, about 10 minutes, then remove from the heat.

4. Place a fine-mesh strainer over the bowl with the butter, then pour the egg mixture through the strainer, discarding any cooked egg that collects in the strainer. Stir the butter and curd until well combined. Place a sheet of plastic wrap directly on top of the curd to prevent a skin from forming and refrigerate for 2 hours.

5. In a stand mixer fitted with the whisk attachment, add the cream. Starting on low speed and gradually increasing the speed to medium-high, whip the cream until it holds a stiff peak when you pull the whisk out of the bowl, about 2 minutes. Fold the whipped cream into the chilled curd. Cover with plastic wrap and refrigerate.

6. To assemble: Using a serrated knife, slice each cream puff in half horizontally. Put the whipped cream/curd mixture in a large piping bag or zip-top plastic bag. If using a zip-top bag, cut a ½-inch hole at one corner of the bag. Pipe the filling into the bottom of each cream puff and gently press on the top. Use a fine-mesh sieve to sift powdered sugar over each cream puff. Serve immediately or refrigerate until ready to serve.

7. Store in an airtight container in the refrigerator for up to 3 days.

TIP: To chill the curd faster, cover the bowl and place it in an ice bath for an hour.

Makes 20 cream puffs

Chocolate Crème Brûlée

PREP: *15 minutes*   **COOK:** *1 hour*   **COOL:** *3 hours*

Chocolate is my flavor. There are some desserts I love that don't have chocolate, but the ones that give me that weak-in-the-knees feeling usually do. For this reason, I learned to make my own version of chocolate crème brûlée. My kids love a traditional crème brûlée and I make that for them plenty. But when I'm craving a chocolate version, this is the recipe I turn to.

2 cups heavy cream

½ cup plus 4 teaspoons sugar

1 teaspoon pure vanilla extract

1¼ cups semisweet chocolate chips

6 large egg yolks

1. Preheat the oven to 285°F. Place four 8-ounce ramekins in a 9 × 13-inch baking dish and carefully fill the dish with 1 inch of water, making sure not to get any water in the ramekins.

2. In a small saucepan, combine the cream, ¼ cup of the sugar, and the vanilla over medium heat. Cook, stirring occasionally, until the sugar dissolves and the cream is just starting to simmer. Place the chocolate chips in a medium bowl and pour the cream mixture over them. Let steep for about 2 minutes, then stir until the chocolate has melted and been incorporated evenly.

3. In a medium bowl, whisk together the egg yolks and ¼ cup of the sugar. Temper the egg yolks by adding a small amount of the chocolate mixture at a time and whisking constantly until all the chocolate mixture has been added. Using a strainer over a clean bowl, strain the mixture to remove any lumps.

4. Divide the mixture evenly among the prepared ramekins.

5. Bake the dish with the ramekins and water until there is a slight jiggle in the center of the ramekins, 50 to 55 minutes. Carefully remove the ramekins from their water bath and let cool at room temperature for 1 hour. Refrigerate for 2 hours.

6. Before serving, sprinkle 1 teaspoon of sugar on the top of each ramekin and gently jiggle to evenly coat the top. Carefully use a kitchen torch to melt the sugar and create a hard, caramelized top. Serve immediately.

7. Store leftovers in the refrigerator for up to 3 days.

Makes 4 servings

Toffee Cakes

PREP: *45 minutes*   **COOK:** *30 minutes*   **COOL:** *15 minutes*

Every once in a while I come across a dish I love so much that I ask the recipe creator if I can share it, which is exactly how these toffee cakes came to be in this book. We were on a family vacation in Telluride, and we went out to dinner one night at a local restaurant named Allred's. I had one bite of their toffee cake and couldn't put it down. It was so delicious that we went back to that same restaurant the next night just so we could order it again.

CAKES

Nonstick baking spray

8 ounces pitted dates, chopped

1 tablespoon pure vanilla extract

1 teaspoon baking soda

8 tablespoons (1 stick) unsalted butter, at room temperature

1 cup granulated sugar

2 large eggs

1½ cups all-purpose flour

2 teaspoons baking powder

TOFFEE SAUCE

1 cup heavy cream

½ cup packed light brown sugar

4 tablespoons unsalted butter

1 tablespoon Myers's dark rum (optional)

Whipped cream, for serving

1. To make the cakes: Preheat the oven to 325°F. Spray two 12-cup muffin tins with nonstick baking spray.

2. In a medium saucepan, combine the dates and 1½ cups of water and bring to a boil over medium heat. Boil for about 2 minutes. Stir in the vanilla and baking soda. Let cool for about 10 minutes.

3. In a stand mixer fitted with the paddle attachment, cream the butter and sugar on medium-high speed for about 90 seconds. Add the eggs, one at a time, mixing well after each addition. Lower the speed to medium and gradually add in the flour and baking powder, mixing until the batter is smooth, about 30 seconds.

4. Using an immersion blender or conventional blender, puree the date mixture. Add the date puree to the mixer and mix on medium speed until all the ingredients are well combined.

5. Fill only 18 cups of the prepared muffin tins two-thirds full with the batter. Place a piece of parchment paper over the top of the cupcake tins, then place a baking sheet on top.

6. Bake the tins with the baking sheet on top until a toothpick inserted in the center comes out clean, 16 minutes. Carefully remove the baking sheet and parchment paper from the top of the cupcake tins. Turn the cakes out onto a wire rack to cool for about 5 minutes.

7. To make the toffee sauce: In a medium saucepan, combine the cream, sugar, butter, and rum (if using). Bring the ingredients to a boil over medium-high heat and cook, stirring constantly, until the sauce has thickened and darkened in color, 6 minutes.

8. Plate the cakes and pour the warm sauce over the top. Serve with whipped cream.

9. Store cake and sauce separately in airtight containers in the refrigerator for up to 2 days.

Makes 18 servings

Chocolate Molten Cakes

PREP: *15 minutes*   COOK: *15 minutes*   COOL: *5 minutes*

The last couple of years I've noticed there are certain foods I consider "restaurant foods." In other words, foods that I enjoy eating but would never try to make at home, mostly because they appear too complex. Chocolate molten cake is certainly on that list, but I love chocolate so much that I had to try. It took a couple of times to get the textures right, but it was so fun to see the surprise in my kids' eyes when they dug into the cake and discovered I had learned to make the one with the warm and gooey middle. I still like to order chocolate molten cake in restaurants but I also enjoy that I can make it on my own.

Nonstick baking spray

4 ounces bittersweet chocolate, chopped

8 tablespoons (1 stick) unsalted butter

3 large eggs

½ cup granulated sugar

¼ cup all-purpose flour

1 teaspoon pure vanilla extract

1 teaspoon instant coffee granules

½ teaspoon kosher salt

4 tablespoons powdered sugar

1 pint vanilla ice cream, for serving

1. Preheat the oven to 400°F. Spray 4 ramekins with nonstick baking spray and place them on a baking sheet.

2. In a medium microwave-safe bowl, add the chocolate and butter. Microwave on high in 30-second intervals, stirring thoroughly between intervals, until the mixture is completely melted and smooth. Let cool slightly, about 5 minutes.

3. Whisk the eggs and granulated sugar into the cooled butter mixture. Add the flour, vanilla, coffee granules, and salt and whisk until the ingredients just come together.

4. Evenly divide the batter among the prepared ramekins. Bake until the sides are set and the center is still a bit wet, 12 to 14 minutes.

5. While the cakes cool for 1 to 2 minutes, portion 4 scoops of ice cream. Carefully hold an individual serving plate on top of each ramekin and flip over, letting each cake release onto the plate; remove the ramekin. Dust the cakes with powdered sugar and place the ice cream on top. Serve immediately.

Makes 4 servings

Carrot Cake

PREP: *40 minutes*   COOK: *40 minutes*   COOL: *1 hour 15 minutes*

When I host brunch in the spring, I love to have a carrot cake on the table. Its not-too-sweet quality is a nice complement to more savory dishes. Whether you serve this cake on its own or as part of a more complete menu, I've always found it to be an easy win. The texture of the carrots, nuts, and raisins keeps every bite interesting.

CARROT CAKE

Nonstick baking spray

4 cups all-purpose flour

1 tablespoon ground cinnamon

1 tablespoon baking powder

2 teaspoons baking soda

½ teaspoon kosher salt

6 large eggs

1½ cups vegetable oil

1 cup granulated sugar

1 cup packed light brown sugar

1 tablespoon pure vanilla extract

3 cups finely shredded carrots

1 cup chopped walnuts

Cream Cheese Icing (page 331)

1. To make the carrot cake: Preheat the oven to 350°F. Spray two 9-inch round cake pans with nonstick baking spray.

2. In a medium bowl, sift together the flour, cinnamon, baking powder, baking soda, and salt.

3. In a stand mixer fitted with the paddle attachment, combine the eggs, oil, granulated sugar, brown sugar, and vanilla on medium speed until the mixture comes together, about 2 minutes. Reduce the speed to low and gradually add the flour mixture, then add the carrots and walnuts. Increase the speed to medium and mix until the ingredients are just fully incorporated, about 1 minute.

4. Divide the batter evenly between the prepared pans.

5. Bake until a toothpick inserted in the center comes out clean, 35 to 40 minutes. Let cool for 15 minutes in the pans before turning them out onto a wire rack to cool completely, about 1 hour.

6. Place one cake layer on a large plate. Dollop about ½ cup of the icing on the center of the cake. Using an offset spatula, carefully spread the icing toward the edge of the cake, making an even layer. Place the second layer on top of the icing and dollop the rest of the icing on the top. Carefully spread the icing toward the edge of the cake, then spread it down the sides, keeping the icing very thin until the cake is fully covered.

7. Store in an airtight container in the refrigerator for up to 5 days or at room temperature for up to 2 days.

Makes 10 servings

Chocolate Chip Bundt Cake

PREP: *25 minutes*   **COOK:** *45 minutes*   **COOL:** *40 minutes*

When my friends have birthdays, I love to bake them cakes. This recipe was created because I have a good friend who doesn't like cake icing. I wanted to make her a cake that would still have the right amount of sweetness and feel special even without the flourishes of icing on top. She loved it, and over time I discovered other people did, too. It has since become a go-to cake when we want something sweet. Served with or without candles, it can make any day feel like a celebration.

Nonstick baking spray

3 cups all-purpose flour

2 teaspoons baking powder

1 teaspoon baking soda

1 teaspoon kosher salt

½ cup plain whole-milk Greek yogurt

¼ cup whole-milk buttermilk

¼ cup vegetable oil

1 cup (2 sticks) unsalted butter, melted

1 cup granulated sugar

½ cup packed light brown sugar

4 large eggs, at room temperature

1 tablespoon pure vanilla extract

10 ounces mini chocolate chips

1. Preheat the oven to 350°F. Spray a 10-inch Bundt pan with nonstick baking spray.

2. In a medium bowl, sift together the flour, baking powder, baking soda, and salt. In a small bowl, whisk together the yogurt, buttermilk, and oil.

3. In a stand mixer fitted with the paddle attachment, combine the melted butter, granulated sugar, and brown sugar on medium-high speed for about 1 minute. Reduce the speed to low and add the eggs, one at a time, and vanilla and mix until well combined, about 2 minutes.

4. With the speed still on low, alternately add half of the buttermilk mixture and half of the flour mixture, letting the ingredients incorporate for 30 to 45 seconds between additions, until all is added and well combined.

5. Increase the speed to medium and add the chocolate chips, mixing until well distributed.

6. Pour the batter into the prepared pan, distributing evenly, and tap the pan on the counter a few times to level out the batter.

7. Bake until a toothpick inserted in the center comes out clean, 45 minutes. Let cool in the pan for 10 minutes, then turn the cake out onto a wire rack, carefully removing the pan. Let cool for 30 more minutes before serving.

8. Store in an airtight container at room temperature for up to 3 days.

Makes 10 to 12 servings

Butter Cake

WITH ROASTED STRAWBERRIES AND BALSAMIC

PREP: *15 minutes*   **COOK:** *45 minutes*   **COOL:** *40 minutes*

The balsamic reduction on this cake makes it feel unique. Some days I look forward to that finishing detail, but if I'm being honest, most of the time I crave the simplicity of a butter cake that doesn't need anything else to be delicious.

Nonstick baking spray

8 tablespoons (1 stick) unsalted butter, at room temperature

2 cups sugar

½ cup whole milk

2 large eggs, at room temperature

1 teaspoon pure vanilla extract

1 tablespoon fresh lemon juice

1 teaspoon freshly grated lemon zest

1½ cups all-purpose flour

1 teaspoon baking powder

½ teaspoon kosher salt

2 cups sliced fresh strawberries

2 cups whipped cream (see page 263), for serving

Fresh whole mint leaves, for garnish

¼ cup balsamic reduction

1. Preheat the oven to 375°F. Spray a 9 × 9-inch baking dish with nonstick baking spray. Line a baking sheet with parchment paper.

2. In a stand mixer fitted with the whisk attachment, whip the butter on medium-high speed until fluffy and lighter in color, 3 minutes. Add the sugar and milk and whisk for 1 minute. Reduce the speed to low and add the eggs, one at a time. Increase the speed to medium and mix in the vanilla, lemon juice, and zest, 30 seconds. Turn off the mixer and scrape down the sides and bottom of the bowl with a spatula. Mix again on medium speed for 30 more seconds.

3. In a medium bowl, stir together the flour, baking powder, and salt.

4. With the mixer on low, add half of the flour mixture to the butter mixture and mix for 1 minute. Add the other half and mix until thoroughly combined, 1 more minute.

5. Pour the batter in the prepared baking dish.

6. Bake until a toothpick inserted in the center comes out with a crumb coating, 25 to 30 minutes. Let cool on a wire rack for 30 minutes. Leave the oven on and increase the temperature to 400°F.

7. Scatter the sliced strawberries on the prepared baking sheet. Bake until the strawberries are softened, 12 minutes. Let cool for 10 minutes.

8. Cut the cake into 12 equal squares. Top each piece with roasted strawberries, whipped cream, and a mint leaf, then drizzle with a teaspoon of balsamic reduction.

9. Store the cake in an airtight container at room temperature for 3 days. Store the whipped cream and strawberries in separate airtight containers in the refrigerator for 3 to 5 days.

Makes 12 servings

Confetti Sugar Cookie Sandwich

SERVED AT SILOS BAKING CO WACO · TX

PREP: *30 minutes*   **COOK:** *15 minutes*   **COOL:** *20 minutes*

I'm a believer that dessert of any kind can make a day feel special. But there's something about sprinkles specifically that can make an ordinary moment feel like a party. Anytime you have something big or small to celebrate, I recommend this dependably delicious sugar cookie recipe, loaded up, of course, with sprinkles.

CONFETTI COOKIES

1 cup (2 sticks) unsalted butter, at room temperature

1½ cups granulated sugar

2 large eggs

1 teaspoon cake batter extract

½ teaspoon pure vanilla extract

2 cups cake flour

1 cup all-purpose flour

1 teaspoon baking soda

½ teaspoon baking powder

1 teaspoon kosher salt

⅓ cup rainbow sprinkles, plus more for sprinkling

VANILLA FILLING

9 ounces (2 sticks plus 2 tablespoons) unsalted butter, at room temperature

1½ teaspoons pure vanilla extract

3¾ cups powdered sugar

1½ tablespoons whole milk

1. To make the confetti cookies: Preheat the oven to 350°F. Line two baking sheets with parchment paper.

2. In a stand mixer fitted with the paddle attachment, cream the butter and sugar on medium-high speed, until light and fluffy, about 1 to 2 minutes. Add the eggs, one at a time, and mix until thoroughly incorporated, then add the cake batter extract and vanilla and continue mixing. Slowly add both flours, the baking soda, baking powder, and salt. Mix until all the dry ingredients are incorporated, then mix in the rainbow sprinkles.

3. Using a 1-ounce scoop, portion the cookie dough into balls and place at least 2 inches apart on the prepared baking sheets. Sprinkle the tops with a few more sprinkles.

4. Bake, swapping the placement of the pans halfway through, until the edges start turning a golden color, 10 to 12 minutes. Let the cookies cool on the baking sheets for at least 5 minutes, then transfer to wire racks to cool completely.

5. To make the filling: In a stand mixer fitted with the paddle attachment, cream the butter on high speed until light and fluffy, 3 to 4 minutes. Beat in the vanilla.

6. Reduce the speed to low and slowly beat in the powdered sugar, about ¼ cup at a time, then beat in the milk. When the mixture is smooth, increase the speed to medium, mixing until thoroughly combined and fluffy, about 2 more minutes.

7. Set the cookies up in pairs, with the bottom of one of them facing up. Using a small scoop, place about 1½ tablespoons of the filling on the bottom of the upside-down cookie. Place the second cookie on top, right side up, and sandwich them together, pressing just enough to spread the filling to the edges. Repeat to make the rest of the sandwiches.

8. Store in an airtight container at room temperature for up to 5 days.

Makes 16 sandwich cookies

Lemon Tea Cookies

PREP: *15 minutes*   **COOK:** *15 minutes*   **COOL:** *25 minutes*

These bite-size desserts are perfect to bring to a shower or serve for a special occasion, though my favorite way to enjoy them is as a simple afternoon delight paired with tea. They have a bright taste that's refreshing, and their smaller size makes them easy and light to snack on.

1 cup (2 sticks) unsalted
   butter, at room
   temperature

2 cups powdered sugar

1 large egg yolk

⅓ cup fresh lemon juice

1 tablespoon freshly
   grated lemon zest

1 teaspoon vanilla bean paste

3 cups all-purpose flour

1 teaspoon baking powder

1 teaspoon kosher salt

1. Preheat the oven to 350°F. Line two baking sheets with parchment paper.

2. In a stand mixer fitted with the paddle attachment, cream the butter and 1 cup of the powdered sugar starting on low speed and gradually increasing to medium-high for about 2 minutes. Turn off the mixer and scrape down the sides and bottom of the bowl with a spatula. On low speed, slowly add the egg yolk, lemon juice, lemon zest, and vanilla bean paste and mix until incorporated, about 2 minutes.

3. In a medium bowl, whisk together the flour, baking powder, and salt. With the mixer on medium speed, slowly add the flour mixture to the butter mixture. Mix until just combined and a dough forms, about 1 minute.

4. Using a 1½-tablespoon scoop, portion the cookie dough into balls and place them about 1 inch apart on the prepared baking sheets.

5. Bake until the bottoms of the cookies are golden (the tops will still be very blond), 15 minutes. Let the cookies cool on the baking sheets for 10 minutes.

6. Place the remaining 1½ cups powdered sugar in a medium bowl. Roll the warm cookies in the powdered sugar to coat them completely, then transfer to a wire rack to finish cooling, another 15 minutes.

7. Store in an airtight container at room temperature for up to 5 days.

Makes 32 cookies

Brownie Cookies

PREP: *25 minutes*   **COOK:** *35 minutes*   **COOL:** *1 hour 25 minutes*

These delicious cookies are a bestseller at the bakery. They have a soft rise and just the right amount of gooeyness. We are a house divided when it comes to cookies versus brownies, so this two-for-one combination is an easy win for everyone.

2 ½ cups semisweet chocolate chips

8 tablespoons (1 stick) unsalted butter

1 cup all-purpose flour

2 tablespoons Dutch-process cocoa powder

1 teaspoon baking powder

½ teaspoon kosher salt

3 large eggs

1 cup granulated sugar

⅓ cup packed light brown sugar

2 teaspoons pure vanilla extract

1. In a medium microwave-safe bowl, combine 2 cups of the chocolate chips and the butter. Microwave on high in 20-second intervals, stirring thoroughly between intervals, until the mixture is completely melted and smooth. Scrape the chocolate mixture into the bowl of a stand mixer fitted with the paddle attachment and let sit at room temperature for 20 minutes to cool.

2. While the chocolate mixture is cooling, sift together the flour, cocoa, baking powder, and salt in a separate medium bowl. Preheat the oven to 375°F. Line two large baking sheets with parchment paper.

3. Add the eggs, granulated sugar, brown sugar, and vanilla to the cooled chocolate mixture and beat on medium speed until thoroughly combined. Reduce the speed to low, slowly pour the flour mixture into the chocolate mixture, and mix until all ingredients are thoroughly combined. Add the remaining ½ cup chocolate chips and mix briefly to incorporate fully.

4. Using a 1-ounce scoop, portion the dough onto one prepared baking sheet. You do not need to space them out. Chill until firm, about 45 minutes.

5. Working in batches, place the chilled cookies 2 inches apart on the other prepared room-temperature baking sheet.

6. Bake until the edges are set, 12 to 14 minutes. The centers of the cookies will appear and feel soft when hot but will set as they cool. Let cool on the baking sheet 5 minutes, then transfer to a wire rack to cool completely. Repeat with the remaining cookie balls.

7. Store in an airtight container for up to 5 days.

Makes 35 cookies

Blonde Brownies

PREP: *15 minutes*   COOK: *40 minutes*   COOL: *20 minutes*

This is a classic chocolate chip cookie, but in brownie form. So extra moist, extra chewy, and extra delicious. Because the recipe doesn't take much time, it's an easy choice for an afternoon treat.

Nonstick baking spray

1 cup (2 sticks) unsalted butter, at room temperature

1 cup packed light brown sugar

¾ cup granulated sugar

2 teaspoons pure vanilla extract

3 large eggs, at room temperature

2¼ cups all-purpose flour

1 tablespoon cornstarch

1 teaspoon baking powder

1 teaspoon kosher salt

¾ cup semisweet chocolate chips (optional)

1. Preheat the oven to 350°F. Spray a 9 × 13-inch baking dish with nonstick baking spray.

2. In a stand mixer fitted with the paddle attachment, cream together the butter, brown sugar, and granulated sugar on medium-high speed until light and fluffy, about 3 minutes. Reduce the speed to low and add in the vanilla and eggs, one at a time, mixing well after each addition.

3. Turn off the mixer and scrape down the sides and bottom of the bowl with a spatula. On low speed, slowly add the flour, cornstarch, baking powder, and salt. Increase the speed to medium and mix for about 1 minute, then reduce the speed to low and add the chocolate chips (if using). (You can also do this step by hand with a spatula.)

4. Scrape the brownie mixture into the prepared dish and spread so it is evenly distributed.

5. Bake until the edges are golden and a toothpick inserted in the center comes out clean, 35 to 40 minutes.

6. Let cool for 20 minutes before cutting into 12 equal pieces.

7. Store in an airtight container at room temperature for up to 5 days.

Makes 12 brownies

Pecan Bars

PREP: *15 minutes*   **COOK:** *1 hour 15 minutes*   **COOL:** *2 hours*

Pecan pie is a staple in Texas, especially in the central part of the state where a lot of pecan orchards can be found. The only drawback is that when it comes time to serve, the slices are often too heavy and can get messy. So if I'm hosting a gathering, I tend to serve these bars instead. They are so easy to slice up and stack. I like to prepare them in a large baking pan, and I'll often add mini chocolate chips to half of the batch. Having two varieties makes serving the bars all the more fun.

CRUST

Nonstick baking spray

2 cups all-purpose flour

8 tablespoons (1 stick) unsalted butter, cold, cubed, plus 5 tablespoons melted

½ cup sugar

¼ heaped teaspoon kosher salt

PECAN FILLING

1 cup mini chocolate chips

4 large eggs

2½ cups coarsely chopped pecans

1¾ cups sugar

1½ cups light corn syrup

2 teaspoons pure vanilla extract

½ teaspoon kosher salt

3 tablespoons unsalted butter, melted

Whipped cream, for serving (optional)

1. To make the crust: Preheat the oven to 350°F. Spray a 9 × 13-inch glass baking dish with nonstick spray to coat all sides and line with parchment paper, allowing the paper to hang over the sides to use as handles later.

2. In a food processor, pulse the flour, cold butter, sugar, and salt until well combined. Slowly pour in the melted butter while pulsing, until the mixture crumbles like sand, about 1 minute.

3. Using your hands, press the mixture evenly into the glass baking dish, covering the bottom completely.

4. Bake until the crust is light brown, 25 minutes. Remove from the oven and leave the oven on.

5. To make the filling: Sprinkle the chocolate chips over half the crust.

6. In a medium bowl, whisk the eggs. Add the pecans, sugar, corn syrup, vanilla, and salt and mix well to combine. Slowly stir in the melted butter until well combined.

7. Evenly pour the mixture over the warm crust.

8. Bake, tenting with foil halfway through to prevent overbrowning, until the center is slightly puffed and set, 40 to 50 minutes. Let cool for 2 hours.

9. Carefully lift the bars out of the dish using the parchment paper handles and cut into 20 squares. Serve with a spoonful of fresh whipped cream, if you like.

10. Store in an airtight container at room temperature or in the refrigerator for 3 to 5 days.

TIP: These are a fun packed-lunch item or a great brunch or shower addition.

Makes 20 squares

Spiced Honey Orange Peanut Brittle

PREP: *5 minutes*   **COOK:** *15 minutes*   **COOL:** *2 to 3 hours*

PEANUT BRITTLE

Grated zest of 1 large orange

2 teaspoons ground cardamom

¼ cup boiling water

1½ cups sugar

¼ cup honey

1 cup raw peanuts

2 tablespoons unsalted butter

1 teaspoon baking soda

TOPPING (OPTIONAL)

8 ounces chocolate candy melts

¼ cup finely chopped peanuts, raw or roasted and lightly salted

1 teaspoon ground cardamom

Grated zest of ½ large orange

Flaky salt

1. Line a baking sheet with a silicone baking mat.

2. In a mug, cover the orange zest and cardamom with the boiling water. Stir, then let steep for 7 minutes. Using a fine-mesh sieve or coffee filter, strain the mixture over a medium saucepan, retaining the liquid in the pan. Add additional water to make ¼ cup, if needed.

3. Add the sugar and honey to the saucepan with the liquid. Bring to a boil over medium heat, stirring occasionally and scraping down the sides of the pan with a rubber spatula to ensure the sugar does not burn. Do not walk away from the pot. Use a candy or kitchen thermometer to check the temperature frequently. Immediately clean off the thermometer with a folded kitchen towel so the sugar doesn't harden onto it. Once the mixture reaches 240°F, add the peanuts and stir constantly until the mixture reaches 300°F.

4. Once the mixture reaches 300°F, immediately remove the pot from the heat and carefully stir in the butter and baking soda until the butter is completely incorporated. The mixture will foam and double in volume.

5. Quickly pour the mixture onto the prepared pan and use a spatula to spread it evenly. (It does not have to fill the pan entirely.) Let cool at room temperature for at least 2 hours.

6. Carefully break the cooled brittle into chunks using a sharp knife or your hands.

7. To decorate the brittle, if you like: Line a baking sheet with parchment paper.

8. Melt the chocolate candy melts according to the package directions.

9. Dip each chunk of brittle halfway into the chocolate and set on the prepared pan.

10. Immediately sprinkle with chopped nuts, cardamom, orange zest, and flaky salt (if using). Let the chocolate set at room temperature for at least 1 hour or in the fridge for a maximum of 20 minutes.

11. Store at room temperature in an airtight container lined with parchment paper for up to 1 week. Do not refrigerate.

Makes 12 servings

Flavored Popcorn Trio

PREP: *5 to 15 minutes*   **COOK:** *5 minutes to 1 hour*   **COOL:** *up to 20 minutes*

BASE POPCORN

½ cup popcorn kernels

4 tablespoons clarified unsalted butter, melted

2 teaspoons kosher salt

CHOCOLATE PEANUT BUTTER

½ cup semisweet chocolate chips

¼ cup creamy peanut butter

½ teaspoon pure vanilla extract

1 batch base popcorn (above)

1 cup powdered sugar

RANCH

2 teaspoons powdered buttermilk

½ teaspoon dried parsley, crushed

¼ teaspoon dried dill, crushed

¼ teaspoon mustard powder

¼ teaspoon onion powder

¼ teaspoon garlic salt

1 batch base popcorn (above), butter and salt reserved

CARAMEL

1 cup (2 sticks) unsalted butter

1 cup packed light brown sugar

¼ cup light corn syrup

1 teaspoon pure vanilla extract

1 teaspoon kosher salt

1 batch base popcorn (above)

BASE POPCORN

Place the corn kernels in an air popper and pop according to the manufacturer's directions. In a large bowl, toss the popped popcorn with the butter and salt.

CHOCOLATE PEANUT BUTTER

1. In a small microwave-safe bowl, melt the chocolate chips and peanut butter together, stirring every 30 seconds, until fully melted. Stir in the vanilla until well combined.

2. Pour the chocolate peanut butter mixture over the popcorn and toss to coat. Sprinkle the popcorn with the powdered sugar and toss again to fully coat the popcorn.

3. Store any variation in a sealed bag at room temperature for up to 5 days.

RANCH

In a small bowl, combine the powdered buttermilk, parsley, dill, mustard powder, onion powder, and garlic salt to make ranch seasoning. Pour the reserved butter and salt and the ranch seasoning over the base popcorn and toss together to fully coat the popcorn.

CARAMEL

1. Preheat the oven to 250°F. Line a baking sheet with parchment paper.

2. In a medium saucepan, melt the butter over medium heat. Add the brown sugar and corn syrup and stir constantly until the sugar dissolves, then stop stirring. Boil the mixture without stirring for 4 to 5 minutes. Remove the mixture from the heat and carefully stir in the vanilla and salt.

3. Pour the caramel mixture over the base popcorn and stir to coat. Evenly spread the popcorn onto the prepared baking sheet.

4. Bake for 1 hour, stirring carefully every 15 minutes. Allow the popcorn to cool for 20 minutes. Pour the popcorn into a clean bowl, breaking up any large chunks.

Each variation makes 4 to 8 servings

Homemade Chocolate Sauce

PREP: *10 minutes*   **COOK:** *10 minutes*   **COOL:** *none*

Since I was a kid, I remember my dad always topping his vanilla ice cream with chocolate sauce and walnuts. I love to top mine the same way, so I've been a fan of chocolate sauce for a very long time. What you can buy at the store is good, but homemade chocolate sauce is next-level delicious. It's such a treat, and something people so rarely think to make for themselves. I love to bottle this sauce and gift it to friends, especially around the holidays.

12 ounces evaporated milk

1½ cups sugar

½ cup unsweetened cocoa powder

1½ teaspoons instant espresso granules

½ teaspoon kosher salt

8 tablespoons (1 stick) unsalted butter, cold, cut into 1-inch cubes

1 tablespoon pure vanilla extract

1. In a medium saucepan, combine the evaporated milk, sugar, cocoa, instant espresso, and salt over medium heat. Bring the mixture to a boil, stirring occasionally. Boil for 5 minutes, stirring constantly, making sure the chocolate does not stick to the bottom and burn.

2. Remove from the heat and carefully whisk in the cubes of butter and vanilla, until the butter is fully melted. Serve the chocolate sauce warm over your favorite dessert.

3. Store in an airtight container in the refrigerator for up to 3 weeks. Reheat in a small saucepan over low heat, stirring frequently until warm.

Makes 3 cups

Hot Chocolate Bombs

PREP: *55 minutes*   **COOK:** *none*   **COOL:** *40 minutes*

A tradition at the Gaines household every year is a hot chocolate bar. Last year, I thought I would step it up a notch and make these hot chocolate bombs. There's something so fun about the experience of dropping one into hot milk and watching the chocolate magic unfold. They were a hit with the whole family, and something I'll definitely bring back for years to come.

¾ cup dry milk powder

¼ cup sugar

¼ cup unsweetened cocoa powder

1 tablespoon instant chocolate pudding mix

1 pound chocolate candy melts

Silicone mold with six 2½-inch-diameter half-sphere cavities

⅔ cup mini marshmallows

1. Preheat the oven to 300°F. Place an empty baking sheet in the oven.

2. In a medium bowl, whisk together the dry milk powder, sugar, cocoa, and chocolate pudding mix until well combined.

3. Melt the chocolate candy melts according to the package directions. Put 2 tablespoons of melted chocolate into each mold, then, using a paintbrush or a spoon, evenly spread the chocolate all the way up the sides to the top. Place the mold in the freezer for about 10 minutes. Gently remove the chocolate from the molds and place the half spheres on a piece of parchment paper. Repeat this process until you have 20 chocolate half spheres.

4. Take the baking sheet out of the oven and set it next to your work space. Working in pairs, carefully place the rims of two chocolate half spheres on the hot baking sheet to melt away the jagged edges. Working quickly, fill one of the half spheres with 2 tablespoons of the cocoa mix and about 1 tablespoon of marshmallows. Take the second half sphere and place it directly on top, rim to rim. The melted chocolate will act as a glue to seal the two pieces together to make a sphere. Continue melting and forming spheres with the remaining chocolate, cocoa mix, and marshmallows.

5. To serve, place a hot chocolate ball in a mug and slowly pour hot milk over it. Stir the mixture together and enjoy!

6. Store in a sealed container at room temperature for up to 1 week.

Makes 10 bombs

Chocolate Meringues

PREP: *20 minutes*   **COOK:** *1 hour*   **COOL:** *2 hours*

I like to describe these chocolate meringues as "airy brownies." Even though the chocolate taste is rich, it never feels heavy. My favorite way to serve them is with whipped cream and berries on top.

4 large egg whites

½ teaspoon cream of tartar

1¼ cups sugar

½ teaspoon kosher salt

⅓ cup unsweetened cocoa powder, sifted

2 teaspoons pure vanilla extract

1. Preheat the oven to 225°F. Line two baking sheets with parchment paper.

2. In a stand mixer fitted with the whisk attachment, mix the egg whites and cream of tartar on low speed until combined. Gradually increase the speed to high and slowly pour the sugar and salt into the mixer. Continue mixing on high until the egg whites are white, glossy, they hold a stiff peak when you pull the whisk out of the bowl, and the sugar has completely dissolved, 5 to 8 minutes.

3. Using a spatula, gently fold the sifted cocoa powder and vanilla into the egg whites until just incorporated, making sure not to deflate the mixture.

4. Using a ¼-cup scoop or two large spoons, portion the mixture onto the prepared baking sheets, spacing the meringues about 1 inch apart.

5. Bake for 1 hour. Without opening the oven door, turn the oven off and allow the meringues to cool in the oven for 2 hours.

6. Store in an airtight container at room temperature for up to 5 days.

TIP: Serve with whipped cream and fresh berries.

Makes 18 meringues

Peanut Butter Cookies

PREP: *25 minutes*   **COOK:** *15 minutes*   **COOL:** *25 minutes*

My first-ever batch of peanut butter cookies nearly burned down my childhood home. I was eight or nine years old and I'd decided that I needed a peanut butter cookie right away, so I got a cupful of peanut butter, mixed it with a little bit of flour and sugar, and set it in the microwave. What came next was mostly smoke and regret and the realization that I had some learning to do. My cravings for peanut butter cookies haven't changed much since then; they still come on fast and furious. Only now I've learned how to bake a really delicious batch without the smoke. Here I'm sharing my go-to recipe for whenever the mood strikes.

1 cup (2 sticks) unsalted butter, at room temperature

1½ cups smooth peanut butter

1¾ cups granulated sugar

1 cup packed light brown sugar

3 large eggs

2 teaspoons pure vanilla extract

2¾ cups all-purpose flour

1 teaspoon baking powder

1½ teaspoons baking soda

1 teaspoon kosher salt

1. In a stand mixer fitted with the paddle attachment, mix the butter, peanut butter, 1 cup of the granulated sugar, and the brown sugar on medium-high speed until fluffy. Turn off the mixer and scrape down the sides and bottom of the bowl with a spatula. On low speed, beat in the eggs, one at a time, then add the vanilla.

2. In a medium bowl, whisk together the flour, baking powder, baking soda, and salt. On low speed, add the flour mixture, about ½ cup at a time, into the butter mixture, beating until combined.

3. Line two baking sheets with parchment paper. Place the remaining ¾ cup granulated sugar into a small bowl. Using a 1-ounce scoop, portion the dough, then roll into balls using your hands. Press the tops of each ball into the sugar, completely covering the tops, and set 2 inches apart on the prepared baking sheets. Using a fork, gently press in two different directions onto the top of each cookie, creating a crisscross pattern.

4. Preheat the oven to 350°F. Refrigerate the cookies for about 15 minutes before baking.

5. Bake the chilled cookies until the edges turn a golden color, 11 to 12 minutes. Let cool on the baking sheets for 10 minutes, then transfer to a wire rack to cool completely. Repeat with the remaining dough.

Makes 48 cookies

Classic Vanilla Bean Soufflé

PREP: *45 minutes*   **COOK**: *25 minutes*   **COOL**: *none*

The timing on these soufflés needs to be precise, and you really can't make them ahead. But I've found that when guests know you are prepping something as special as soufflé, they don't mind your absence at all. In fact, it tends to build anticipation, which makes the final dish all the more appreciated.

6 tablespoons unsalted butter, at room temperature

¼ cup plus ⅓ cup granulated sugar

4 large eggs

2 tablespoons bread flour

1 cup whole milk

1 tablespoon vanilla bean paste

½ teaspoon kosher salt

¼ cup powdered sugar

1. Preheat the oven to 375°F. Brush the bottoms and sides of six 5-ounce ramekins with 4 tablespoons of the butter. Divide ¼ cup of the granulated sugar among the ramekins and turn them to thoroughly coat the butter on the bottoms and sides with a dusting of sugar, discarding any excess. Place the ramekins on a baking sheet.

2. Separate the egg yolks from the whites, placing the yolks in a medium bowl and the whites in the bowl of a stand mixer. Whisk the yolks together.

3. In a small saucepan, melt the remaining 2 tablespoons butter over medium heat. Sprinkle in the flour and whisk until incorporated. Slowly pour in the milk, vanilla bean paste, and salt and continue whisking until the mixture thickens, 4 to 5 minutes. Remove the saucepan from the heat. Temper the egg yolks by adding ¼ cup of the milk mixture at a time and whisking constantly until all the milk mixture has been added.

4. In a stand mixer fitted with the whisk attachment, whip the egg whites until they start to get foamy, then sprinkle in the remaining ⅓ cup sugar. Continue whipping the egg whites on medium speed until they hold medium-stiff peaks when you pull the whisk out of the bowl and the consistency resembles whipped cream, about 3 minutes.

5. Using a spatula, fold about half of the egg whites into the yolk mixture, carefully lifting from the bottom and folding over the top. Fold in half of the remaining egg whites, then the last of the egg whites, taking care not to deflate the mixture.

6. Divide the mixture among the prepared ramekins.

7. Bake undisturbed until the soufflés have risen over the top of the ramekin rims and the tops are golden brown, about 15 minutes.

8. Using a sifter or fine-mesh sieve, sift the powdered sugar over the soufflés immediately as they come out of the oven. Serve immediately.

Makes 6 servings

Coconut Cream Cake

PREP: *30 minutes*   **COOK:** *30 minutes*   **COOL:** *1 hour 10 minutes*

When the craving for something extra sweet strikes, this cake is a welcome salve. I like how the crust offers a balance for the dessert and keeps the richness of the coconut cream from going over the top. With the pretty whipped topping, this cake makes a nice finishing touch to any summer table.

Nonstick baking spray

4 large eggs

1½ cups superfine or granulated sugar

1 cup whole milk

8 tablespoons (1 stick) unsalted butter

2 cups all-purpose flour

2½ teaspoons baking powder

¼ teaspoon kosher salt

2 cups sweetened shredded coconut

1 tablespoon vegetable oil

1 teaspoon coconut extract

1 teaspoon almond extract

15 ounces cream of coconut, preferably Coco López

2 cups heavy cream

½ cup powdered sugar

1. To make the coconut cream cake: Position the oven racks in the middle and upper positions. Preheat the oven to 350°F. Spray a 9 × 13-inch glass baking dish with nonstick baking spray.

2. In a stand mixer fitted with the whisk attachment, beat the eggs for 1 minute on medium-high speed. Reduce the speed to low and add the sugar. Once combined, increase the speed to medium and whisk until pale yellow and doubled in volume, 8 minutes.

3. Meanwhile, in a medium saucepan, heat the milk and butter over medium heat until the butter is fully melted—remove from heat. In a large bowl, sift together the flour, baking powder, and salt.

4. Reduce the mixer speed to low and add the flour mixture in three additions, mixing well in between each addition, then switch off the mixer.

5. Add 1 cup of the shredded coconut, the oil, coconut extract, and almond extract to the saucepan with the warm milk mixture and stir together.

6. Temper the milk mixture by adding 1 cup of the batter to the saucepan and whisk to combine. Repeat with another cup of the batter, whisking again.

7. Turn the stand mixer to low speed and add the tempered milk mixture to the cake batter, mixing until well combined, 10 seconds. Using a spatula, scrape down the sides and bottom of the mixer bowl. Mix on low for another 5 seconds.

8. Pour the batter into the prepared baking dish.

9. Place the dish on the middle rack of the oven and bake until slightly underdone, when a toothpick inserted in the center comes out with some crumbs (but not wet with batter or clean), 25 to 30 minutes. Let cool for 10 minutes. Leave the oven on for toasting the coconut.

CONTINUED FROM PAGE 329

10. While the cake is slightly warm, use the blunt end of a wooden spoon to poke 12 holes in your cake (3 rows of 4 holes). Set aside 1 tablespoon of the cream of coconut and reserve it for the whipped topping. Pour the remaining cream of coconut over the top of the cake and let it seep into the cake. (If the cream of coconut is solid at first, just spread it smoothly on top and allow it to settle.) Let cool completely, at least 1 hour.

11. Meanwhile, spread the remaining 1 cup shredded coconut on a small baking sheet. Place on the top rack of the oven and toast, stirring once, until lightly golden, 8 to 10 minutes. Set aside and let cool.

12. To make the coconut whipped cream: In a stand mixer fitted with the whisk attachment, whip the cream on medium-high speed until it begins to thicken, 5 minutes. Add the reserved 1 tablespoon of cream of coconut and the powdered sugar and continue to whip until thickened, soft, and smooth, 2 to 3 more minutes.

13. Once the cake is completely cool, spread the coconut whipped cream over the top and sprinkle with toasted coconut. Serve promptly.

14. Store in an airtight container in the refrigerator for 2 to 3 days.

TIP: This cake is excellent prepared the day before you plan to eat it—just refrigerate the baked, un-topped cake the day prior, then make the whipped cream and assemble just before serving.

Makes 12 servings

Pumpkin Spice Sheet Cake

WITH CREAM CHEESE ICING

PREP: *45 minutes*   **COOK**: *30 minutes*   **COOL**: *45 minutes*

By Thanksgiving it feels like everywhere I turn is another pumpkin pie. It's nice to have a recipe that changes it up a bit. Here, you still get the cozy, nostalgic flavors of the season, but with a cake-y layered texture I've come to prefer over a traditional soft pumpkin pie.

PUMPKIN SHEET CAKE

Nonstick baking spray

8 tablespoons (1 stick) unsalted butter, at room temperature

1 cup granulated sugar

⅓ cup packed light brown sugar

2 large eggs

1 cup whole milk

1 cup pumpkin puree

2¼ cups all-purpose flour

1 tablespoon pumpkin pie spice

1 teaspoon kosher salt

1 teaspoon ground ginger

1 teaspoon baking powder

½ teaspoon baking soda

CREAM CHEESE ICING

1 cup (2 sticks) unsalted butter, at room temperature

8 ounces cream cheese, at room temperature

2 teaspoons clear vanilla extract

¼ teaspoon kosher salt

6 cups powdered sugar

1. To make the pumpkin sheet cake: Preheat the oven to 350°F. Spray a 9 × 13-inch pan with nonstick baking spray.

2. In a stand mixer fitted with the paddle attachment, mix the butter, granulated sugar, and brown sugar on medium speed until crumbly. Add the eggs, one at a time, mixing well after each addition. Add the milk and pumpkin puree and combine until the mixture looks a little broken, 1 to 2 minutes.

3. In a medium bowl, stir together the flour, pumpkin spice, salt, ginger, baking powder, and baking soda. With the mixer on low speed, slowly add the flour mixture. After all the flour has been added, turn off the mixer and scrape the sides and bottom of the bowl with a spatula. Turn the mixer to medium and mix again until the ingredients are incorporated, about 15 more seconds.

4. Using a spatula, spread the batter evenly in the prepared pan. Gently tap the pan against the counter to release any air bubbles.

5. Bake until a toothpick inserted in the center comes out clean, 25 to 30 minutes. Let cool on a wire rack for at least 45 minutes.

6. To make the icing: In a stand mixer fitted with the paddle attachment, cream the butter and cream cheese on medium-high speed until light and fluffy, about 1 minute. Reduce the speed to low and add the vanilla and salt. Slowly add the powdered sugar, then increase the speed to medium for about 2 minutes. Using a spatula, scrape the sides and bottom of the bowl well. Mix on medium for about 15 more seconds.

7. Once the cake is cool to the touch, dollop the icing in the center. Using an offset spatula, evenly spread the icing over the cake, making sure the cake is fully covered.

8. Store in an airtight container in the refrigerator or at room temperature for up to 3 days.

Makes 12 to 15 servings

Frozen Layered Ice Cream Cake

PREP: *30 minutes*   **COOK**: *40 minutes*   **COOL**: *4 hours 30 minutes*

1 quart vanilla ice cream

Nonstick baking spray

8 tablespoons (1 stick)
   unsalted butter, melted

1½ cups sugar

4 large eggs

4½ teaspoons pure
   vanilla extract

2 cups cake flour

2½ teaspoons baking powder

¼ teaspoon kosher salt

1 cup sour cream

¼ cup whole milk

2 cups heavy cream

¾ cup powdered sugar

Candy and/or sprinkles,
   for decorating (optional)

1. Let the ice cream sit at room temperature for about 5 minutes to soften slightly. Line an 8-inch round cake pan with parchment paper, allowing the parchment to hang over the sides to use as handles later.

2. In a stand mixer fitted with the paddle attachment, add the ice cream and mix on medium-low speed to create a smooth consistency, 30 to 60 seconds. Transfer the ice cream to the prepared cake pan. Using an offset spatula, spread the ice cream into an even layer, from edge to edge, and place in the freezer for at least 2 hours.

3. Preheat the oven to 350°F. Spray two 8-inch cake pans with nonstick baking spray.

4. In a stand mixer fitted with the whisk attachment, whisk the melted butter and sugar on medium speed. Add the eggs, one at a time, mixing well after each addition, then add 3 teaspoons of the vanilla and continue mixing until the eggs are well incorporated. Turn off the mixer and scrape down the bottom and sides of the bowl with a spatula.

5. Sift the cake flour, baking powder, and salt into a medium bowl. In a small bowl, stir together the sour cream and milk. With the mixer on medium-low speed, add the flour mixture in thirds, alternating with the sour cream mixture in halves, mixing well in between each addition.

6. Evenly divide the batter between the prepared cake pans.

7. Bake until a toothpick inserted into the center comes out clean, 35 to 40 minutes. Let cool in the pans for 15 minutes, then turn the cakes out onto a wire rack to finish cooling for at least 1 hour.

8. Once the cakes are completely cooled, level the tops of each round with a serrated knife, if needed. Wrap each cake layer with plastic wrap and freeze for at least 2 hours. (Working with frozen cake rounds will keep the ice cream from melting too quickly while assembling the cake.)

9. In a stand mixer fitted with the whisk attachment, combine the cream, powdered sugar, and remaining 1½ teaspoons vanilla. Starting on low speed, then gradually increasing the speed to high, mix until fluffy and the whipped cream holds a stiff peak when you pull the whisk out of the bowl, 3 to 5 minutes.

CONTINUED

CONTINUED FROM PAGE 333

10. Unwrap each cake layer and remove the ice cream from its pan. Set one cake layer on a 10-inch board, then set the layer of ice cream on top, in the center. Add the second cake layer on top of the ice cream.

11. Using an offset spatula, fill the gaps on each layer with the whipped cream, working it all around the cake. Place the remaining whipped cream on top of the cake and spread over the cake and down the sides to make sure the cake is completely covered. Decorate with candy or sprinkles, if you like. Place the cake back in the freezer for 30 minutes before serving.

12. Store, covered, in the freezer for up to 1 week.

Makes 10 to 12 servings

Acknowledgments

The life that unfolds around our family's table is the reason I love to cook. So thank you to Chip, Drake, Ella, Duke, Emmie Kay, and Crew for your taste testing, your ideas, and your support over the months and months we've spent creating this book. It's a joy to cook for each of you.

I couldn't do this work without our amazing food team here at Magnolia. Becki Shepherd, Jamie Collier, Ashleigh Starchman, Holly Robb, Abigail Law, and Victor Hernandez, I loved every step of the process and am grateful to have you alongside me in the kitchen.

Beyond the recipes is a team of talented creatives who bring each page to life through words and design. Alissa Neely, Anna Mitchael, Kaila Luna, Kelsie Monsen, and Heidi Spring. And to the photographers, stylists, and editors who truly made this book beautiful. Amy Neunsinger, Kate Martindale, Frances Boswell, Billy Jack Brawner, and Elinor Hutton.

Thank you to the Meredith food team in Birmingham for double-, triple-, and sometimes quadruple-checking these recipes, and for helping us get each one over the finish line. Allison Lowery, Melissa Gray, Katie Barreira, Blakeslee Giles, Alyson Haynes, Pam Lolley, Ali Ramee, Paige Grandjean, John Somerall, Jasmine Smith, Anna Theoktisto, Marianne Williams, Olivia Dansky, Nicole Hopper, Julia Levy, Britney Alston, Liz Mervosh, Karen Rankin, Amanda Stanfield, Callie Nash, and Meredith Butcher. As always, thank you to Byrd Leavell at United Talent Agency and our team at Harper for believing in this project and working alongside us from beginning to end. Matt Baugher, Liate Stehlik, Marta Schooler, Ben Steinberg, Lynne Yeamans, Susan Kosko, Pamela Barricklow, Rachel Meyers, Anwesha Basu, and Kayleigh George.

I have saved the best for last because my biggest gratitude is for you. Being a part of what unfolds around your own table is such a gift. Thank you for inviting us in and for trusting us with the meals you serve those you love. My hope is that this book is one you savor always.